The Life Crimes and Hard Times of

RICKY ATKINSON

The Life Crimes and Hard Times of

RICKY ATKINSON

Leader of the

DIRTY TRICKS GANG

A TRUE STORY

RICHARD ATKINSON

WITH JOE FIORITO

Publishers of Singular
Fiction, Poetry, Nonfiction, Translations and Drama

Library and Archives Canada Cataloguing in Publication

Atkinson, Richard, 1955-, author
The life times and hard crimes of Ricky Atkinson : leader of the Dirty
Tricks Gang : a true story / Richard Atkinson with Joe Fiorito.

Issued in print and electronic formats.
ISBN 978-1-55096-674-9 (softcover).--ISBN 978-1-55096-675-6 (EPUB).--
ISBN 978-1-55096-676-3 (Kindle).--ISBN 978-1-55096-677-0 (PDF)

1. Atkinson, Richard, 1955-. 2. Thieves--Canada--Biography.
3. Bank robberies--Canada. 4. Dirty Tricks Gang.
I. Fiorito, Joe, 1948-, author II. Title.

HV6653.A85A3 2017   364.15'52092   C2017-901180-4
                                                 C2017-901181-2

Text design and composition, and cover by Michael Callaghan
Typeset in Janson, Trajan and Cochin fonts at Moons of Jupiter Studios
Published by Exile Editions Ltd / Ontario, Canada ~ www.ExileEditions.com
Printed and Bound in Canada by Marquis

We gratefully acknowledge the Canada Council for the Arts,
the Government of Canada, the Ontario Arts Council,
and the Ontario Media Development Corporation
for their support toward our publishing activities.

Canadian sales representation:
The Canadian Manda Group, 664 Annette Street,
Toronto ON M6S 2C8   www.mandagroup.com   416 516 0911

North American and international distribution, and U.S. sales:
Independent Publishers Group, 814 North Franklin Street,
Chicago IL 60610   www.ipgbook.com   toll free: 1 800 888 4741

To Angela Mezzacappa Casey,
who encouraged me to finish at all costs that which I promised:
a life free of crime.

INTRODUCTION

BY JOE FIORITO

Ricky Atkinson is the most famous crook you've never heard of, which makes sense if you figure that you can't be a good crook and have everybody in your business.

I knew of him before I met him.

His father, Sonny, was an influential black community organizer who did his best to clean up Alexandra Park when it was a haven of guns and gangs. He was so good at it that, when the housing project was restructured, they called it The Atkinson Co-op in his honour.

Thing is, Sonny's boy was a gangster.

Ricky and his crew, the Dirty Tricks Gang, had a daring record of criminality in Toronto during the Seventies and Eighties; dozens and dozens of bank and credit union robberies, not counting jewellery heists, and a lot of high-level drug running. No other gang in the country has managed to achieve such a record.

I also knew that the Tricksters were the first to use a spike belt – a length of rubber hose, poked through with long sharp nails – because it is on display in the Toronto Police Museum. Cops commonly use spike belts now during high-speed chases. But the Dirty Tricks Gang, led by Ricky, pioneered their use.

Against the cops.

I met Ricky through one of his confederates, a guy who'd read my columns in the *Toronto Star*. This particular Trickster had just been released from prison, and as a member of the Dirty Tricks Gang he was Toronto criminal royalty. He said he had a manuscript that he wanted to wrestle into shape as a way of explaining his life to his kids.

That book didn't happen.

But word got to Ricky about me and he also had a book, and would I agree to read it? The result is what you are holding in your hands.

So, who is Ricky Atkinson?

I still don't know what to make of him. He is one of the most alert people I've ever met, and one of the hardest to read. He is also one of the most enigmatic, probably the most fearless, and surely the most comfortable in his own skin.

He threw himself into crime for a very long time, in spite of the fact that he kept getting thrown into prison. He's spent half his life inside bars.

The thrill of the score was his drug.

He is also painfully aware, in middle age, that he wasn't all that successful as a crook, not really, not considering how often he got caught and how much hard time he did, and how much of his life he lost.

Thing is, I like the guy.

He never, as far as I know, hurt anyone during the commission of a crime. And he was born with a set of gifts which, in other circumstances, would have made him successful as a CEO, if he'd gone that route.

Was he pushed into crime?

I won't make that case. You can draw your own conclusions. All I will say is that most of us are not the product of a hard father whose background is black and native, and a mother who is white. Most of us are not fearless. Most of us are not smart. Most of us have never been called "nigger." And most of us, when shoved, do not push back.

If you think he is the author of his own misfortune, he is also the author of this book. The stories in it are his alone, and they contain lessons in wit and cunning. Or maybe the better word is leadership. I'm glad I never met him when I was a young radical. I'm also glad I know him now.

Rare are those who live their lives at the top of their professions, for whom every day is a lesson in risk and reward. He has seen things, and done things, that most of us can never imagine. And so there are lessons to be learned here from a man who has, I believe, learned his lesson.

IN THE BEGINNING

The first memory is crime followed swiftly by punishment. I was four years old. It was my birthday and I wanted cake and a celebration. A light-skinned kid lived a few doors away. His name was Gaylord Baldwin and it was his birthday, too. The party for both of us was at his house. At the time there was a commercial jingle for a Gaylord the Dog pull toy: "Gaylord, he looks kind of crazy, moves kind of lazy."

I sang that jingle to tease Gaylord and he punched me, so I threw one of my shoes in his direction. I missed him with the shoe but I broke a window in his house. My mother saw the shoe fly onto the street and came out to see what was up. I got a spanking right there, from my mother, on the street. I didn't care. My first lesson was that there's a reward in not caring about punishment when you're fighting back.

Happy birthday.

Another memory from that time is one I carry with me every day. There was a hot comb on the stove, glowing red – I guess someone was planning to straighten their hair. That happened all the time in a house that was home to so many aunts and uncles and cousins. You rubbed straightening cream into the hair and then pulled the hot comb through it – hissing and stinking – but giving that long, pretty, white folks' kind of hair desired by many non-whites then and now.

My younger brother Dwane took the comb by the wooden handle and laid the hot metal on my hand. Sizzle, howl! I don't have to try very hard to remember the smell of my burning skin. I threw the comb back at him and it hit his bare chest, sticking there for an instant. Also sizzle, also howl.

My mother said, "Look at you two, burning each other up. You better learn to get along because you will be sharing this house until your sixteen. Come and put this ointment on your burns." I learn the lesson of "getting along with my brother" every time I look at that faded scar on the back of my hand.

These are just the first of the memories that linger. Not long afterwards, with my hand still bandaged, we gathered in the backyard getting ready for Thanksgiving.

We were a big mixed-race clan, black, native and white, from Nova Scotia. Five uncles, nine aunts, and all us kids, including my older brother, Danny, and the younger ones, Dwane and Russell, plus little sister, Brenda. I had forty-five cousins, some in the yard that day. My second cousin Junior MacDonald and his mother came because they were close to us.

It was turkey-killing day. With so many of us to feed, we had three turkeys, live ones because it was cheaper than buying them killed and gutted from the market. My father, Sonny, beheaded them himself, and my brothers and I helped. It was his way of teaching us about life.

Sonny laid the neck of the first bird on the chopping block while Dwane held its body firmly in place. Down came the axe, thud; up rose the headless bird with hot blood spurting from its neck, flapping its dead wings furiously and flying sightlessly but straight at me.

I hid behind my uncle Biggy until the bird landed, spun around and finally died on the grass.

"Next," said Sonny.

He meant the next bird and he meant me.

Meanwhile my grandmother, Edith, sat in the background, nodding her approval, trying to hurry things along so she and the others could get the birds gutted and plucked. Edith, of Mi'kmaq/black blood, was the matriarch of the clan and the one who did the cooking. My grandfather was nowhere in sight. He was out on the streets, forbidden to come to the house because he was drunk all the time and wouldn't leave the girls alone, including his teenage daughters and their friends.

"Come on," said Sonny. "Can't wait all day."

This was downtown, in Toronto, in the Fifties. We were country people, black and native, killing turkeys and doing whatever else we did, in large numbers, right there in the heart of town.

I don't know what the neighbours thought, but the business of meat and blood was not new to me. I'd seen Sonny skin the rabbits he shot in Mississauga so that we'd have food on the table, just as I'd watched him crack a pig's head with a hammer so that the women could make head-cheese.

Even so, I was afraid because this was the death of a living thing.

"Get over here, Ricky. Help me with this bird," my father ordered. I froze. "I ain't going to ask you again, get your little butt over here."

Shakily, I crept over to the chopping block. My father grabbed my hand and forced it firmly on the turkey's chest. The bird fluttered I could feel its heart beating. My father smiled and I smiled back nervously, knowing that the smile on his face was really a smirk. Then *swoosh* – the bird's head flew off. Its heart seemed to jump against my palm, wings flapping madly. I tore my hand from my father's and jumped back, racing across the yard to hide behind Uncle Biggy. Kids and women were shrieking when the bird fluttered their way, until it collapsed and died. I looked at my hand to see if it was bloodstained. It wasn't and I relaxed a bit.

Once the last bird was beheaded, we were sent out to play in the park close by the station where the streetcars turned around. Five minutes later, a car pulled in. I guess the driver thought we were too close to the tracks. "Hey, you little half-breeds, get out of here."

Half-breeds?

We ran home and told Sonny what the driver had said. My father picked up his axe, still red with blood, and hurried out the laneway to the park with a hard look in his eye.

No one ever messed with my father. If you were talking shit, he'd smack you, adult or child, as simple as that. Anyone calling us "half-breeds" was clearly talking shit.

The driver of that streetcar had no idea how lucky he was that he'd caught the light and was too far away to chase. I remember looking around then and seeing my grandfather sitting on the sidewalk by the liquor store, drunk as usual.

Happy Thanksgiving.

And then there were the killings that were averted.

Dwane was four years old and I was five. We were playing William Tell in the backyard, not with a bow and arrow, but with my father's .38 calibre revolver.

Dwane stood there with an apple on his head while I took aim. I was William Tell, Robin Hood and John Dillinger all at once. The gun was big and full of bullets, far too heavy in my hand.

I had taken it from my father's dresser drawer. My mother hadn't seen me do it, and I didn't know that what I was doing was wrong. One thing I did know was that pulling the trigger was not supposed to be hard. It was supposed to be easy, just like in the movies.

"I told you it wasn't real," said Dwane, who finally tired of standing still. The apple rolled off his head but I was not going to give up. I slapped the gun against my thigh, bent over and banged it hard against the ground. I fiddled with it and I fumed. Then all the banging somehow freed the safety and the cylinder clicked easily as I turned it. Almost intuitively, I knew that the bullet in the chamber was ready to be fired.

I told my brother to take up his position against the wall and once again he balanced the apple on top of his head. "Don't move. I don't want to miss." I raised the gun carefully and took aim. I could feel the trigger begin to move beneath my finger, and...

"Ricky!"

My mother's voice, urgent, louder than I had ever heard it before. I turned to see her looking at us through the open kitchen window. There was something wrong about the way she called my name. I froze. The gun fell at my feet and once again the apple rolled off my brother's head.

Mother came running out the back door and raced toward me. I put up my arms and tried to stop her, but she slapped me hard across the face with a hand still soapy and wet with dishwater. I was crying as she picked up the gun, wrapping it in her apron, before any of the neighbours could see what had just happened.

"Dwane and Ricky, get in the goddamned house right now!"

We followed her, dragging our feet in the dirt, my harmless little game spoiled. Before I could stop crying, my mother grabbed the razor strap from where it was hanging and she took my pants down and she struck me across the backside, over and over again.

"Don't you ever *(slap)* ever *(slap)* ever *(slap)* touch your father's gun again." Before she had finished hitting me, I twisted from her grasp and ran into the living room, pulling my pants up as I ran.

Dwane, who was innocent, was punished just the same, and we were crying together on the couch as my mother dialled my father's number. I couldn't hear a word she said until she hung up the phone, and then she said what I feared the most. "You little bastards, you get up to your room and wait until your father gets home."

I knew from experience that, no matter how hard my mother had hit us, my father's punishment was going to be worse.

He worked a few minutes away, at the Army and Navy Club. It wasn't long before I heard the screech of braking tires, the slamming of the car door, and the sound of his heavy footsteps.

"Where are those little hard-headed bastards?"

Dwane and I doubled our tears as my father ran up the stairs, two at a time. The bedroom door flew open, and his entry was so violent that plaster fell from the wall. He took off his belt and slapped it across his palms, to get the feel of it.

"Which one of you was in my room and found my gun?"

I howled a confession.

"Dwane, you was with him, boy?"

My brother shook his head, and so my father grabbed me by the shoulder and spun me around, whipping my ass again and again.

I writhed in pain but his grip was too strong to escape. I screamed as loud as I could, flopping around like a fish out of water, hoping that my grandmother, who lived a few blocks away, might hear me and tell him to stop.

But he didn't stop, not until his arm got tired and I fell to the floor, holding my little burning bum. We had to stay in our room, without supper, until the next morning, a familiar part of the punishment. It was a full week before my father looked at me as if he didn't want to spank me some more. He never stopped telling Dwane how foolish he had been to let me persuade him to stand still, with an apple on his head, while I had a gun in my hand. He was right.

I'd have killed him.

The truth is that if I'd known about the gun, and known how to use it, I surely would have taken it and killed a six-year old blond boy a few weeks earlier. We had just moved to Niagara and King Street from Queen and Bathurst. It's not so far away, but when we were kids it might as well have been a million miles.

Sonny pulled up to the curb in his big black 1955 Buick, with my white mother, Anne, in the front seat and a carful of half-breed, mixed race, Afro-Metis kids in the back.

People stared at us.

The new house was near a corner. The air was filled with the wine-scented smell of tobacco from a cigar factory not far away, and the ammonia stink from the doomed pigs in the nearby slaughterhouse.

Following my dad's car were my five uncles in a ten-ton moving truck piled high with everything we owned. As the truck pulled up to the curb, my uncle Biggy and my uncle Ronny – everyone called him The Bear – jumped out of the truck with smiles on their faces.

The Bear pointed and said, "Hey, Sonny, your boys got a park to play in down the street."

My father said, "Boys, go play in the park and stay out of the way." He wanted to finish the move without us kids underfoot, but I wanted to watch the unloading of the truck so that I knew which boxes held my toys. I stopped wondering about toys when Sonny jumped on the back-loading platform of the truck and made sure I understood what he'd just said. "I ain't playing with you boys. Now get the hell out of the way."

My mother held my one-year-old sister in her arms, and they went into the house as I headed for the park, followed by my brothers Russell and Dwane. The park looked like paradise, full of happy kids splashing in a wading pool and playing on the slides and swings. We raced over to join them.

After a few minutes I noticed three blond white boys staring at us and talking to each other in dark whispers. I could tell they didn't like us.

I hopped off a swing and was leading my brothers over to one of the slides when the oldest of the blond boys stepped in front of us. I sure wished my older brother, Danny, was with us. He was whiter and bigger and knew how to handle a situation like this one. He was away, visiting my mother's mother up north in Sudbury.

Now all of the blond boys were staring at me and I stared back, waiting for them to make a move. The biggest was about the same age as me, but smaller boned.

I wasn't afraid of him but if a fight broke out I was on my own. There was no one in the park who was going to help me, just some kids on the swings and no adults. The blond boy said, "You people ain't allowed in this park."

You people?

I looked down the street. My father and my uncles were hard at work unloading the truck. I said, "You don't own the park." He said, "Niggers ain't allowed in this park."

I was five years old. I didn't know if there was a law that could keep us out of the park, although I knew that there were such laws in Nova Scotia. And as young as I was, I remembered hearing my relatives talk about how it was in the United States, where white people lynched black people in parks that I imagined were just like this.

Nigger?

I'd heard the word spoken when my uncles were drunk and horsing around. I'd heard it when white people drove past our house as my parents sat side by side on the front steps. I'd heard it from storeowners and I'd heard it from the police when they stopped my father in his car.

I'd never heard it said to my face by a kid.

It looked like I'd have to do something about it. All I could think to say was, "You're not allowed to call us names." He pushed me. I fell back, and as I did I knocked three-year-old Russell over. He started crying.

All the white kids were watching to see what I would do next. As I reached down to help Russell, I saw a stick on the ground. For the first time in my life I knew I had to defend myself – not just because I was being bullied, but because I was being bullied on account of the colour of my skin.

I brought that stick crashing down on top of the blond boy's skull. That was good enough to make the point. He held his head with both hands and started crying, and he was still crying as I led Russell and Dwane out of the park and back down the street to our house.

My father stopped what he was doing in the truck as soon as he heard Russell's sobs. "What the hell is wrong with your brother, and why is you boys in our way?"

I pointed down the street to the park. The three blond kids were still staring after us, and the one who was holding his head was now holding the stick I'd hit him with.

"Those boys said niggers ain't allowed in the park."

My father sighed and Biggy shook his head; that sort of trouble had followed them all their lives. The Bear snarled. "You go mess those boys up, Ricky."

That's when Dwane spoke up. "Ricky hit that boy in the head with a stick because that boy pushed him, and Ricky fell and he knocked Russell down."

The Bear laughed. "That's the way you do those white boys." It looked like what had started long ago for my father and his brothers was just starting for us.

Biggy was about to say something when my father held up his hand. I knew what he was thinking. He said, "Ricky, we too busy for this shit. Go in the house, or play in the backyard, do something, but stay out of our way." Biggy reached into his pocket for a dime and patted me on the head. "Here, go on over to the store around the corner."

But that wasn't the end of it.

My father always met racism with a snide remark or with aggression. Either way, at over six feet and muscled hard from years of working on his family's farm, he was big enough to back up what he had to say.

He'd also been a drill sergeant during the Korean War, serving two terms. He was a boxer. He'd worked in the mines and he'd been a bar manager. I mean to say he knew how to handle trouble.

When we came back from the corner store with our mouths full of candy, I saw two men and a woman approaching us, with the three blond boys following behind. One of the men was holding the stick I'd cracked over the kid's head.

I knew I was in some kind of trouble, but I didn't know – and couldn't tell – what my father was going to do. I stepped behind Uncle Biggy for protection as my father looked down from the truck at the white people.

"What do you want, mister?"

"Your son hit my son on the head with this stick." My father stared at him, hard and quiet. His stare, I knew, had made other men walk away. My mother was standing in the doorway, and she called out to us.

"What's going on over there?"

My father raised his voice so she could hear him. "One of these boys called Ricky a nigger, and pushed him down on top of Russell, and Ricky licked that boy on the head with a stick."

My mother looked from me to the kid who was crying. Having married into my father's huge multi-racial clan in the Fifties, she had experienced more racism than anyone she knew when she was growing up in Sudbury. Now as the Sixties began, she had to raise her Afro-Metis kids so that they would fit into a society that barely tolerated them.

One man started: "No, but—"

My father cut him off. "But what? Your kids didn't learn that nigger shit on their own. If they continue to harass my kids, my kids will slap the shit out of them every time they open their nasty little mouths."

By now a crowd had gathered to watch the commotion. And then, for some reason my father's voice grew friendlier, and he smiled.

"Mister, kids are kids and they'll work this stuff out on their own if we don't push them to do something stupid. Let's leave our personal prejudices to ourselves. As you can see, my brothers and I are busy. We can all get to know each other better later on."

My father was waiting, but the boy's father didn't have the nerve to push the issue, because he and everyone in the crowd sensed that my father meant what he had just said. If my father said "Later on," he meant later on.

The man threw the stick aside angrily and walked away, but he didn't turn around, nor did he stop to say anything to antagonize an already tense situation.

"Damn right," growled The Bear.

Not long after that, the blond boy I'd nearly brained with the stick became my friend. In years to come we'd smile at each other in various prisons every time we met.

Another life lesson for a young mixed-race kid: not all white boys who used the "N" word are racist, but anyone who did had to be put in his place at once. If it took a bit of violence to get respect, so be it.

A word about my father.

Sonny didn't talk much about his early life, or what he'd done to make a living, or where he went to school, or who his influences were. Everything I knew about him, I learned second-hand, from family or from friends.

We were never close in the white-bread, Fifties-television, father-and-son sense. He did not confide in me, and I did not confide in him.

But I knew he'd nearly killed a man.

He was sixteen years old at the time, working on a merchant ship in the Atlantic Ocean when two men, armed with stevedore's hooks, got him alone and cornered him. "No black nigger is gonna work on this ship, not while I'm alive," said one of the men. Sonny had no choice.

He fought them for his right to work. He fought to provide for his thirteen brothers and sisters. He fought to be equal. He fought to win.

When it was over, one of the racists was left for dead. Sonny went to jail for a couple of years.

These days, Toronto may be the most racially mixed city in the world but, when I was growing up, the sight of a white woman on a black man's arm was a recipe for tension. Plus, I had a black father who had taken down a white racist with brute force, so that raised the stakes for me.

My mother often told me about the times they drove down home to Nova Scotia to show us kids off to Sonny's family. She remained bitter as she told me about the restaurants and hotels along the way, the ones that refused them for no better reason than the colour of their skin.

She once pleaded with a woman in a motel to let them in so that the youngest one of us could get a bath, and the rest of us might get a bite to eat. The woman took pity on us, but she told my mother that we had to be gone by 5 a.m., before any of the other guests woke up to see a mixed-race couple and their half-breed kids.

The Atkinsons were from a white town, Windsor, Nova Scotia, yet we were at once black, brown, red and light-skinned. We were the centre of the racist bull's-eye. My father was constantly angry at the way we were treated.

That's why we moved to Toronto originally.

A year after I brained the blond kid with the stick, we moved again. This time, we had the first floor of an old brown-brick social housing complex that took up an entire block of Dundas Street, not far from Spadina Avenue.

The nearby Kensington Market was the largest open-air bazaar in the country at that time. When the windows of our apartment were open, we could smell fish on ice, and blood – fresh and dried – and some other smells I could not name.

It was a busy place, especially on the weekend; people came from all over town to look at the live fish in barrels, as well as the ducks and chickens and rabbits in cages, all of them destined for the frying pan or the pot. They could be killed and skinned or plucked for you on the spot, as you wished. On the sidewalk stands and in the shop windows there were more kinds of nuts and bread and cheese and fruit than I have ever seen anywhere else.

My mother used to say that Toronto was the most multicultural city in the world, and at that time, Ryerson Community School was the most racially mixed school.

I didn't have far to go to get to school on time. The school was thirty feet from my bedroom window. The first thing I learned was not reading or writing – it was how to hustle. Whether it was playing marbles, shooting baseball cards against the school wall, or whirling chestnuts on a string – a game some kids called conkers; it seemed as if everyone had an angle, a smart mouth and the nerve to back it up. Used marbles could be traded for cash or candy at local stores. Baseball cards were sold in pawnshops and comic book stores that littered the area. We were shooting cards for nickels and hitting chestnuts for dimes. Everyone hustled to make money at Ryerson Community School.

That neighbourhood, in the Sixties, had a heady mix of blacks, Eastern Europeans and Chinese, but the Jewish people were predominant. They were the ones who owned the shops and the factories in the garment district. They ran the corner stores and managed the movie theatres. Even the bar my father managed was Jewish-owned. As a kid, I could tell by words – silent or spoken – which of the ethnic groups in Kensington accepted our big, black and mixed-race family. The storeowners were generally friendly, and they gave us plenty of opportunities to earn a dime or two if we were willing to do honest work.

There were no Jewish gangs running the streets or hanging around in the bars and poolrooms.

The biggest gang in the city at that time was the Spadina Spooks. They were mostly Nova Scotians, a mixed-race group, a generation or two older than me. They hung out at the Hub Pool Hall, next to Shopsy's Deli. I knew them as teenaged bikers, thieves, pimps and mobsters.

I was a precocious kid, and it wasn't long before I joined in with a loose gang of my cousins and their friends. Right from Grade One, I had a relationship with guys in every other gang in the area. I still know those guys.

My first crime?

My mother says it was the theft of some bananas from Kensington Market, when I was three and half and we had just moved to Toronto from Sudbury. I don't remember that but do remember my first crime at age four. My seven-year-old brother, Danny, had a girlfriend named Twinkle. She lived above a furrier on Bathurst Street, across from us. Danny would sing, "Twinkle, twinkle, little star" to her as she hung out her window, listening to him. I wanted to up his game with his love, so stole a bouquet of flowers from a delivery truck at the loading dock that faced our backyard, giving them to him for Twinkle.

Mostly, I stole candy from stores and other little things, but my first major theft ended in a murder.

It started with an egg. I'm not sure why I wanted that egg. It would have been easier to take one from the Market. Maybe the guy who owned the coop said something to us that he shouldn't have when we walked by his place on our way to school.

I was with Dwane and my friends, Owen, Junior and Demetro. We discussed what to do and how to do it. I picked the gate latch with my pocket knife and made my way into the yard. I hadn't gone very far when a damn chicken flew out of the coop and into my face.

I had no intention of killing anything. That bird belonged to someone and it was a living thing, but I had my knife in my hand and reacted instantly, sticking the chicken in mid-air.

Then I pocketed an egg and we took off, all of my gang complicit in the murder I'd just committed. That act made us a crew, then and there.

We were on our way to school when the egg broke in my pocket and the goopy mess dripped down my pant leg, making it look like I'd wet myself.

I kept thinking everyone knew what I'd done. A cop car passed by and slowed down. I was sure I was going to be pinched. The car moved on.

My little gang was really just a crew of five guys who hung around together because we lived in close proximity in the vibrant downtown core. Naturally, it started with family. I was six and my brother Dwane was just a year younger than me. He had just as much moxy, curiosity and bravado as I did and we naturally had each other's backs.

Our youngest brother, Russell, was four when we put him to the test, urging him to jump from one roof ledge to another on a building at the northeast corner of Kensington and Dundas. That jump became a test for anyone who wanted to be in my gang and follow me. Russell refused to do it. As brothers, he and I were never that close. He also never had the misfortune of spending time in jail with me. That day, Dwane and I dissed Russell and left him to the wind. It was the same treatment I gave to any others who couldn't – or wouldn't – play "Follow the leader." All of the guys who succeeded in making that ledge-leap ended up doing time.

Owen Crookendale was a short, dark, powerful-looking kid with a large flat nose, big ears and thick lips. He excelled in all sports and that's how we met. He challenged a couple of Asian guys to a fight after a floor hockey game. Owen grew up in Chinatown and knew the Chinese word for monkey. Every bully he met called him that. He didn't need my help that day. The way he punched, kicked and bit those boys, I knew they wouldn't be calling Owen a monkey again. He appreciated that I had his back and we became friends.

Owen was just a year older than me, and he'd laugh and joke as easily as the rest of us but if you crossed him he turned into a hurricane of fists and punches. His mother was dead. She had moved back to New York to be with her American family, and she died a few days after arriving. Owen lived with his father, whose booming Trinidadian voice said nary a good word about anything or anybody.

If Owen's father was miserable, his white stepmother, Jewels, was his match. When Jewels was sober she was pretty much like anyone else's mother, but when she was drunk she was both racist and violent. Owen often had to leave the house to escape the nasty fights, finding food wherever he could, and sleeping in friends' basements or abandoned buildings. Now and then, his father was drunk for a few days.

Owen did what he had to do to survive.

One day, Dwane and I were out walking with Owen when Demetro Shapansky jumped out his front door and very nearly knocked Owen down. Owen jumped up just like that and pulled a knife. They circled each other for a minute, and then the skirmish dissolved into laughter.

Demetro was Ukrainian, very big and very white. He was the class clown and sat in front of me at school. We had a culture in common, since my maternal grandparents were immigrant Ukrainians from Baluczyn, Poland. He had the nerve to bend over and look up our First Grade teacher's dress each time she walked the room. Miss Evans never caught him. We became friends.

Demetro's mother was huge, maybe 350 pounds. Her kind heart was as big as her body. Mrs. Shapansky was often seen in the Market walking around with Demetro's mentally challenged sister.

Although we hung out together all the time, we could never play at Demetro's house because his father hated blacks. He threatened Demetro, telling him that, if he ever brought any of us home, he'd give us all spankings. Still, we went up to the Shapansky apartment often when Demetro's father was at work as a baker at the Mars Diner on College Street. Demetro always carried a knife and we often practised throwing it at targets on his bedroom wall when his parents weren't home. He rarely missed.

Junior MacDonald's mother, Verna Allison, was my aunt and she seemed to always be at my house – drinking, joking and telling stories that had my parents laughing. Junior's father lived on Spadina Avenue and was married to another woman. We often sat with his dad on their rooftop, looking down at the hustle of people on the street, while he drank a cold beer after work.

Junior and his mom lived a month here and several months there, moving all around the Market district. It wasn't unusual to knock on his door and have a strange man answer. Aunt Verna was a small dark-skinned, skinny woman who was quick to fight and often beat up the men who came to her house. Drunken fights, yelling and screaming at all hours were common. Junior often slept at our house when the madness at his was too much for him.

A good-looking kid with a big Afro ahead of its time, Junior was a year ahead of me at school. Even in Grade Two, he attracted girls from all the grades. They brought him little presents, things the rest of us could not afford. He was bright, his smile was disarming and he loved to tease. He was also a habitual liar and nobody believed anything he said until it was proven.

He carried a knife with him, too. When his mood changed, as it did quickly and often, he could be dangerous with it. Junior was only eight years old, but he'd already stabbed a couple of older boys in the neighbourhood.

Whether we were a gang or just a gaggle, we stuck together in pretty much everything we did. It was winter, fresh snow fell overnight, and we planned to meet in front of Demetro's apartment building with our shovels before school, to earn a few bucks shovelling shop owners' sidewalks

The plan was to work both sides of the street heading for Lottman's Bakery on the corner of Kensington and Baldwin Street. Mr. Lottman liked my father. He always gave us kids a chore to do in return for a sweet bun or a couple of nickels. Even if no one wanted to pay us for shovelling a walkway, Mr. Lottman would. He liked kids who got up early to hustle a buck.

Walking up Augusta Street toward the Market, Junior asked if we had heard about the whore who had been murdered that night behind the Victory Burlesque Theatre on Spadina.

We looked at him suspiciously.

He looked directly at me, "I overheard one cop say she was working for your uncle Glen."

Owen and I looked at each other, knowing that if it were true, my father would have said something to my mother, and she would have spread the word around the city - quickly.

We weren't buying it, so Junior tried again.

"A cop said she had a thick roll of money that she dropped as she was trying to get away. We should go over to Spadina and look for it."

"Bullshit!" said Owen.

Demetro said, "And if she did drop it, and the cops didn't get it, all our moms would be out there looking for that dead whore's money."

As predicted, we ended our snow-shovelling enterprise in front of Lottman's Bakery, where we all chipped in to clear the long lane. That morning, each of us earned around two dollars – a winter windfall. Getting into a movie only cost fifteen cents and a prized Switzer's corned beef sandwich was fifty cents.

After school, and before I had to go home for supper, I had a few back walkways to shovel for folks I promised that morning. Nobody went home to play. The apartments were too small and crowded.

I walked over to the St. Christopher House, a local community centre. St. Chris' was a sanctuary from the racial problems we coloured kids suffered from in Toronto's inner city at the time. Nobody there ever said chink, Jew boy, nigger, wop, pork chop, wagon burner or honky. Many of my mixed-race cousins went there, so I got to see family I normally didn't hang with otherwise. I felt safer there than anywhere else.

The centre had a gym, rooms for art classes, cooking classes, music lessons and counselling. There was even a ballroom where they held dances on Friday nights.

The place seemed to be run by two men – a karate expert named Bob Opperman and a big, black man named Bob Ellis.

Opperman was a native man who had played on Canada's national lacrosse team. He was in charge of all the sports, and his lacrosse teams won championships at all levels of play. He provided a physical outlet for inner city kids who had nowhere else to vent their energy or their anger.

Ellis helped with the sports, but mostly he looked after the social activities. He managed to master the art of mediation between the various ethnic gangs who gravitated toward St. Chris'. The place was neutral territory and everyone agreed to abide by the rules he set.

There was no fooling: if you broke any of the rules, you were banned, and no one wanted to be banned.

By the age of nine, I was tough and streetwise. I knew Kensington Market like the back of my hand. I was also aware, even at that age, that there were few opportunities for people of colour. There were very few black firemen, policemen, lawyers, teachers, and bus or streetcar drivers.

I knew of only three black businessmen: my father, who managed the Army and Navy Club, Jay the barber, and the junk man, Charlie Fowler.

Charlie hauled an old wooden cart around town looking for anything he could clean up or fix up and sell. He drank. The rumour was that he'd had a hard time during the Second World War and there were things he didn't want to remember.

He made an adequate living as a junk man, raising his two sons and Elizabeth, the finest, coal-blackest daughter a man could ask for.

We all liked Charlie for his kindness. He was always fixing things for us to play with. More than that, we all took turns trying to get next to Elizabeth. It wasn't until I reached my teens that I could officially call her my girlfriend.

Jay the barber was an anomaly, a black man with a shop in a Jewish neighbourhood. My father and his brothers were over there often. Jay let our crew run errands for some of the men that hung out there. Most of them wanted food from one of the many diners or delis around. We did it all – whether it was shining shoes, taking a jacket to the cleaners or fetching a special newspaper at one of the international newspaper stores on Spadina. Jay also let us return his discarded pop bottles to claim the deposit. The place was a gold mine for a pint-sized hustler.

Jay's was also a social hub. You didn't just go to get a haircut; you went to pick up all the gossip in the black community. It was where you learned who was new in town, which kids were in trouble, and who was doing good or harm. Jay also ran a little craps game in the basement and that drew hustlers from all over town. If you had a new suit, a big car or a hot woman, that was where you went to show off. It wasn't unusual to see cars with Michigan or New York plates parked out front. I knew all about players and hustlers. They spent freely and tipped well.

Pimps were not pariahs in those days. They went out of their way to be noticed. If you were a serious player, you drove a Cadillac with white-wall tires, and you wore a mink hat, diamonds and gold. Cops nodded at you.

At that time, many women who worked as prostitutes got to choose their player, not the other way around. A whore had power. Her persona was her livelihood. A pimp never walked up to a woman and said, "Girl, I want you to be my bottom woman." Any woman who really knew her power knew she could choose which peacock she wanted to pay.

The plain fact was that working girls outnumbered players. If a girl tried to go solo and take a prime spot on one of the busier corners, she needed a pimp to back her up or the other working girls might just scratch her eyes out in a hoe fight.

High-class prostitutes often worked as secretaries or nurses by day. Only rich men could afford them. They didn't need a player to boost their egos and take their money. As for the others, I knew most of them as next-door neighbours, and some of them were my close relatives.

One Saturday, I went over to Jay's to collect bottles and run errands for the players. The door was locked, but there was the usual assortment of flashy cars parked outside. That was unusual, and it meant trouble of some kind. Everyone understood that what happens in Jay's stays in Jay's, and Jay never called the cops. So I went over to the nearest car, sat on it and waited.

Before long, an angry pimp stormed out of the shop and over to me. He threw me off his car, cursing and muttering about the trouble I was in, while he checked the car for scratches. He was reaching for me again when Jay appeared.

"What's going on?"

"This little yellow nigger was sitting on my car."

"That's Sonny Atkinson's kid. You might just as well pack up and get out of town if you don't leave that boy alone." The man took a moment to digest that thought, and then he reached into his pocket and peeled a fiver off his roll.

"Listen, son, my car is all I got. Don't sit on it again." He patted my head, and Jay called me over and gave me a pop. I had no idea why there'd been a problem.

But I knew I was Sonny's boy.

As for the rest of it, Jay's was back up and running – full of hustlers getting haircuts and talking about the usual things – girls, cops, and boxing. What could be wrong with any of that?

What I liked most observing the ebb and flow of inner city hustlers hanging around Jay's were the guys everyone called "rounders." They were guys – and some women – who lived the criminal lifestyle as if they were born into it, as if they had been called by a higher power. I heard talk of Pete-men (safecrackers) second-storey men (housebreakers) pick-pockets, car thieves, jewel thieves, fences (sellers of stolen goods) and hijackers (with stolen trucks laden with furs, cigarettes, booze and anything else average people wanted at a bargain with no questions asked or taxes paid).

Armed robbers usually specialized in banks. Then there were card sharks and loan sharks and the feared arm-and-leg men (debt collectors). The gamut ran from contract killers to pimps and gigolos.

Rounders were the consummate hustlers of the criminal underworld. They were the jacks-of-all-trades, doing anything to make a buck or two and refusing to succumb to a square job. Working for a paycheque was a sign of failure to a good hustler, unless one had too much heat from Toronto's cops.

At the top of their game, they seemed free spirited – never bowing to authority, other criminals, or the mob. When pinched, they were supposed to stand tall and take the beef, or fight it in a court of law. Rounders didn't rat anyone out. Their reputation was based on their ability to secure a loan, get a gun, hide out and find crimes to commit.

Toronto has always had one of the world's best police forces. Beating them at crime isn't easy but it's what rounders loved to do. I listened to these hustlers talk about how good and long their run at a certain criminal adventure lasted before they were pinched by the cops or forced to shut down whatever hustle they were up to.

My uncle Glen was a rounder other rounders looked up to and I wanted to be just like him. He applied himself to whatever hustle he had going on any given day, but he never worked a day in his life. He never called anyone boss, sir or master. He owned nothing in his name, but many envied him. He drove an expensive car, lived in a nice place, wore nice clothes and had lots of friends. More importantly, he always seemed to have a fat roll of cash on him at all times.

Every rounder had a crew around him. Even at my young age I was starting to get my crew of young hustlers together so that I, too, could play the cat-and-mouse game against the cops that rounders loved.

Near the end of the summer, not long before I'd enter the third grade, I came home one day, tired from hours of hustling with nothing to show for it. I'd been walking in and out of stores and knocking on doors of people we knew, asking if there were any errands to be run. Mr. Lottman usually gave give me a donut for going to get his Jewish newspapers, but not this day. A woman who lived across the street and made delicious bagels in her kitchen would give me one for taking out her garbage, but not this day. Some of the older, Jewish fruit storeowners would give me twenty-five cents for carrying their large baskets of fruit into the store, but there weren't any on this day.

I opened the door and my brother Dwane stepped out and punched me in the face with a boxing glove on his fist. It felt like my head was exploding and I heard adults laughing. I stumbled backwards down the stairs as Dwane jumped up and down with his gloves held high, shouting that he was the winner.

Uncle Glen hurried downstairs after me, picked me up and shoved a pair of boxing gloves on my hands.

"Stop crying, get up there and fight."

My father's cousin, Stewart Gray, and my uncle Donny Upshaw had come over to play cards, when talk of boxing came up. My brother butted in, claiming he could beat me. That's all it took. Bets were made and money flashed. We were a fighting family that produced champions. Everyone waited to see Dwane and I go at it, while a card table was set up. Both Stewart and Donny were boxing champions, with Stewart subsequently dying from injuries in the ring. Those gloves were not toys.

I ran upstairs and began punching and I didn't stop until my brother was crying in defeat. Uncle Glen gave me fifty cents, patted me on the back, and collected his winning bets from Stewart and Donny. I'd just had my first "professional" fight and my heart was filled with pride.

Fighting makes you hungry. Or maybe when you're hungry, you fight that much harder. My brother and I were starving, so we walked over to Switzer's Deli to split a corned beef sandwich. The walls were plastered with pictures of all the famous movie stars who'd ever had a sandwich there. Half a sandwich is not enough, so we headed over to Owen's house. It was Friday, and Spadina was overflowing with shoppers picking up groceries on their way home from work.

Owen hushed us when we got there. His stepmother, Jewels, was asleep. She'd been drinking, and you never knew with her. We tiptoed into the kitchen, where there was a big pan of fried chicken on the stove. I had a weak spot for her cooking but, Jewels being who she was, I rarely got a chance to eat it. I asked Owen if Dwane and I could split a piece.

Jewels must have heard us smacking our lips and licking the crumbs from our fingers, because she burst out of her bedroom, reeking of booze. She screamed at Owen: "Get your ugly black ass out of my house and take those chicken-eating half-breeds with you."

We walked over to Grossman's Tavern, where a group of black blues musicians were unloading their equipment. I'd forgotten all about Jewels until she stuck her head out of the apartment window, pointed down at us and started to rant.

"Hey, I can see you chicken-eating bastards down there. I hate you people, you're good for nothing." She paused, and then started up again, as if explaining herself to a larger audience: "You don't understand these black bastards like I do. All they want to do is eat and eat."

The musicians stopped what they were doing, stunned. They thought she was yelling at them. One of them said, "I should go up there and slap that white bitch in her nasty mouth." That meant Owen had to stick up for Jewels, who was the only mother he had ever known. He explained who she was and got an apology.

One of the other musicians said, "Man, I thought I had the blues. I may be from Mississippi, but you got me beat." He reached into his pocket and handed Owen a shiny little harmonica.

We were too young to go in and listen to them play, so we drifted off, walking down Spadina, taking turns on the harmonica, trying to find a tune and singing the blues as best we could.

MY FIRST PINCH

One hot Sunday morning in the summer when I was ten, my little gang and I rode our bikes up to Casa Loma. We liked the place because it really looked like a castle. It was fun to sneak in without paying admission by climbing over the stone walls. After we fooled around inside checking out the secret passages and the suits of armour on display and other stuff, we rode over to the Sealtest Dairy Company to drink chocolate milk from the no-charge vending machine that was supposed to be for truck drivers only. After we had our fill, we headed home, with a stop-off at the Salvation Army donation depot. Rich people left piles of junk at the big back doors on Richmond Street and it sat there all weekend. You never knew what you might find.

On this day there was nothing worth hauling home, so Demetro and Dwane left. My cousin Junior and I took our time, nosing around the nearby factories until we ended up in front of Sherman's Hardware, at the corner of Queen and Augusta.

Mr. Sherman kept a display of twenty new bikes chained to the sidewalk at the side of the store. When the business was closed, he covered them with a long, heavy tarp. Junior began to play with his big ears, which is what he did when he was nervous. He leaned down and peeked underneath the tarp. Then he reached over and rang the bell on the handle of my bike. I knew he wanted a bell just like it. He jumped off his bike, reaching into the tool pouch hanging from his seat and told me to keep my eyes peeled in case I saw a cop car.

My heart raced. The street was crowded with people who were coming out of the Catholic church a block and a half away, but I was sure we would be noticed. I pedalled across the street, leaning my bike against the wall of a bank while Junior smiled and slipped under the tarp with his tools. Whatever he was doing under there, it seemed to take forever. A cop car passed by, but there was no reason to suspect anything was going on. I held my breath anyway.

Then I felt a hand on my shoulder.

I spun around in fear.

If I knew one thing, I knew cops, and the one grinning down at me like a wolf was Bert Novis. A former Toronto Argonauts football player, Novis joined the police force in the Fifties and worked his way to detective.

In his neatly pressed brown suit, Novis stood six-foot-four, weighing in at over 200 pounds – all of it muscle. He was the most feared man in a part of town where most men feared very little.

Policing was different back then. It wasn't unheard of for a cop with a beef to walk into your house and punch you in the mouth just to send a message, without making any arrest. Novis was that kind of cop. When he tightened his grip on my shoulder, it felt as if he was crushing me.

"What are you and Junior up to, Ricky?" Of course, Novis knew who we were. My father was a well-known businessman. Sonny also had an aversion to paying parking tickets, and every couple of months Novis or some other cop would haul him off to spend a weekend at the Don Jail over unpaid fines. Novis had also broken up a fair share of drunken brawls at Junior's house.

I couldn't let Junior get caught. I was supposed to be watching out for him.

I called out our Eastern Woodland Metis signal, "Heroo, heroo!"

The big detective lifted me off the ground with one hand and shook me hard to shut me up. Junior scrambled out from under the tarp and looked around. Our eyes locked. He dropped the screwdriver and bicycle bell and started to run, leaving his bike behind him.

He didn't get far. A man in a cheap grey suit stepped out from behind a lamppost and caught him by the jacket. Junior twisted around, trying to escape. Then he started to scream.

"Help! Kidnapper! Child molester!"

A couple of passing cars stopped to look as my cousin kicked the man in the shins. One driver got out of his car and walked over to help a kid in trouble. The man in the grey suit flashed his badge.

"Police."

That was all he had to say. Traffic kept moving along. Novis hauled me across the street and collected the bell and screwdriver. People were staring. I was embarrassed and afraid.

Novis handed the bell to the other cop, and I heard those words for the first time.

"You're under arrest."

I'd been stealing little things, pop and candy and so on, ever since I was in the first grade, but this was new. I started to shake, because I thought maybe they were going to take us down to the waterfront and beat the shit out of us, which we knew happened all the time.

Novis made us lock our bikes and he put us in his car. Like his suit, it was big, brown and unmarked. He must have spotted us sorting through junk at the Salvation Army, which was just across the street. We had been too preoccupied with finding something worth lifting to notice a couple of plainclothes cops on the watch. Junior and I sat in the back seat, sneaking sad little glances at each other.

Novis looked at me in the rear-view mirror. "You know, Ricky, stealing that bell was a stupid thing to do."

Why was he talking to me? I hadn't tried to steal anything. But I looked at the back of his thick red neck and nodded, trying to hold back the tears.

The cop in the grey suit addressed Junior, "Yeah, you little black monkey, and resisting arrest was just as stupid."

Junior twisted his ear nervously, protesting, "I didn't know who you were."

The cop had the last word. "Shut your lying mouth."

Novis drove along Queen Street with his prize, pint-sized crooks, in the back seat. When he turned up Claremont Street, toward the police station, my heart stopped. Not a hundred yards away, I saw my father dancing on the sidewalk with my aunts and uncles. Music came from a record player perched on my grandmother's window ledge.

"Look at those assholes," said the cop in the grey suit. "We should go over there and arrest them for something." I looked at Novis and he looked back at me. Neither of us said a word.

The Atkinson clan eyed the car suspiciously and I ducked down so they wouldn't see me.

At the station, Novis took me to his office and pointed to a chair. "Sit down." I did as I was told. Junior's cop took him to another room.

Novis put the stolen bell and the screwdriver on the table in front of me. I looked around the room. It was bright, orderly, bare and clean. I wondered where the glaring light was, the one they shone in your face when they worked you over for a confession.

The big detective pulled arrest forms out of a cabinet, dropped them on his desk and asked if I wanted a bottle of pop. I nodded, and he left me alone to contemplate my sins.

Alone, looking at the wanted posters and mug shots plastered on the walls, I wondered if my picture would soon be there. I knew I didn't want to be fingerprinted. They kept prints on file forever.

Novis came back and handed me a cold orange pop. I raised the bottle to my mouth and couldn't stop my hand from shaking.

Novis wriggled his large frame into the seat at his desk and, without looking up at me, said, "It was really stupid of the two of you to steal that bell. You could easily have earned the couple of bucks it cost, couldn't you?"

"Yes," I whimpered.

He began to type, and was about to ask me a question when I was startled by a loud crash and bang coming from the room where my cousin was. I looked at Novis, frightened. He kept typing, creating my file, unmoved by the noise.

"Your father is going to kill you for this."

I put the pop bottle on the table, wondering what was happening to Junior.

Novis asked where I lived, what grade I was in, how tall I was. He asked if I liked school and what I wanted to be when I grew up. I told him I wanted to be a professional boxer, like some of my relatives.

At that, Novis smiled. "For a ten-year-old kid, you're big and tough. You can probably box, if you try. You just have to promise me you won't do anything stupid like try to steal bike parts anymore."

I promised him I would never steal again.

"Well," said Novis, "the judge won't go too harshly on you for this." He sounded nonchalant, but my heart stopped and my head went numb.

"I've got to go to court?"

Most of the kids I knew who got caught stealing things were simply taken home to their parents. Only the worst delinquents went to court. I wondered if there was anything I could do to get out of the mess I was in. I would have gladly worked all week, for free to pay for the bell.

A thousand different scenarios went through my mind. My father knew Mr. Sherman, and I thought he might get him to ask the court to go easy on me. If I had to go to jail, I wondered if I could go with my father when they took him in for unpaid parking tickets. I could sleep on the floor under his bed, just for a day or two. My mind raced. Maybe I'd get probation, maybe not. The only certain thing was that I was in big trouble.

But my fate was in Novis's hands. As afraid as I was, I also hated the sight of him because of the power he had over me. Lessons from my family's history taught me that I was now deep in the white man's world, and there was not a black or brown face anywhere in Toronto Police Division 14 to help a poor mixed-race kid like me.

I snapped to when the other cop appeared in the doorway with Junior. His face was puffy from being smacked and his eyes were red from crying. It hurt to look at him.

There was nothing we could do now but take whatever medicine was coming our way, including the beatings we were surely going to get from our parents.

"Your mother home?" Novis asked. He ripped the arrest form out of the typewriter and stood up. "Finish your pop. I didn't buy it for nothing." I raised the bottle to my lips but couldn't drink, so I handed it to Junior.

"This asshole doesn't get any treats," announced the other cop, grabbing the bottle out of Junior's hand and slamming it down on the desk. A stream of pop shot out of the bottle and splashed him. He hissed at Junior as if the spill was Junior's fault and pulled a handkerchief out of his pocket.

Booking us for our first arrest took less than an hour. We weren't photographed or fingerprinted. Apart from the slap to Junior's face, we weren't worked over the way I'd been certain that we would be.

The cops drove us home in the big brown car. My aunts and uncles were still there at my grandma's, dancing on the sidewalk. They never saw us pass by. The cop in the grey suit said, "Look at those coloured fools. They think they own the sidewalk." And so I knew, at that age, how the world worked – if it ain't white, it ain't right. I was young and wrong.

The car turned up Vanauley Street and pulled to a stop in front of the house. My mother came out, wiping her hands on her apron. She looked at Junior and me and asked Novis, "Why do you have my boy in your car?"

He explained what happened and handed her a thin brown envelope with our charge sheets in it. My mother took it and gave him a long hard look.

Junior and I were led out of the car by the cop in the grey suit, who glared at my mother.

"Mrs. Atkinson, can you give Junior's papers to his mother?" Novis asked. He knew that if my mother explained the situation, Aunt Verna, who could be unpredictable after a night of partying, might go a little easier on her son.

It was a nice gesture.

The cops climbed back into their car and, as they pulled away I heard the other one say, "If that little crook ever kicks me again, I'll slap the black off of him."

My mother took her time reading the charge sheets and then said, "Junior, get home. Ricky, you get upstairs and wait for your father." I looked at Junior, thinking it might be the last time I'd see him. I was sure our fathers were going to kill us.

When Sonny came home, he called me downstairs and asked me to tell him what happened. I told him everything, including the part about Junior getting slapped. All that my father said was that I should go and get my bike, come home, and stay in my room for the rest of the night.

I wondered why he didn't spank me for being arrested. But I also knew that sometimes it took a day or two for his anger to ripen. I stayed out of his way for a week.

Soon enough, it came time to go to court. We stood around waiting, watching some of the lawyers laughing and others bent over in conference with concerned families. I couldn't help noticing that many of them greeted my father with respect.

Surprisingly, I wasn't really afraid. After all, I was an Atkinson and it seemed almost everyone in my father's family had been to court.

My father's boss, Mr. Birnbaum, allowed us to use his lawyer. Uncle Glen said Birnbaum's lawyer must be good because Birnbaum had money, and money bought the best lawyers – a statement as true then as it is today.

All it took was a minute.

The judge handed us over to our parents, and said we were free to go. No fine, no training school, nothing. I shook the lawyer's hand – it was soft, but firm – believing at the time that I would never see the inside of a courtroom again unless it was as a lawyer, which was on my mind now that I had seen how powerful they were at dealing with the system.

A CHANGE OF SCENE

Suddenly, all the homes around us were being abandoned, having been expropriated by the City. The turn-of-the-century homes that had been a cheap refuge for the Polish, Ukrainian and Afro-Metis community were going to be levelled and replaced with a new way of housing the poor, popularly dubbed Housing Projects. We were told we'd be moving out of our old place and into a new home that the city was about to build. The old neighbourhood quickly became a ghost town – in other words, a place to play.

Our little group of adventurers began exploring the abandoned houses, running around the empty rooms of people we knew and looking at the stuff they'd left behind. Each house had the smell of the people who had just moved, but after a while they just began to smell like all the others – old and empty.

Dwane and I decided to hang around the Richardson place across the street from us. Adam Richardson, the youngest boy in a white family of six, was my friend and he was in the same grade as Dwane, but his family was slightly different. Adam's father seemed to have buckets of money and he didn't live with the family. He had his own playboy-style apartment near Bloor and Spadina.

Mr. Richardson owned a mining and prospecting company, with an office in the bank towers on Bay Street. He had dozens of people working for him and Adam sometimes took us to visit. Mr. Richardson didn't judge us. Once, we arrived at his office dressed in our bathing suits and riding wooden stick ponies. We were met with looks of horror and disgust from all of the white people who saw us hopping into the elevator of the prestigious building. However, Adam's father greeted us warmly and sent us to a fancy Bay Street restaurant. Dwane, Junior, Adam and I sat there almost naked among the finely dressed lawyers and judges who frequented the place. I'll never forget the look on the restaurant manager's face when he tried to stop us from entering and Adam said, "My dad is Mr. Richardson. He'll be calling you."

What I liked most about Mr. Richardson was that he collected guns. His apartment was loaded with them. We often went there when he wasn't home, just to hold the guns in our hands and feel their power.

One hot July evening before the Richardson family home was cleared out for demolition, Dwane and I went over to see how they were doing. Adam's sister, Velvet, was still there, hanging around and talking to one of her girlfriends. I waved to her and she smiled back, running her long slim fingers through her bright blonde hair. I was only eleven but knew the kind of girls I liked and Velvet fit that profile. Her grandparents lived in the posh Forest Hill area on Russell Hill Road and even though they were rich, they never looked down on us poor mixed-race kids when we visited their home.

On one of those hot summer days I got an unexpected lesson in race relations. All the kids on the block were wearing bathing suits and squirting each other with water guns, so Dwane and I joined in.

The old white man next door was laughing at our antics. He seemed to want in on the fun, so he aimed his garden hose at Adam. We all screamed, ducking and dodging and doing our best to spray him back. After fifteen minutes, the old man had enough, so he put his hose down and retreated to the front door of his home.

Dwane and I ran up to him one last time and emptied our water guns at him. He laughed as he slammed the door shut, looking at us from the window and sticking his tongue out like a kid.

Turning away, I noticed my father's car slowing down. He had an angry look on his face. Jumping out of the car, he shouted for us to get into the house.

As soon as we were inside, he whipped off his belt and began shouting. "You little bastards, lay down on the floor." We did as we were told, wondering why he was so angry. My mother pleaded with him to go easy on us. He wasn't listening.

"I tried to raise you bastards right, didn't I?" We nodded. "Then why were you bothering that old white man?" Before we could answer, the belt came down on us again and again. "I've tried to show you how to live in this white man's world, but you just won't listen." His blows were like punctuation. "If I ever see you bothering any white man again. I'll whip you both to death."

My mother screamed for him to stop. He wasn't disciplining his sons anymore; it was something more personal, something that had nothing to with us. She grabbed his arm, which she had never done before. He stopped swinging, looking at her angrily, breathing heavily, his jaw clenched tightly. My brother and I ran upstairs.

From that day on, I looked at my father differently. I knew he was filled with anger. When I think about it now, I suppose I know why. He was strong, fearless, smart and capable. He was also Afro-Metis from the east coast, poor, under-educated and powerless, with a big family to support. He could have become a robber or lived off of the avails of prostitution like some of his brothers and friends, but he didn't. The result was frustration, without the prospect of a happy future.

The lesson of the belt? Be careful around white people.

My parents fought often that summer, in part because an extended province-wide beer strike crippled Sonny's bar business at the Army and Navy Club. Sometimes he came home late, reeking of booze and broads. As time went by, that began to bother my mother more and more. She picked at him, she nagged and nattered, and she wouldn't let up. He'd come home happy, doing a little dance. She'd be suspicious and she'd start in, going at him until he reached the breaking point. Then he'd hit her. I still wince thinking about it.

My parents fought for days at a time. Both of them spanked us for trivial things. A few times we went to stay with relatives when Sonny needed space to cool off.

It all came to a head some months later. I was sitting in the kitchen, and had done or said something that angered my mother, who was screaming obscenities at me. Time seemed to slow down as she came at me with a hockey stick in her hand. "You hard-headed bastard, I can't take this shit anymore."

I had no idea what shit she was talking about.

She pointed the stick at me menacingly. I moved back, wondering what was wrong with her. She said, "I'm going to take Danny and Brenda to go live with my mom, and leave you, Dwane and Russell with your father. See how long you last before you're in prison or stuck in Children's Aid."

I wish she had just hit me with the hockey stick and said nothing. As young as I was, at that precise moment, I felt that I had to prepare to live alone. I knew that my relatives in Sudbury would take me in but life wouldn't be the same without my friends.

When Junior and Owen had family strife, they retreated to sleep in abandoned or vacant garages they called "forts." I started to look for forts of my own and found a couple of good ones in the downtown core. We stocked our hideaways with stolen army cots, lanterns, camping stoves, radios and canned goods. Any time we wanted or needed to retreat from the world, we headed for one of our illegal hiding places.

Sonny never beat me the way he had that hot summer day of the water guns and the white man. It took decades for me to stop hating him. I think now that he was trying to steer us toward a better life than the one he had. He just wanted everyone to get along, without prejudice of any kind.

At the same time, I started to change, becoming very selective of the white people I looked up to. I felt contempt for the Uncle Toms, those blacks who smiled and jived with white folks, whether they liked them or not.

I even stopped listening to the Beatles and the Rolling Stones, turning to soul music to soothe my pain. As a mixed-race kid, I was most comfortable in the company of other kids like me – ones who shared the same pain, the same social class and the same uncertainty over whether we were more black, white or red. I had to find a way to sort out my confusion.

The only white adults I looked forward to seeing were my mother's relatives in Sudbury. Her brother Tom – yes, I had an actual Uncle Tom – was a Sudbury cop who was always friendly and made us feel comfortable in his home.

My mother's sister, my Aunt Jen, was married to Sam Baldelli, a stocky Italian with a bright smile and a kind heart, who we nicknamed Uncle Sambo. The two of them lit up with joy every time we rolled into town. I loved Jen so much that I named my first daughter after her.

Jen and Sam's only son, Randy, grew up to become a prison guard. His sister, Carlene, married a union steward who worked in the Sudbury jail.

My father was still in the army when he went to Sudbury to visit his sister and met my mother. At the time, his position as a drill sergeant made him the highest-ranking black in the army, charged with training black troops who were heading for Korea. Sonny never went to Korea, though. After meeting my mother he quit the army and went AWOL, which is how I ended up being born in Sudbury.

Even though my mother's family was filled with the law-abiding and the law enforcing, they had as much fun partying as the criminals on my father's side of the family.

Family aside, my hatred for rich white folks or white folks with power over me began to grow. My attitude was "us against them," and we got daily lessons in this matter. On one occasion, the cops shook Junior and me down and found matches in our pockets.

"What are you doing with these?" one cop asked, holding up the matches. "Are you the two little niggers burning down these empty buildings?" We both shook our heads.

"You're a bunch of liars. You two and are under arrest for arson!" We were put in the police car and forced to abandon our bikes on the sidewalk.

In the interrogation room at 3 Division, one of the cops grabbed me and slammed me against the wall, trying to get me to talk about my uncles, Glen and Ronny. I knew enough to never talk about my uncles and it was clear that Junior and I were never their real targets.

That cop might have hurt me but I had no fear of him, just pure hate.

"My dad's going to punch you out for hitting me."

He grinned and said, "I'll shoot your dad if he raises a hand."

Word spread quickly, and minutes into our interrogation our parents came to get us, accompanied by a dozen or more of my relatives. They swarmed the station, screaming blue murder.

"Where's Ricky? Let him fucking go." "He's a fucking kid!" "What the hell is this?" All of it at the top of their lungs. If that happened today, there would have been blood spilled, theirs and ours.

The cops let us go, but when we returned to the scene of the so-called crime, the bikes were gone. I'd spent a whole month shining shoes after school and Saturdays at a leather shop next to the Horseshoe Tavern to earn the money for that bike. My father talked about that incident until the day he died.

From then on all of us – Junior, Owen, Dwane and the rest of the neighbourhood kids – took to the streets to take our revenge on the world. We put burning bags of shit on doorsteps, rang doorbells and scattered. We set booby traps using long fluorescent lighting tubes discarded by factories and rigging them on rooftops with fishing line so that we could send them exploding down on white passersby. Bottles of piss were rigged the same way.

We snatched purses, vandalized cars, slashed tires, smashed windows and set fire to abandoned houses. We learned to swarm anyone who had the nerve to threaten us and we cut people with knives – all in the name of fun. Becoming bullies on a grand scale sometimes got confusing and we ended up confronting each other. Junior stabbed me and I ended up taking twelve stitches to a baby finger at Sick Kids Hospital. Later, I stabbed him back.

We roamed rooftops with the ease of cats. Like phantoms of the alleyways, we were able to crawl into the most unlikely hiding places. Learning the ins and outs of the neighbourhood served us well in later years.

It isn't as if we never tried normal social stuff as kids. At one point, my whole crew joined the Boy Scouts to keep out of trouble and learn to get along with others. That lasted until one of the scout leaders called Owen a monkey. When we beat him up, they kicked us out. There is no badge for that, but there ought to be.

An army of construction workers were readying to raze the old houses in the neighbourhood and we were forced into temporary housing a block away. Before we moved, my mother gained her strength and confronted my father. "The kids are too big to see us fighting all the time," she said firmly. "Don't you ever put your hands on me again or I'll take you out."

My father saw something in her that woke him up, because he got all soft and cuddly with her, wrapping his arm around her and kissing her. Their relationship stayed that way, changing overnight, giving our household a chance to breathe and appreciate the thought of having a new home after being in so many rat-invested hellholes.

They called the new neighbourhood Alexandra Park.

Many of the new kids who were moving in were strangers to us and my father advised us to be friendly with them, no matter what colour. He went out of his way to be nice to all of the parents who would soon be our neighbours. If they didn't show signs of racism, they stayed friends for life.

We were the first family to move in. Sonny warned us all against writing graffiti or destroying property by telling us what the government told him – that one day soon, we would own these homes. He didn't want to see them devalued.

Soon, people in the shops and stores up and down Spadina began to refer to us as "Project kids." We hung anywhere that was free to kids twelve and under – the Art Gallery of Ontario, the Royal Ontario Museum and the gym at the University of Toronto.

We tended to overstay our welcome wherever we went and at times we were a bit unruly. They got to know us and began to kick us out.

One night we were thrown out of the gym at the Settlement House behind the art gallery for kicking basketballs at some Asian kids. What to do? Brink's security firm had its garage and headquarters nearby, a place of obvious interest.

Once before, on a dare, I rode my bike right through the garage. Nothing to it. I just tucked my bike alongside a truck that was on its way in and rode alongside until I could safely peel off into the street.

I can still remember looking at a row of tall black safes, which I figured were full of treasure. With nothing better to do, we went to Brink's and hung around. It was cold and dark when we saw a big grey truck backing up in the laneway. One of the guards walked over to the entrance of the building carrying a duffle bag and a clipboard.

The driver finished parking and walked to the back of the truck. I thought he was going to take a leak. Instead, he slipped a key into the lock and opened the back of the truck. Our eyes widened.

Owen nudged me, pushing a small stick into my hands and grinning mischievously.

"Watch this," I said. "I'm going to scare the shit out of that guy."

Demetro put his hand over his mouth to keep from laughing. Junior tugged an ear and pulled his knife.

Unaware, the guard jumped on board the truck and a second later he was backing out with a white canvas bag in his hand. He never saw me coming.

I jabbed the stick in his ribs.

"Freeze, mister!"

He raised his hands but he didn't drop the bag. I figured he would turn around, see me and start laughing. Instead, his hand dropped to his gun and he wheeled around, scaring the shit out of me.

As soon as he saw me, he slapped my face and I started crying.

"You can't hit me," I wailed. "I'm telling my father. He's going to kick your ass. We were only joking."

He wasn't laughing. "You little bastards, I could have shot one of you. Come over here, the lot of you. I'm arresting you."

Before he could finish the sentence, I was tearing down the laneway with the others on my heels. I heard him yell for his partner. We circled the block and came back, staying hidden while they searched for us. Why had I taken the stick from Owen?

Various reasons. Because I was angry? Maybe. Because we were bad? No. We were seen as bad simply because of who we were and where we lived. The idea, "You think I'm bad, then I'll be bad," raged through me.

By the time I was twelve, we had graduated from sticks to guns. Junior and I joined the army cadets at historic Fort York and learned how to shoot rifles and other military skills. One of the corporals took offence to Junior screwing his sister, so we beat him up. That got us kicked out but it didn't stop us from smelling gunpowder.

We stole pellet guns and .22 calibre rifles from department stores and sporting goods stores. We did it by cutting holes in our pocks and sliding the rifle barrel down a pant leg. Then you just had to walk out limping stiffly, as though you had a broken leg. In one store, I pretended to slip on the floor and crawled behind the counter, reaching up to snatch a box with a compact .22 calibre handgun.

We used guns to rob old Eastern European and Italian men playing cards in the park. We hazed any strangers we saw as trespassers. We held up delivery boys and we robbed cab drivers of their fares. We threw rocks at passing streetcars and cop cars.

It got so bad that streetcar drivers refused to stop if there were groups of teens on a corner. None of the stores, factories or Market shops was safe – but I never robbed a black or brown person of any age.

I'm sorry to say it now, but old people suffered because delivery vans stopped coming, and taxis were reluctant to pick up fares at night. Even ambulance drivers were wary of the Projects.

As part of the renewal of the neighbourhood, 3 Division, the police station I knew best, was converted into a fire hall, and a new station was built to replace it.

The new station, now called 14 Division, developed a reputation for having the meanest cops in the city, perhaps because its boundaries also had the highest crime rate in the city. You can make of this what you will, but I think part of the problem was that they staffed 14 Division with cops from the suburbs who didn't identify with the neighbourhood and couldn't understand the anger of us kids. They preferred to bully us and push us around.

We saw them as goons sent to oppress us.

I don't want to soft-pedal the situation, but most of us were guilty of little more than being poor and hanging around in groups for the twin purposes of comfort and safety. Even though we were bad, we weren't bad all of the time. As a group, our numbers swelled with kids at risk from far-flung regions like Africa, Brazil and the West Indies. If a minor crime was going to go down, many kids just went home or figured out ways to avoid the sightlines of conflict. It's only natural that there were gangs and where there are gangs there is rivalry.

The Spadina Spooks tested my little crew all the time. The oldest of them was at least five years older than the oldest of us and some of them had kids of their own. I knew every one of them and was related to some of them, but that didn't prevent them from kicking our asses for infractions real or perceived.

Some of the emerging kid gangs put up with it but we were different. I began stealing guns and stashing them here and there in the neighbourhood, ready to pull them on anyone who threatened me. Once, I corralled Junior and Owen into helping me break into the armoury at Fort York to steal machine guns, but an alarm went off and we ran like hell. The Spooks were bad news, but not many of them had ever done hard time for robbing or shooting anyone.

The truth is that the gang responsible for most of the criminal activity at that time was a small one, younger than the Spooks. And I was their leader.

I became more and more estranged from my parents. Our Alexandra Park house was new but we were poorer than ever. My mother was forced to take a job at Eaton's department store, which meant leaving us kids at home alone during the day when school was out. At least Mom was there to make us supper. We had a TV to watch and a basement to play in. Now we were only sleeping two to a room. Other families had it a lot worse.

There was a kind of camaraderie among the first families who moved into the neighbourhood. Very few households had locked doors, day or night, even when there was no one home. Our house was never broken into, no one stole our bikes and everyone looked out for everyone else. Adult neighbours became surrogate aunts and uncles, making sure we were safe from sexual predators, bullies or strangers.

The crime rate might have been high, thanks in large part to me and my little crew, but the Atkinson house was the safest fortress in the city.

That said, the business of unlocked doors was not without incident. One night, our whole family was sitting in the living room watching television, when a drunk staggered into our house. He was surprised and then angry and upset to see us. .

"Why are all you niggers in my house?"

My father looked at him evenly, but we all laughed, knowing that the drunk was in a whole lot of trouble for using the N-word. Sonny stood up with a kind of smile on his face. He'd seen his share of drinkers of all stripes.

"Mister, you got the wrong house. Let me escort you out."

The man began to struggle, shouting racial slurs. He took a swing at my father, who promptly blocked the punch and knocked him out with a short right to the chin. Sonny carried the man out of the house and laid him on our front lawn. We all went back to watching television as if nothing had happened. The drunk slept it off on the lawn.

I confided to my brother that I thought I should sneak outside and teach that man a lesson by cutting him with a knife. Dwane said, "If dad wanted him hurt, don't you think he would have done it himself?" He had a point.

In the morning, the wandering stranger woke up and dusted himself off, looking bewildered, wondering why his jaw was sore. He headed for home unsteadily, not knowing how lucky he was to be heading anywhere.

He was the only outsider ever to come into our home without an invitation – or a warrant.

My father began to talk about the promise, made by the city, that we would soon own the houses we lived in. That was a lie, of course, but the dream turned into an obsession that drove him to dedicate himself to the neighbourhood. He worked long and hard, risking his life trying to keep Alexandra Park from being vandalized by frustrated kids.

Twenty-two years later the residents took over the housing project for themselves and turned the place into a co-op. It was the first of its kind in Canada and they named it The Atkinson Co-op.

AS REAL AS IT GETS

I was thirteen years old in 1968, when Martin Luther King was shot dead by James Earl Ray. On TV every night afterward, we saw the tanks on American streets, the riot police and the smoke from the fires as cities burned. We had no idea Ray was hiding out in Toronto for a time, visiting bars like my father's. My whole crew felt the shock waves.

Black rage was not just an American thing. One of the white kids in the neighbourhood said, "If a race war begins, remember me – I have a lot of black friends." That made me laugh. I also remember laughing when I saw a Chinese man on the news, running around with a sign that said, "Don't burn my store – I black, too."

Toronto began filling up with people – white and black – who fled the United States, bringing with them stories of Jim Crow lynchings, segregation and racial alienation. That helped us put a perspective on the nightly news.

We were told that when there was trouble in black America, the cops never did anything to help. We were also told that when cops picked up blacks, they were given a choice: jail or Vietnam.

So we took up their chant in Toronto – the cops were pigs. They were racist oppressors and imperialists.

Sometimes we would surround a cop car and shout slogans at the frightened cops inside. They responded by increasing their brutality towards us, uniting us even more. Round and round it went.

It was a time of rock concerts, drugs and long-haired hippie protests. The sit-ins at the University of Toronto convinced me that everyone was fed up. If the rallying cry among white kids was, "Don't trust anyone over thirty," then the soundtrack of the times for black kids was James Brown's "Say it loud – I'm black and I'm proud."

Not that the cops gave a damn.

One night Owen and I were picked up by a couple of 52 Division cops who berated us and told us they had a mandate to keep the downtown area between Jarvis Street and University Avenue "nigger-free."

When newcomers got a taste of the racism and a whiff of the unrest, they soon gravitated toward our methods of retaliation. That's how downtown Toronto became a hot spot for smash and grabs, and a place where pickpockets and robbers roamed freely.

The Black Panther Party, and the Nation of Islam, started selling newspapers on Toronto streets. That was new. I began to hear the first whispers of something harder. There were people now talking about wanting to kill a cop, as if that act might help free the world from tyranny.

The cops sensed something was up and so they sent their best, toughest and most cunning policemen, including some who broke as many laws as they enforced.

I often saw Bert Novis with Julian Fantino, racing around the downtown core trying to catch bad guys. Fantino rose to become Toronto's police chief before going into politics. I learned about the hard cops – Barry King, Pat Kelly, Frank Barbetta and "crazy" Mike Burke – names that were soon on the lips of all the criminals I knew.

In the midst of all this, the Project boys I hung with began to play a game that would give us street credibility and a city-wide reputation. We'd choose a dark, secluded corner and wait like wolves for someone to come along. If it was a black person or a woman, a kid or a really old man, we let them pass. Anyone else, we fought – even an experienced boxer, a karate expert or a seasoned street fighter. We had to fight and win, or get our asses kicked.

If a cop turned the corner, those of us with the biggest balls would taunt him, call him names or even challenge him to fight. Cops in those days were tougher than they are now, or so it seems to me. Every once in a while, a cop would take on a mouthy, aggressive teenager in a fist fight, and not bother to arrest him afterward.

Reputation is what gangs are all about, and I developed a reputation for leading from the front, never backing down no matter who walked into my path. One evening I was tested hard in front of about fifty kids. While crossing the street into Alexandra Park, a cop car almost ran me down. I still remember seeing it swerve toward me.

As I leaped out of the way, the cop behind the wheel shouted, "Walk on the sidewalk, burrhead!"

Everyone heard him and I had to save face. In a matter of seconds, I put together a plan that the others agreed on. We ran into Kensington Market and grabbed boxes of empty bottles, along with as many rocks as we could find. We hid them behind the cement wall that ran along Dundas Street. Then I asked Owen to slip into one of the little stores and steal a couple of pairs of nylons to mask our faces.

One of our guys volunteered to phone the police and say that his parents were fighting. To make sure the cops showed up, he cried into the phone: "My mother, she's white, she's getting her ass kicked by my black stepfather, everyone is watching, please hurry, he's crazy!"

Within minutes, the same cop car that almost creamed me raced around the corner and headed into the Projects. The cop drove slowly, looking for a crowd of people watching a black man beating a white woman. When the car was close enough, I jumped up from behind the wall and yelled, "Get the fucking pigs!"

I threw my bottles. They shattered loudly against the side of the car. Within seconds the rest of the gang pitched in, hurling bottles and rocks down on the cop car. Windows shattered and dents began appearing on the side of the car.

The cops ducked under the dashboard for protection as their car slowly rolled up on the sidewalk and caved in the front door of a Mac's Milk store, setting off alarms.

Most of the kids fled then, running for the safety of the maze of streets in Alexandra Park, but Owen and I held our ground, holding our bottles, looking at each other with smiles on our faces. Filled with rage we ran at the cowering cops. I tossed a bottle through the shattered windshield, screaming, "Fuck you, pigs." And then we ran away, too.

About a hundred feet from the cop car, I could see big Mrs. Peyton standing in her doorway, watching me. She was holding back her two daughters and four sons with her strong arms. They all wanted to join the action that night.

The image of her standing there, protecting her kids, is burned into my memory. She didn't know it then, but she would live to see all four of her sons die in one prison or another. Her pretty eldest daughter would spend forty years on the streets, running every kind of hustle she could to pay the rent, score some dope or buy a meal.

The sound of sirens snapped me into alertness, as cop cars, fire trucks and ambulances all came screaming toward Alexandra Park. Owen and I walked into my house as if nothing had happened. We went up to my room, and then out the window and up on the roof.

Standing there in the dark, we watched the shadows below us, cops shining their flashlights, chasing the shadows deeper into the maze of streets that made our neighbourhood so dangerous for them.

It wasn't long before I spotted Bert Novis and his gang, looking for evidence, looking for suspects, looking for us. My crew was smart enough to stay indoors during the sweep. We knew that Novis would beat the shit out of anyone he thought was responsible for such a blatant attack on civic authority.

Novis found nothing. And that was the virtue of our tight little neigh-bourhood: everyone knew everyone. We all had to get along and nobody was a rat.

My crew and I kept reasonably cool for the rest of the summer, partying and doing the occasional smash and grab at jewellery stores. Both of my parents were working and there was a lot more joy in our home. I was becoming a man. I'd been stabbed twice before I was twelve. I'd been shot at and I shot a big black teen from a nearby gang. I believe that summer-time was the last time I was really free.

About the kid I shot.

Ezzard was big and dark. He boxed at Benny D'Amico's gym on College Street but his home turf and his gang were based about a block west of Alexandra Park. Once, he had the nerve to punch me, when I was walking through the Projects.

I'd been with some of my guys and he was with some of his. He sucker-punched me. Then my crew picked up two-by-fours and so did his. It ended in a standoff but I recognized it as a warning. He wanted in on the action at St. Christopher House, especially the dances. I had to do something.

Ezzard's gang was multiracial and ahead of its time, in that it was made up of guys and girls. There was no point in attacking him directly, which is what he was expecting. Instead, I figured I'd get at him by letting him think he was getting what he wanted.

The dances at St. Chris' had the prettiest girls, the sharpest dressers, the smoothest players and the best dancers in the west end. The music was Motown and R&B, provided by one of the Spadina Spooks, Dwight Johnson.

I knew a tall, pretty Polish girl who travelled between my gang and Ezzard's. She loved sniffing nail polish remover. When she was high on Cutex fumes, she'd screw anyone. So, I stole six bottles of nail polish remover from a drugstore and offered her the lot if she'd tell Ezzard that I was too scared to go the dances at St. Chris' after our standoff. With all that nail polish remover to make her happy, I knew she'd be extra friendly when she cornered him. The next night I headed to the dance with some of the boys. We waited behind the community centre, staring down the dark laneways that led back to the basketball court.

If Ezzard smelled a trap, he was too tempted to resist. He and his crew snuck past the laneways and hopped over a tall fence right into the basketball court. They came unarmed, to avoid being kicked out of the dance if they were searched at the front door. I had a .22 short, nickel-plated ten-shot, with a pearl handle and a two-inch barrel that I traded for a stolen car. It made a loud bang and shot out little bullets that made their point.

We were waiting and they were trapped. As soon as Ezzard landed on the ground, I stepped from the shadows with the small gun in my hand. He made a split-second calculation to run. As he was scaling the fence I ran up to him, pressed the gun against his ass and pulled the trigger. He dropped, jumping around and yelping like a puppy.

I stuffed the gun in my pocket and planted a solid right to his ribs. He dropped to the ground. Then I grabbed him by the hair and yanked his head back. "If you ever fuck with me again, it won't be your ass that takes the bullet."

He nodded to show he understood. What he really understood was that he'd met someone who would not stand to be sucker-punched.

Then my crew went to the dance while Ezzard scaled the fence with a small bullet hole in his ass, accompanied by his crew. I had taken a calculated risk and now everyone around me knew what I was capable of. After a few weeks of healing and some mediation between gang members, Ezzard's crew joined ours. Suddenly, we were the largest, multiracial teen gang in the city.

I stayed friends with Ezzard for years.

At the end of the summer, I started Grade Eight at Ryerson Community School and was surprised to see a smiling black woman standing in the doorway of my classroom. It didn't take long to realize that Miss Smith was not just competent; she was also fun. I began looking forward to class.

Two weeks into the first term, I got into a fistfight during recess with a kid who ran a gang in Chinatown. This kid knew karate or some other martial art that made him tough to nail. We fought long and hard, with neither of us able to get the upper hand.

During a break, I looked up and saw Miss Smith watching us. When I got back into class, she pulled me aside and said I'd get into trouble if I ever fought like that off school property.

She was right. It was safer to fight on school property because out on the street there were no rules and you were at the mercy of your opponent. If that Chinatown kid and I had not been able to take care of our problems at school, with our fists, there's no telling what might have happened to either of us on the street.

For me, school was a reprieve from home, as it is for many kids. Like most teenagers I knew, I hated my house and the way we lived and the hypocrisy I perceived in my parents. One day my uncle Biggy dropped off twenty boxes of grapes that had obviously fallen off a truck somewhere. So it was all right for us to benefit from whatever Biggy was up to, but it wasn't all right for us kids to catch such a break with all of the clothes and jewellery in the stores surrounding us that we could easily "make available." My cousins' parents were not so strict and it bothered me that they walked around looking flashier than I did because I had a far better idea of what to steal and how to pull it off. To get my parents off my back and to justify some of the stolen things I had, I took a job after school at a local grocery store stocking shelves.

I never stole a dime from the store while I worked there and I wouldn't let my friends steal when they came in. I have never stolen from anyone who put me in a position of trust, including my parents and relatives. I never stole from storeowners who treated us the same way they treated white kids. I was a thief, but I had principles and they have stayed with me for life.

I'd had lots of jobs throughout my young life. I sold everything from newspapers on the corners to pop and candy at the stock car races. One summer I worked at the Canadian National Exhibition running a kids' ride. I shined shoes and helped old people load things in their cars. Zeroing in on the many Jewish people in the neighbourhood, I did things they couldn't do on the Sabbath. I hustled to make a buck and sometimes as I hustled I broke a few rules.

That was all normal to me. I could hustle and keep a straight job on the side; both things were legitimate to me. However, I quit stocking groceries on shelves after a month. The minimum wage pay of seventy-five cents an hour paled, compared to what I could make on the street. It just didn't make sense to me.

My parents began riding me even more, urging me to get my life together. Owen and Ezzard both had their own apartments and I thought about moving in with them.

The problem was that I was fourteen. The rule was that you had to be sixteen to be on your own or truant officers could pick you up, take you off to court and send you to training school for delinquents.

Eventually, Miss Smith sent me to a guidance counsellor, in preparation for the many high schools available to students in the downtown core. It didn't go as either of us hoped.

The counsellor seemed friendly enough, with an office filled with colourful brochures. I already had a plan. Harbord Collegiate Institute had courses in legal studies for high-school students to prepare them for law school. I thought I could have a career helping kids like me get through the legal system and move on to productive lives. I dreamed of being a lawyer, like the one with the soft hands and the nice suit who helped me through the stolen bicycle bell incident.

Instead of helping, the guidance counsellor told me I should go to a vocational school and become a carpenter.

"There are no black lawyers," he said matter-of-factly. "The chances of you becoming one are slim to nil. Do what your father does, work with wood; blacks can get work in that area easily."

I wish I could remember his name. I'd send him a list of blacks – male and female – from our neighbourhood, who made it through law school.

I had a couple of incidents with guns, both of them eerily similar. I had just turned fourteen and I stole a .22 pistol from a sporting goods store. All I wanted to do was shoot a few Coke cans in the alley – *pop, pop* – and take a little target practice. Owen and Junior stole a couple of gas-powered .22 calibre pellet guns and we'd get together and pretend we were like the great white hunters we saw on TV killing animals in Africa, only our prey was assorted squirrels, pigeons and rats.

One night we tried to take out a streetlight in the lane. I know I hit it, but nothing happened. A brown car drove slowly past the lane and out of sight as I was firing for a third time. The car came back and a white man in a dark suit got out and ran to the far side of the car. He was about fifty feet away and I could see a gun in his hand. Instinctively, I fired in his direction. So did Owen and Junior. Everything seemed to happen in slow motion after that. The man crouched and levelled his gun, firing six times. I heard the *zip, smack* as each bullet flew past me, thudding into the garage door behind us. The bullets scared me less than the words that came out of the shooter's mouth: "Stop, police, or I'll shoot."

He had already shot, so there was no upside to stopping. We ran, vanishing into the laneways we knew so well. After that night, none of us mentioned that shoot-out with the cop, but sometimes I went to that garage door and looked at the bullet holes, contemplating how lucky I was to have survived being so stupid.

A little later, I was walking with my crew to the Market when we passed a grocery store. It was long past closing time, but the lights were on. We pressed our faces to the window and couldn't see any signs of staff.

Twelve-year-old Mike the Polack shinnied up a lamppost and lowered himself into the store through a skylight. Soon, we saw him dancing on the counter with a bottle of wine in each hand and a string of sausages around his skinny neck.

We tapped on the window and he pointed to the back of the store where he let us in. We often broke into local stores, stealing just enough to have a party back at Alexandra Park without cleaning the store out. This was no different. We ran around shopping for our favourite stuff and filled two boxes, which we dragged outside and slithered through the darkened alley, ending up in a back lane across from Western Hospital.

We were splitting up the loot when Mike reached into the box of goodies, pulled something out and handed it to me. I felt the cold metal of a gun in my hand.

"It was in a desk drawer in the back office," he explained.

I handed the gun off to Dwane and reached into the box to see what else was there when, out of nowhere, a grey car drove slowly past. The driver was white. He looked our way.

At that moment, a soft rain began to fall. We ignored the car and the rain and went back to dividing up the goodies. Then the grey car returned and the driver opened his door. Before we saw the gun in his hand, we all knew that he was a cop just by his demeanour. All of us had various items in our hands, and one of us had a gun. Without warning, a loud boom like a shotgun going off filled our ears and a flash of lightning lit up the lane.

The officer ducked reflexively. He must have confused the thunder with the sound gunshots and assumed we were firing at him. He fired one shot into the air and shouted: "Police. Stop or I'll shoot." Then he ran for cover behind a garage wall, where he squeezed off six rounds. The bullets whizzed over our heads.

This was as real as it gets.

I knew I could outrun anyone and this cop was no different. I gave it everything I had, racing between houses, jumping a fence, cutting across a couple of backyards and slipping behind a car like I'd done a thousand times.

I waited for what seemed like twenty minutes, listening to cop cars skidding around the lanes, while the warm rain soaked my clothes in the darkness.

Why had I let myself get caught up in this situation when there were so many other things to do in life? I hadn't learned the lesson: if you don't want to get chased by the cops, don't do things the cops will chase you for – like stealing food.

It sounds simple now.

My musings were interrupted when the back door of a nearby house opened and a barking dog came bursting out. I heard a woman's voice: "Officer, there's someone behind that car." I could see her in the light of her doorway, pointing in my direction as the dog came at me. The woman and the dog weren't a problem. The cop with the gun was.

Before he could fire off another shot, I jumped a fence and raced toward a wooden gate. There were rusty nails sticking out of the top of it, hammered in to stop guys like me from climbing over. I found a space between the nails and pulled myself up but, when I went to jump down, my pant leg snagged. I hit the ground hard.

I got up slowly, my head spinning, stunned, but not too stunned to see the cop burst out of a laneway and come racing up the street, shouting madly, waving his gun.

I ran across the street to the hospital and burst through the thick glass doors, knocking aside anyone who stood in my way. My wet shoes made sucking noises on the floor as I picked up speed. I didn't get twenty feet before hearing, "Police, stop or I'll shoot!"

I wasn't going to stop for a trigger-happy cop who just might be stupid enough to take a pot shot in a hospital. I kept on going. Glancing over my shoulder, I saw a young black intern running after me, following me down the corridor, gaining on me. I sped up. So did he. I was getting farther away from the cop, but the black intern was getting closer. He tackled me just inside the Bathurst Street exit. We struggled.

"Get off me, brother, these pigs are KKK."

Nothing doing.

The cop took over, kicking me and punching me until I was cuffed. Other cops showed up.

"Get the monkey up!"

I looked at the intern as they hauled me to my feet. "Told you so, brother." He turned sheepish as the cops led me out and shoved me in their car. Four of them piled in around me. They said nothing as we sped off, down the street and around a corner where ten other cars were waiting.

Two cops jumped out, joining the search for evidence of a shooting. I saw another car speeding towards us, and I could tell from the size of the driver that Bert Novis was now in charge. Novis opened the door of the car, and leaned his big frame against it.

"How you doing, Ricky?"

I didn't say anything.

His big hand shot out and slapped me on the back of the head, crushing me into the other side of the car.

He shouted, "Where's the gun?"

"Mr. Novis, what are you talking about?"

"The gun, the goddamn gun. The officer said you shot a gun." He pointed to the cop who had opened fire on me twenty minutes earlier.

"Mr. Novis, what gun are you talking about? It must have been lightning and thunder," I implored. "Look, it's starting to rain."

Just then, God spoke to Bert Novis on my behalf. A flash of lightning filled the sky, followed by a blast of thunder. It sounded like a shotgun and it shook the car. "See? I'm too young to have a gun."

"You better not be shitting me, son."

He looked up at the sky and walked over to the other cops, who were busy shining their flashlights up and down the laneway. Five minutes later, I was being raced over to 14 Division.

They let me stew in the interrogation room for six hours, and then they charged me with break and enter and possession of stolen goods. They found no gun and no shell casings. I figured there was a good chance I'd be out on probation the next day with nothing more than a slap on the wrist to go along with the slap to my head.

I was wrong. Instead of a slap on the wrist, I was hustled out of the interrogation room and taken upstairs. They put a hood over my head and worked me over, swinging pillowcases filled with phone books at my face, at the back of my head and in the ribs. They worked me over for an hour.

Then I was taken to a holding area for juveniles, where I was introduced to a cop named Schultz – all six-foot-four and 300 pounds of him. I was five-foot-eleven and 178 pounds and still a kid.

"Oh, Atkinson? You related to Perry?"

"He's my cousin."

"Come here."

Schultz punched me hard in the face and sent me flying. He and Perry must have had some beef. I jumped up, ready to fight, but three cops grabbed me and held me, while Schultz beat me black, blue and bleeding. Then they let me alone overnight.

Later, when the door opened for lunch, I saw Ezzard, who had also been pinched for break and enter over a box of meat he had picked up in the alley after my gang ran. We went downstairs together. I told him I was going to swipe a knife from the lunch tray, for protection. He said they counted the knives, so I stole a fork. I hadn't counted on being searched after lunch.

They found the fork and stripped me to my shorts for another beating. Don't ask about my pain threshold. I'll just say I didn't want to give them any satisfaction.

Ezzard and I went to juvenile court the following Tuesday. He was released. The judge bought his story about innocently walking along and finding a box full of neatly packed meat lying at his feet. I wasn't caught holding anything and I was pronounced guilty and sent up the river until I was eighteen.

While Ezzard waited for his paperwork, I worked out an escape plan. Going over it a few times with him, I impressed on him that I had to get the hell out of there.

The plan was nothing short of daring.

I would make my way out of a small, exercise yard by running straight up the wall, grabbing support bars and pulling myself up to stand on a basketball net ring. From there I'd grab the top of the wall and get over it – with a little help from my friends.

A day or two later, I was walking alone in the cement-walled yard, when I heard our gang call. My heart was beating wildly. I knew it was my brother Dwane. Then I heard more calls. Owen, Junior and Ezzard were on the other side of the wall, too. I gave our signal back, causing everyone in the yard to look at me. Then I saw three sets of black hands gripping the top of the wall, and Junior hoisted himself up with a knife held between his teeth like a pirate. Owen and Ezzard's heads appeared next, their eyes wild and looking around. They all shouted at once seeing me.

Thing is, the guards also saw them and pushed the alarm button. Then they rushed me. When I got up I had a whole new set of bruises. The boys outside the wall were long gone.

I would be gone soon, too.

TRAINING SCHOOL DAYS

Since I was sentenced to remain a ward of the province until my eighteenth birthday, the government was my new mommy and daddy. First stop, Bowmanville School for Boys, just outside the small Ontario farming town of the same name. It was a reception centre where all delinquent Ontario boys, from seven to sixteen years of age were classified before being forwarded to training facilities. I knew I wouldn't be there long, and I instantly recognized the acres of closely mowed lawns and flowerbeds.

When I was eight, my father drove us to this place along with five carloads of his brothers and sisters. We had a barbecue with his youngest brother, my uncle Ronny, while he was waiting for placement in a juvie prison. Now here I was, following in the family footsteps.

I was handcuffed and shackled when the police cruiser pulled up to the one-storey, red and white administration building. I had been told this facility dated from the Second World War, when it was used as a prisoner-of-war camp for Germans. It was still run like a military operation and I could see boys walking around in military formation, heading to or from the freshly painted buildings. I wasn't afraid, just was curious.

At the reception area, I was stripped, searched, showered and interviewed by a nurse. A staff member gave a long speech about the futility of escaping or breaking any rules. I was given bedding and a rule book and turned over to a prison escort who took me to my prison barrack. Surprise, my escort turned out to be my friend from kindergarten, Demetro Shapansky, who had been in the system for a while. He had worked his way up to a position as trustee and was in charge of escorting new boys and tracking down those who tried to escape.

He told me my cousin Perry had escaped a couple of weeks earlier and hadn't been caught.

Demetro giggled, "If you want to split let me know. I'll tell you the best time and direction."

What a comfort to see his smiling face.

I spent the rest of the day locked in my barrack studying the rule book.

On my second day, I noticed some white greasy guys eye-fucking me at dinner. They were from Regent Park, and they knew my reputation. I asked Demetro if he'd sharpen up a butter knife from the kitchen so I could jump the one who wanted to test me.

The next afternoon I went to the mess hall with the little knife in the waistband of my pants. I spotted the guy I was after and he sensed that I meant business, so he stood up.

When he saw the knife he started screaming for his crew and began to back away. But his crew just sat there, unwilling to gather their balls for a beef they had nothing to do with. My target picked up a cup and threw it at me. Demetro knocked over a table and everyone jumped to their feet screaming, "Fight! Fight!"

I dropped the knife to the floor. I wasn't afraid of any white boys throwing cups. Within seconds, ten officers swarmed in and grabbed me. I'm not saying that the system is tilted, but no one grabbed the white kid who threw the cup.

I was sent to solitary for a week. Nobody found the knife. I was not charged with assaulting another inmate, which was fortunate because, while I was in there, I had a visit from the warden. He'd read the report about the size and seriousness of my gang; the report contained an outline of how I could be helped if I was removed from them.

It was signed by Bert Novis.

As a result, I was sent to Glendale Training Facility, near Simcoe, in the heart of tobacco country. Glendale was new and intended for gifted boys. Most of the staff had degrees in child psychology. The warden, for example, had a PhD. He told me I'd been sent there because I had so many relatives and gang associates in all of the other training schools. He agreed with Novis that – if isolated – I could be turned into a productive member of society.

Glendale wasn't as rough as some of the other boys' training schools. A kid might get slapped around, but usually only if that kid was a bully, or if he attacked a staff member. Rape, by inmates or by staff, was a rare thing, whereas years later other schools in the system would be rocked by accusations of brutality and sexual assault by chaplains, guards and other inmates.

The plan Novis set in motion was to isolate me from my Afro-Metis roots and any connection to my old neighbourhood and culture. Being isolated from all that is familiar makes some kids crazy, others docile, others violent. Some kids ran away, others hurt themselves or lashed out. The smarter ones poured their energy into sports or school. Evolution theorist Charles Darwin observed first-hand that isolation and time can change a species. I know I changed and not for the better.

When you are separated from your family and deprived of choice – where to go, what to do, what to eat, when to sleep, when to wake and who to see – you might as well be dead.

The only way I was going to see the street again was by being a model prisoner. It wasn't easy. Some of the kids were racist, a cast of mind they usually picked up from their parents. After I beat the shit out of one or two of them, things quieted down. Every now and then, somebody would stroll in and challenge me to a fight, if for no other reason than to gain a reputation.

Most of the guys who tried to fit in by being tough and sounding racist were from small towns where people of colour didn't exist. They weren't willing to go all the way, like I was. If there were times when I didn't want to fight, it was not because I was afraid I'd lose, but because I was afraid I'd kill. As the days dragged on, I became lonelier than I'd ever been. The loneliness made me bitter. To demonstrate my unhappiness, I refused to show any compassion to anyone who was white – staff or inmate.

The only black people I saw were my parents, who drove up once a month to take me out for a bite to eat – a rare and precious privilege. But those visits were strange because they were nothing more than an illusion of freedom. Wherever we went in those small southern Ontario towns, we stood out.

On one of those occasions a group of white kids called my father a nigger and then sped off in their car down a one-way road. This was a definite mistake. Sonny hammered his car in reverse and chased after them, driving backward at sixty mph until the boys stopped to confront him.

Sonny got out of the car with a hammer in his hand. I stood by his side, carrying a knife from the fishing tackle box he habitually carried with him. I was grinning, but Sonny was dead serious. The kids had the good sense to apologize. I'd have cut them up.

Lunch afterward was tense. I think if I had so much as asked my dad for the pepper shaker, he'd have snapped.

I sat there with mixed emotions–glad to be free but horrified by the notion that my freedom had subjected my father to a racist confrontation that could have cost him his freedom.

As I picked at my food, I thought of an earlier time and a family trip we'd taken. Ten carloads of our mixed-race clan stopped at a small town to do some fishing. The cars pulled over and I jumped out, running across the road and over a small dam, heading for a store on the other side. We were inside for less than a minute when a small white boy my age rushed in, racing around the corner and behind the register where his mother was standing.

"Mom, Mom," he shouted. "There's a circus come to town. A whole bunch of niggers just pulled up in cars across the river." Needless to say, that store suffered significant inventory losses on that long summer day.

In all, I spent one full year in training school. The average stay was six months. And what I'm about to tell you is hard for me, even now.

I was out on a pass but still reporting to a probation officer, Lou Taylor. He was a tall, well-educated black man from Windsor, Ontario, who ultimately became the head of probation services in Toronto. I was rarely in the company of such a dignified man, so when he laid out his plan to save me I didn't question his logic.

He knew a white family in the east end of Toronto who fostered kids. He reasoned that if I was with a foster family, out of my element and in a white neighbourhood, I might slow down a bit and change.

Taylor took me to my parents' house with a writ in his hand and had the discussion with my parents about taking me away. It was not much of a discussion, however, since that writ was law.

I felt angry and worthless at the same time.

Sonny said nothing until I was about to leave. "Hey, boy," he called. "Don't let anything happen to you. Something happens, you just come home."

Meanwhile, my mother made up a suitcase. Inside she stuffed a card along with a piece of a brown sugar pudding cake. The card read: "I love you. Don't cause any trouble. Come home soon."

She stood on the sidewalk with the writ in her hand, crying as Taylor drove me away.

My new family were a couple of well-meaning fat people with two fridges full of food. All of their relatives came to meet me. It was an uncomfortable surprise, because the kids who were my age were all members of the east end gang my crew was used to beefing with.

I decided I needed a gun.

The first Sunday night I spent in foster care ended up with me picking a lock to a gun store. A Chinese guy saw me. I wondered if I should run. The lock was stubborn. Two cops came and grabbed me as I walked along the curb and took me to 55 Division. They smacked me around. I tried to stand up for myself. They smacked me around some more. The next morning, a judge at the juvenile court was lecturing me about what a risk to society I was.

"Your Honour, I'm only fifteen years old," I said in my defence.

The judge looked at me askance. I wasn't done.

"Your Honour, they beat me, and they fingerprinted me."

That caught the judge's attention. It was against the law to print a juvenile. His attitude changed immediately. Sternly, he told the police to destroy the prints and he dismissed the charges.

"Let him go."

I thought I could just walk away and go home to my parents, with the foster parents out of the way because I had embarrassed and frightened them. Not so fast. My probation officer stuck his nose in and said I should be sent back to Glendale for my own good. I was "out of control."

Not long after my return, I decided to escape.

I had relatives in Montreal. I figured it would be easy enough to go there and blend in. It was not hard to persuade some of the others to run with me.

Glendale was a lot like a modern boarding school. It held 120 guys in four units. Each of us had our own room and we had access to a library, a well-stocked kitchen and a big gym. More importantly, there was a huge yard surrounded by farmers' fields with no fences of any kind.

The escape plan was simple. One of my chores was cleaning the laundry room. When I asked a lazy guard to open the door for me, he threw me the keys, as I knew he would. By melting a candle from the institution chapel, I made a small wax pad that I used to make an impression of the key, picked up an armload of towels and left, locking the door behind me. The next morning, I fashioned a rough key in the machine shop where I had a vocational training class.

We made our move on a Friday night. Young and fit, and we ran the five miles to the nearest town to steal a car. By the time we got there, sirens were howling. We hid behind some houses while one of the guys went to find a car. In minutes he came running back, followed by two gun-wielding cops.

We hightailed it, jumping fences and cutting down lanes until we came to a supermarket parking lot where we were greeted by those two winded cops and some of their pals, all with guns drawn.

Freedom lasted less than an hour.

Not one of my better plans.

Glendale was progressive but sometimes progressive is weird. Normally, after an escape attempt, you'd end up in the hole and lose your privileges for a long time. But the warden seemed impressed with my intellect, and my thirst for knowledge, so he decided to try a little experiment. He wanted me to spend my days locked in a glass booth with my books and my nights in the hole.

Every morning at 7:00 a.m., I was escorted to the glass booth; inside, I had a chair and books, and that was all. I was on public display. If I needed a glass of water or had to use a toilet, I tapped on the glass.

Staff sneered at me; inmates snickered and mocked me at the risk of being punished. Others discreetly tapped their left shoulders in solidarity.

I was the only non-white in the place and I began to feel diseased by the colour of my skin. I knew I could cut my hair and "act" white to lessen the social stigma. I knew others who easily passed as Italians or Arabs. But I was too much my father's son to deny my blackness. That was never going to happen.

When my time in the glass booth was up, I continued paying the price for my attempt at freedom by doing a month of breakfast kitchen service.

One morning, I was lined up to get my white kitchen service uniform and someone kicked me lightly in the butt. Instinctively, I wheeled around and horse-kicked the idiot in the chest.

It was no idiot. It was a guard named Winnery. He was two years out from serving in Vietnam. I thought he was a bit of a psycho. In an instant, he had me on the floor, twisted into knots of pain.

"Son, you ever strike me again, I will end your life." He knelt over me and pushed his elbow into my neck. "Got it?"

I got it, and I got sent to the hole. I was surprised when Mr. Winnery came to visit me. He was quiet, with the dangerous air of a mob debt-collector. It turned out he was also an intelligent and caring staff officer.

We talked, and he shared some of the shit he went through as the only white guy in a platoon of black and Hispanic soldiers.

"'Private white boy' is all I heard for two years over there," he said. "I signed up for it so I had to take it. You signed up for this so you've got to learn to take it also."

I respected him, but I had not voluntarily signed up for anything. He let me out of the hole later that day.

I found that I'd moved up in the pecking order as a result of having stood up for myself with him. I will explain: boys of all shapes, creeds and colours would walk into prison and ask, "Who's the rock of this place?" The rock was often, but not always, the toughest guy in the place. Sometimes the rock was simply a guy who wouldn't take shit from anybody else.

After I got out of the hole every guy in the place knew that, if I'd gone after Mr. Winnery, I'd be likely to react to anyone else the same way. So I became Rick the Rock.

The tag came with responsibilities, not unlike wearing the white hat or the black hat in a western movie. I welcomed challenge.

One night in my cell I heard a new kid ask, "Who's the rock on this range?"

He was obviously aware of adult prison lingo – a "range" being a reference to a basic cellblock with open doors, allowing the inmates to roam around like so much fenced livestock, with guards on the watch. Glendale was nowhere near that formal, but we did roam around our cellblock freely.

"It's the big coloured boy in room fifteen," someone answered.

Then came the challenge: "Hey, coloured boy, get off the range by supper or get ready to shine my shoes with your face."

I stepped out of my cell. "Who's asking?"

"I did, I'm in number ten." I walked over and yanked open the door. Inside was a runt of a kid who curled up into a little ball and began to whine as soon as he saw me. "Please, don't hurt me, I didn't know you were so big."

I let him be.

The merciful rock.

Sometimes, a rock would wait for someone young and fragile, and make a move on him. If you were weak and you went along, you thereafter led the life of a so-called "sweet kid."

Most sweet kids were used for unpleasant chores such as cleaning rooms or washing down the units. Some guys used sweet kids as sex toys, for blow jobs or hand jobs. Sweet kids were bullied or taunted and sometimes they were raped while others kept watch and waited their turn.

But rape didn't happen as often as friendly coercion.

I often had inmates ask to be my kid, just so they'd be left alone. But I was a loner and looking after a weak white boy, protecting him from the predatory games of other white boys, just wasn't part of my thinking.

Hormones run high in adolescents, so life in prison was sexual by nature, but never overtly. Moves were made over time and not violently. If you brushed past someone, you might hear, "Hey, are you giving me an elbow grip?" Or if your foot brushed another's, you might hear, "Hey, you queer, you trying to give me a toe grip?" That was often all it took to start a fight.

If the person who was touched did not react, you might say, "That elbow grip felt good; maybe I can get one later on when we're alone."

Glendale was largely run on the basis of mutual respect, which made it psychologically comfortable, with an attitude of "Don't bother me, and I won't bother you." That's how you get along in any of the prisons I've been in.

The place was like a modern school. It held 120 guys in four units. Each of us had our own room and we had access to a library, a well-stocked kitchen and a big gym. More importantly, there was a huge yard surrounded by farmers' fields with no fences of any kind.

I had been back at Glendale about three months, when I heard a voice outside my cell door announce: "Man, another coloured boy walked in. He's downstairs now."

"I hope he don't come up here, we got too many of those already," another voice responded.

I wondered who the new brother was, hoping he wasn't a punk someone would turn into a sweet kid.

When supper was called, I pushed my way to the front of the line as usual. Things went silent then, so I knew something was up.

"Who's the rock?"

The tone was threatening, but I didn't turn around. I didn't even tense up. I was used to being called out.

"The tall guy at the front of the line. What of it?" someone shouted.

"He'll be my sweet kid before the night is over," came the answer

Some of the guys chuckled, and I chose that moment to set the tone.

"Let the floor hockey whistle be the bell, fool."

When I turned around I was stunned to see it was the new black guy who came in that day.

"Brother," I said, "I'm going to fuck you up real good, so get ready." I heard his name was Johnny Bayliss.

The fight was set in stone. An excitement swept through our unit, knowing a really good fight was about to break the monotony of the daily routine. I would have attacked him then and there, but I didn't want to go back to the hole. Fighting during gym sports like floor hockey was legal. I could wait.

In preparation, I ate lightly. It's no good fighting on a full stomach, and anyone could see that this Johnny knew how to handle himself. He was coal black, in shape with the strong legs of a track star. I wasn't happy about going up against a brother, but I knew we had to fight and I was going to fight to win.

After supper we went back to our cells and I heard Johnny out on the range, making friends. That wasn't hard to do because a lot of guys on the range didn't like me. It was in their interest to have a new tough friend.

As soon as I heard the call: "Gym up!" I headed for the recreation area, knowing I couldn't afford to lose and hoping I didn't kill this new brother in the process.

When I got to the gym, I picked up a floor hockey stick and walked toward Johnny. He had a stick in his hand, too. He pretended to play with the floor hockey ring. As I neared, he surprised me with his speed – cracking me a good one on the head.

My defence was offence. I attacked, hitting him over and over with my stick while he blocked and moved. We went at each other until our sticks were nothing more than scattered pieces on the gym floor.

Then I was on him, with feet, fists and elbows. We were rolling on the floor, fighting like wild dogs. The gym was filled with cheers.

I made a move, pulling Johnny's ear close to my mouth as though I was going to bite it off. Instead, I hissed: "Brother, all these white boys sure are getting a kick out of us putting on a show."

Johnny instantly stopped fighting and looked at me as though he had just awakened from a deep sleep. "Then let me the fuck up."

I relaxed my grip and we got up slowly.

"Where you from?" I asked.

"Windsor. Who are you?"

I told him my name and that I was from Toronto's west end and that my people were Nova Scotian.

We slapped hands and that was it. Seeing the disappointed faces of the white boys, I knew we'd done the right thing by stopping.

Johnny and I began our friendship playing chess, sharing childhood stories, and putting anyone in their place that even hinted at a racist gaze.

We became the prison track stars, the fastest in the institutional system. Both of us qualified for the southwestern Ontario track championships, me in the high jump and 250-yard dash and Johnny in the 100-yard dash.

Although we lost that competition to athletes who were properly trained, Johnny became a friend for life and a partner in crime for the next several decades. He didn't stay in Glendale long but he did something for me that expanded my intellect tenfold and informed my life.

Johnny had a cousin who had spent a stint. Before he left, he heard that Johnny had been arrested, so he left a box of books for him in the prison library. Johnny shared them with me.

I didn't just read the books, I studied them. *Black Skin, White Masks* by Frantz Fanon and *Black Boy* by Richard Wright – I read the pages off those books. They taught me how to live as a black man in a racist society from various social, political and economic vantage points that I'd never been exposed to.

The source of all my discipline, from then until now, is in *Soul On Ice* by Eldridge Cleaver.

From Cleaver I learned how to conduct myself inside. Everything he did, I did – he went to school, he did his exercises, he told the people around him to leave him alone or he'd kill them – I did the same and guys backed off.

This Cleaver-inspired discipline made me successful, if you can consider the sum of my career, in and out of jail, a success.

The same discipline kept me out of trouble in a world of danger. I knew men who were slaves to drugs and would do anything to get some. I knew men who were slaves to pussy, as addicted as any junkie, spending every cent. Not me.

I only broke with Cleaver when he talked about raping black women as a prelude to raping white women.

That's wrong in every way.

I have never raped, or beaten a woman. My lack of aggression toward women is from my instinctive interest in them: the way they move, the pressure they put upon the earth, the energy that radiates from them That might have been because of my respect for my mother and many aunts, or it might have been the message of the Sixties to respect your revolutionary sister.

When Johnny left he promised we'd meet in Toronto once I got out. So there I was again, lonely and cut off, miserable without an ally, with nothing but my strength and my wits to keep me going. I dreamed of finding an Angela Davis-style revolutionary sister. I figured on getting Johnny's help crossing the border at Windsor into the United States. It was a fleeting thought but it hung there.

Something had to give, and one day I just snapped and made up my mind to get out of there. I made my move in the morning when I reported for mandatory, once-a-month kitchen duty.

The head of the kitchen was a man who had been a top chef at Toronto's elegant Royal York Hotel. He was retired, but he lived close to the prison and he was unhappy about not working at his trade, so he asked if he could teach us kids to cook and bake.

Every kid in the place got a cake on his birthday and they were as good as cake gets. The chef was friendly and polite. He loved teaching us what he knew about the inner workings of the world's best hotel kitchens.

It was a foggy Monday morning and I got to the kitchen early, around 5 a.m. I waited for the chef, ready to greet him with a plan that would make this day different from any other in his life.

I watched him open the walk-in freezer door and enter. As usual, he left his keys in the lock. Quick as could be, I closed the door behind him and snapped the lock shut. He banged on the door, asking to be let out.

"I'm taking off," I told him in a voice just loud enough for him to hear.

"At least you could have left me a coat."

I didn't want to freeze him to death. I liked him more than any other staff member in the place.

"I'll turn up the thermostat."

"No, no, don't do that. Someone will be by in a minute. Just take off. You won't last long, running around this area."

What he didn't realize was that I had his car keys. I also had the key to his office so I could turn off the alarm. He never left his office unlocked and now here I was in it alone and in charge. I wasn't about to get caught running around some small town looking for a place to hide – been there, done that.

I unlocked the back door of the kitchen and stepped outside. The morning fog was so thick I could barely see the cars in the parking lot only twenty feet away.

I did see well enough to find his car. It was a big blue Ford Marquis – the poor man's Cadillac – and a bit too flashy for a getaway car. I figured

I could ditch it and get another in the next town. I hopped in and turned the key. All was good; the cops would have to wait for the fog to clear before they started searching the fields and roads around the prison. A least, that's what I thought.

I hit the highway as fast as I could, but as the fog began to lift I was exposed to anyone driving past me. I figured I'd better do what I could to look older than my fifteen years. So I picked a butt out of the ashtray, stuck it in my mouth and slid the chef's sunglasses on. Passing car after car, I was putting as much distance between Glendale and me as I could.

An hour away from town, a cop car pulled up beside me with his siren blaring and lights on. He waved his revolver, motioning me to pull over.

That's not how I planned to give up.

I hit the gas pedal hard but less than a minute later – with the car veering dangerously – a posse of cruisers boxed me in. All I could do was skid to a halt.

There would be no glass booth this time and no hole. On the way back to Glendale, I lay on the floor of the prison station wagon, hands cuffed behind my back, while the guard in the passenger's seat got up on his knees and did his best to teach me who was the boss. Using the butt end of a baseball bat to inflict as much pain as he could, he dug and churned it into my stomach, legs, back and balls.

I wish he had just hit me in the head and knocked me out but I had to listen to his vitriolic pontificating about my smart-ass attitude, my colour and the punitive tax burden required to maintain incorrigible kids like me. Like my father had done years earlier when he whipped me for squirting water at a white man, this guard punctuated each statement with a blow or a grinding poke. I wanted to kill him.

Later on that day, bruised and filled with rage, I was taken to the warden's office. I heard him talking calmly to my mother on the phone, telling her how I'd been picked up and was okay. When he finished on the phone he leaped up, pointing at me and screaming: "Take this asshole straight to the max in Guelph and let's be done with him; don't take his cuffs off and don't stop for anything."

I wanted to put it to him, "Warden, what good is your Ph.D. if you're not going to use it to help me?" but thought I had already pushed past his comfort zone.

On the road to Guelph I sat in the back of the now-familiar station wagon. Once we got into the city, I memorized every street as we headed for the reformatory, in case I need to be free again.

The facility at Guelph was an entirely different story. There was an adult prison across from it and both had barred cells like you see in the movies. Off the top, everyone had to spend three weeks in the hole. There were only forty-eight of us at the Hillcrest Training School, which accommodated boys from seven to seventeen who had proven themselves the hardest of cases. Without a doubt, it was a no-nonsense training school. As a matter of policy, they let us fight things out on the spot rather than let things fester.

In a way, this created a kind of economics.

For example, you couldn't smoke in jail, but the guards liked to lock down the ranges now and then and watch us fight. I guess it relieved their boredom. One day, I asked one of the guards if I could get a TM – a tailor-made cigarette – if I fought one of the tougher guys from another range. This was a risk. You could get sent to the hole for trying to bribe a guard, but he liked the idea. The fight was set.

After that, every week I was able to fight for cigarettes, which I could then barter for pop or candy. Getting those smokes got me lots of respect from guys who hadn't had a smoke in months.

I only lost once while I was there.

Owen, Junior and many others from my family and from the Projects ended up in the big jail a mile away. It had 1,200 inmates who were all serving two years less a day. I could see their prison from my cell. Naturally, we communicated. I got lots of kites – notes that kept me up to date on family in prison and outside – and they were sent in a variety of ways; messages were stuffed in food containers, in laundry carts, even in loaves of bread and jugs of milk. The warden finally asked my father to take me to visit Owen and Junior to ask them to stop sending me kites. It seems that food products containing foreign objects were deemed contaminated and disposed of, which was costing the institution too much money.

I spent eight months in Guelph, studying, fighting and minding my own business. They had an excellent English teacher, Ms. Rose, who took me on passes to participate in public speaking competitions. A child psychologist talked with me. Many compassionate guards helped out with community recreation programs and work programs, such as spending a couple of weeks at maple sugar farm. These attempts to modify my delinquent behaviour found their mark.

Finally, I guess they figured I was cured of whatever criminality had brought me there in the first place and they told me they were letting me go.

The timing was fortunate. I had been so bored, and so lonely, that I seriously considered knifing someone as soon as I turned sixteen, so that they'd be forced to send me into the adult system. I needed to be with familiar faces – friends and family – people who knew me and understood me.

Before I left, the warden called me to his office to give me a speech about doing the right thing. He was tall and elderly with decades of dealing with tough teenagers behind him. "Follow me," he said, and we went to one of the empty classrooms on the second floor. He sat me down and gave me a pep talk. I still remember what he said.

"Richard, you're smart enough and tough enough to be anything you want to be in this world, but there's little we can do to help you here in this facility. You have to come up with a plan that will guide you into the future.

"If you choose crime, how can we stop you? The prison next door is filled with your friends and family. But I'm betting you won't choose crime. I'm betting that you'll use that brain in your head and strive to stay out of prisons like this one. That choice is up to you, and you alone."

I don't know if he was betting, but he was certainly hoping. With that, he stood up, shook my hand and wished me good luck.

Free at last, free at last.

I walked out of jail, and into my father's waiting white-on-white 1963 Chrysler. I didn't look back as we drove away. My main concern was getting some money.

In prison, I had earned a whopping thirty cents a week, which was used to pay for candies and toiletries. It took three weeks to save enough for a bottle of shampoo. So, I had no savings. All I had in my pocket was a provincial probation order to go see my probation officer, Lou Taylor.

The drive home was awkward.

Sonny was disappointed in me. I thought he was hypocritical. He was not a thief but every now and then he'd buy stolen goods. He wasn't a rat but he beat the hell out of us if he thought we were stealing. I was often beaten for hanging around with my cousins, because my mother and father thought they were bad influences.

They had no idea.

A few of my aunts and uncles were rounders and hustlers. A few of their children grew up to become pimps, whores, thieves and armed robbers. But the truth is that I became the leader of my generation of Afro-Metis in Toronto by turning to crime to get a piece of the proverbial Canadian pie.

I learned fearlessness and other leadership tools in jail. I learned from observing Sonny, not from talking to him and not from him teaching me. We were never close like that. If he really knew what was going on, he'd have known that my cousins should have been beaten for hanging around with me.

As the countryside rolled by, Sonny tried to convince me of the virtues of being a square john and leading a clean life. While he was talking, a Molson's beer truck skidded as it turned onto an overpass high above the 401 highway and it rolled in front of us, spilling hissing kegs of beer.

Sonny jerked the car hard right and left to avoid hitting the kegs. When we stopped and went back to see what had happened, we saw that the driver had been thrown clear of the truck to the highway below, obviously dead.

Whoever he was, he was just trying to do his job. He expected to get home at the end of the day. Death was his reward for being a square john.

So, what difference did it make, I thought, as I looked down at his broken body?

We pulled into Alexandra Park, and I breathed deeply, enjoying the familiar stench of the inner city, glad to be away from the clean country air.

I walked into the depths of the Projects and stopped dead in my tracks: there was a girl I knew standing in her doorway, as lovely as ever. I'd had a soft spot for her. She had her back to me. I called her name. She looked over her shoulder at me and her smile lit up the sky.

When she turned around to face me I could see that she was eight months' pregnant. I was dumbstruck. Later, I found out that the father was one of my friends.

The buddies I had left behind came out to take a look at me. They were all a year older. Some had just been released from adult prison, others had good jobs and would soon leave the gang. For some there was nothing to do but hope for better times ahead with the gang they'd known since childhood.

After his stint in the Ontario Reformatory, everyone called Owen Crookendale "The Crook."

"Welcome back to Hell," he said, greeting me with an impish grin and handing me an expensive knife. Then everybody slapped hands or patted me on the back. My reputation as a solid guy was secure.

Crime is a gamble: some win, but most don't. I saw myself as a winner and I was pretty sure I was going to roll the dice again, even if the probation order in my pocket forbade me from hanging out with guys who didn't respect the law.

I had to be careful if I wanted to stay out of reform school before my eighteenth birthday. I also had to get some money, get some clothes, and find a girlfriend.

Naturally, I hung out with the same guys I'd grown up with, but three new guys came into the Projects for us to befriend.

Everett was a smooth-talking, light-skinned teenager who I met on a school trip to Buxton; a rural community that had black roots similar to Africville in Nova Scotia where some of my relatives lived. He was an amateur boxer, but he was more confident with the knife he carried than he was with his fists. He'd only been in Toronto a week when he met my cousin Marlene. He quickly became her pimp and remained so for the next several years.

Brian Bush was tall, slim, dark brown and athletic. He also had a way with the ladies, and he seemed smarter than most of the crowd in the Projects. His father hung out at my father's bar years earlier, which helped him fit in.

Like me, Brian had a white mother but he didn't live with her. He survived on the street by wits and cunning. He might have been black and unemployed, but lived better than most of us off of the crime available in the Spadina area. He carried a straight razor and had no fear of using it.

In addition to his quick wit, Brian was paranoid – a combination that kept the rest of us alert and busy analyzing the relationships we developed with anyone who came into contact with us. He quickly became a major influence in the gang.

Then my great friend Johnny Bayliss from Glendale showed up. Johnny was like a brother to me. He was renting an apartment near the University of Toronto. I gave him a solid gold, single-shot .22 calibre derringer when he got married. Owen and I stole the derringer from a gun shop on Yonge Street. Guns are better than toaster ovens.

Johnny's wife was a beautiful university student. One night they got into a heated argument that drew the police. He was busted with the golden gun – landing him in jail for thirty days and leaving him with an adult record.

That arrest would haunt us both years later.

Knowing that I needed a car to find a job, my father gave me his Chrysler. A bunch of us piled in and rode around for the day. I woke up in the morning to the siren sounds of fire trucks racing into the Projects. Someone had torched my car.

I became suspicious of everyone and offered a reward for the arsonist, vowing to set him on fire if I found him. It's a good thing I never did.

Before the smoke cleared, the Dorsey brothers from Blind River came to town, wanting to make friends. To me, anything north of Sudbury was the North Pole. I didn't think black people lived that far north.

They were country boys, who grew up using guns to hunt. Guys who knew how to use guns were needed in the Projects in those days, so they had no trouble fitting in.

Levern Dorsey and I became lifelong friends. We rented an apartment together in Little Italy. Soon after, Everett, Junior and Owen moved in. Before long we'd filled every nook and cranny in the place with guns.

With so many armed teenaged boys in the building, none of the neighbourhood tough guys dared to mess with us. We didn't have to worry about anyone breaking in or harassing the girls who came to see us.

Levern loved to till-tap – stealing money out of cash registers while storeowners were momentarily distracted by some ploy.

Our attitude was that everything white people owned was rightfully ours. There was even a slogan for it: "All the white man has belongs to the black man."

We firmly believed that the police and the government existed simply to protect all that had been stolen from us during hundreds of years our slavery.

In the summer of my sixteenth birthday, Sonny tried to get me some legitimate work. He worked on the docks as a stevedore that year. Each morning he went down to the shipyards and stood in line with hundreds of other strong men, hoping to be picked for work that day so he could put food on the table for his family.

I went along out of curiosity and to appease my father for all that he had done for me while I was locked up. I already had more than a day's wages in my pocket that I had stolen the day before from a store till.

We stood in line, father and son amid a throng of hungry men. Within seconds I heard, "Sonny, is that man with you?" My father nodded with a little smirk on his face and off we went through the gate to one of the huge ships anchored there.

The work was steady; it was hard, done by hard men. It could be dangerous but it paid well and was treasured work among those who lined up for it. I knew my dad had connections and wanted me to go further than him. However, his idea of a good blue-collar job as a measurement of success wasn't my idea of success.

All morning I kept wondering how the hell was I going to get out of working beside my father loading and unloading heavy boxes deep inside the sweaty, smelly hold of the ship.

I got lucky when one of four chains hoisting a forklift out of the ship's hold broke, sending two tons of metal flying toward the boxes I was stacking. Men shouted and I jumped out of the way, while the skid of boxes was swept to the holding deck far below lined with metal rebar that stood up like iron spikes. We looked down at the boxes speared like shish kabobs.

"You're one lucky son of a gun," said the foreman, slapping me on the back.

The next day my brother, Dwane, took my place at the shipyard. I went to the bank to open an account with the thirty-two bucks I made. There was no ill feeling between my dad and me.

If you look at Atkinson family photos from Nova Scotia, you see a strong native influence. I consider myself Afro-Metis. It fits me better than mixed race and certainly sounds better than half-breed. The historical differences between my black and native brothers are that the blacks had better resistance to white diseases, worked hard by nature and were imprisoned and forced to work at gun point in a strange land. In contrast, my red brothers were nearly wiped off the face of the earth through warfare, disease and outright murder.

If I suffered any guilt about the thefts I habitually committed, I rationalized it. The native in me whispered that white people could afford to lose a little of what they stole. The black man in me complained that they owed me centuries worth of back pay. The white man in me tried to arbitrate: "Why can't we all just get along and steal together?"

There was another rationalization, derived from reading – this one from Thomas Edison. "Everybody steals in commerce and industry. I've stolen myself. But I know how to steal."

If it was good enough for him, it was good enough for me. There were also multitudes of honest people lining up to buy our stolen goods. We walked the neighbourhood, till-tapping at every opportunity. Over time, we stole thousands of dollars just on our way home from school.

Yes, I was back in high school.

We stuck our noses in factories, on the pretence of looking for work, knowing that black teens with Afros were unlikely to get factory work. In actuality, we weren't asking for jobs. We were casing places, looking at, manipulating and testing alarm systems so that we could come back later and break in, stealing clothes or anything else we could fence.

What we treasured most were the guns we sometimes came across. Levern soon had so many guns he became a dealer. Some of the guns we sold to an arms dealer who worked for mob boss Paul Volpe, known as The Fox.

I got to know Chucky Yanover better in jail, years later, where he regaled me with stories of the international arms trade.

Our gang spent some time ripping off drug dealers in Rochdale College, a residence of the University of Toronto.

At the time, in the late Sixties, Rochdale was the place to be for sex, drugs and rock 'n' roll. Thousands of white, middle-class kids passed through there every month, as if it were Mecca. There were love-ins and lots of white girls loved big, black, inner city tough guys.

Let's face it, hippies were easy marks. We were so busy robbing them that the hippies enlisted a motorcycle club, The Vagabonds, to protect them from gangs like ours. Eventually, there was a meeting and we were asked not to enter Rochdale if we were armed, putting an end to our easy pickings.

The temperature of the times might have been peace and love, but there was also plenty of love and hate. One afternoon I was walking along Dundas with Owen the Crook when I noticed a line of cop cars in front of the wall that ran along the Projects.

Owen chuckled. "Good time to take one of those pigs and kick his head in."

I said, "I'd rather shoot one from a couple of blocks away with my sniper rifle."

We approached slowly, to see what was going on. There was a crowd gathered by the cars and, as we got closer I heard the voice of my aunt Babes, screaming.

I pushed to the edge of the crowd.

A couple of cops were dragging Babes by the hair along the sidewalk toward their car. She was a big woman, full of struggle. The crowd was crazy, seeing her treated as if she were a rabid dog.

Some cops had their guns out, pointing them at the crowd, warning people not to get close. Other cops beat my aunt with their nightsticks while they dragged her along.

My cousin Dewey was in the crowd, sobbing. He told me that his brother, Wade, pushed Bert Novis through a plate-glass window in the building next to their house. Novis was trying to arrest him and Wade ran upstairs to a friend's apartment on the fourth floor with the cops in pursuit.

Wade jumped out the window – landing hard – but he didn't break any bones and limped away. Then the cops went to my aunt's house in the Projects, where they broke down the door and began tearing the place apart.

Babes' husband, my uncle Frankie, was a postman who organized a baseball league to help get kids off the street. He assumed he could reason with the cops. He assumed wrong. They beat him unconscious in his doorway.

Babes, who was loud at the quietest of times and tougher than Frankie at all times, came running to his aid. They beat her down as well. Now they were dragging her off and I could see uncle Frankie in the back seat of a cruiser with his cuffed hands around his head.

I ran home to tell my father, but the news travelled faster than I did. I found my father pushing little bullets into a pearl-handled .22 pistol, the one I'd used the night I shot over the head of the plainclothes officer when I was fourteen.

"This is war, Ricky," he told me. I breathed a sigh of satisfaction. War was what I wanted. Meanwhile, the crowd outside was growing and I knew some of them were carrying weapons. One of our white neighbours kept yelling: "Remember Kent State!"

Just then, a native guy who lived around the corner came walking down the street with two shotguns propped up on his shoulders. He was walking slowly, swaying a little.

"What side you folks on?" he asked.

My father said, "We're on whatever side you're on, friend."

The big native nodded in agreement and kept on walking to the corner of Denison Avenue and Dundas, where two passing cop cars skidded to a halt. They swarmed him, disarmed him and hauled him away.

The crowd did not want to quit and I eagerly joined them. It grew larger as the sun went down and their hatred for the police grew, fuelled in some cases by alcohol. When a streetcar came barrelling along the tracks, someone threw a rock and soon a crowd of people were throwing a hailstorm of stones at the streetcar. The riders inside hit the floor and cries of terror flooded through the open windows.

A radio station put out a bulletin warning people that Dundas Street between Bathurst and Spadina was closed because a streetcar had left the tracks.

That was right but it wasn't the whole story. There was no mention in the bulletin of the cops running wild, no mention of any racial trouble and no mention of a hundred or more angry people – black and white – screaming for revenge.

Is that not racism? Black lives didn't matter then.

I noticed my parole officer, Lou Taylor, walking around, talking to some of the guys he had on his caseload and trying to be an instrument of peace. He stopped to talk to me, unaware that I had a .38 Smith & Wesson tucked under my coat and a knife hidden in my boot. He warned me that I had a curfew and couldn't stay out all night.

When the police formed a protective line, I took off down a laneway and stopped by a musty old garage. I snapped the lock with the blade of my knife, climbed a ladder and went inside to retrieve a canvas bag from behind some loose boards. In the laneway, I pulled out what I'd been looking for – an 8mm German sniper rifle with a scope.

I'd bought it a few months earlier using a stolen ID and hid it for a moment just like this. I knew those laneways cold. I was safe as long as I kept my head down.

I headed for a row of stores and houses on Kensington, climbing fences and leaping along rooftops until I was leaning over the edge of a brick wall, looking down on the crowd and the cops, about 200 yards away. I pulled back the bolt, chambered a shell and flicked off the safety, pressing my cheek against the stock and peering through the scope. Suddenly, it was as if everyone was only inches away. I scanned the crowd, looking for that special someone, knowing that if I did pull the trigger I could get off the roof and across Spadina Avenue before anyone knew what had happened.

Out of nowhere, I heard the roar of the motorcycles. Some thirty black bikers wearing patches from Buffalo, New York, rode up two-by-two, led by my uncle Glen. The crowd cheered and the cops began looking nervous.

Soon, a familiar brown car drove rounded the corner on Dundas not far from the public school. I pulled the rifle tight against my shoulder to steady it, breathing slowly and rhythmically. Four detectives got out of the car. I had what I wanted: Bert Novis, at my mercy.

Novis scanned the crowd and the nearby rooftops, knowing that we often climbed up high to throw bricks and rocks down at them. He didn't look in my direction. He wouldn't have seen me anyway.

But I could see him perfectly.

I adjusted the scope and lined up his big pink face in my sights. I had all the excuse I needed – the cops had beaten my aunt. As I cupped the trigger with my finger, my father, along with Bob Ellis from St. Christopher House and a couple of community leaders, stepped forward and began to talk to the detectives. Damn.

There was my father shaking hands with Bert Novis. Shit. Another cop car pulled up. Novis opened the door and out stepped Babes and Frankie, looking around nervously. Shit again.

My father and Bob Ellis had negotiated the release of my aunt and uncle, saving the city of Toronto from a bloody wake-up call. Unwittingly, my father had also saved Bert Novis's life.

I tucked my handgun inside a small chimney and slid off the roof with the rifle. A quirk of the law at the time meant that if I'd been stopped, frisked and found with a handgun, I'd have been sent straight back to the juvie slammer. The rifle? No problem, as long as I could prove I was sixteen.

I wasn't going to take a chance, so I put it back in its hiding place. The neighbourhood was quiet afterward; the way a house is when there's been a blow-up between a husband and wife.

But not all the tension was gone.

A few days after the near-bloodshed, my friend Demetro strolled into the Projects to check out his old crew. I hadn't seen him since our time together at the Bowmanville School for Boys. Always the bully, Everett took offence.

"We don't want any honkies not from around here, hanging around here, not any more. There's too much shit going down, too many people talking to the cops, too many of us niggers going down."

He drew his knife and challenged Demetro to a fight, then and there. The big Ukrainian wasn't afraid but he didn't know how the rest of us would react if he stood up for himself. He looked at me to see if I would back him up.

I said nothing. If we really were on the verge of a race war, I wanted to keep my position clear. So I lost an old friend, Demetro, as a result of the hatred felt by a new friend, Everett.

That's life in a gang.

THE PANTHERS AND ME

Levern and I were doing well in school. I was always good in the class-room, even when I was hanging out at after-hours clubs until 2:00 a.m. How did I do it? How quickly one can forget. I was a teenager and I could party all night long and still get up in the morning.

I excelled in social studies, in and out of the classroom. I wasn't very good at math – to this day, I rely on a calculator – but I nailed my other courses because I did my homework. I suppose it sounds odd. I had guns, and I was living a very adult life with serious shit going on all around me, but that's a trademark – I do my homework.

I studied as much as I did because I thought school was fun. I never looked on it as non-fun. I always hauled big books around. I even read textbooks, especially when I was in the training school. I wasn't showing off; a novel lasts a day or two, but a textbook lasts a week.

I did not drop out of school. I was taken out of school by the cops.

There were days when one or the other of our gang pulled up to Central High School of Commerce in a stolen car, wearing flashy stolen clothes. I was often armed, but only once did I pull a gun in school.

A kid named Tommy Basker ran into the dressing room, shouting that Levern was in a beef with someone. I trusted Tommy, figured it was seri-ous because he'd backed us in fights since Grade One. I went to look.

Levern and an older black man were circling each other. The man had a knife in his hand, while Levern was armed with a broken pop bottle that his girlfriend, Candace, gave him. I knew something was seriously not right because Candace was crying, and she never cried about anything. Then it hit me – the older man was her father.

I knew I had to do something before things got ugly. I pulled out my gun.

"Old man, this shit stops now or I'll blow off your kneecaps."

The old man put his knife away and walked off. There was a sadness about him. He'd just lost his daughter to the street.

Eventually, the guys I knew in school began dropping out. Every week, more of them chose to get their education in the nightclubs downtown; playing with the girls and keeping their eyes on the older pimps, the robbers, the players and the hustlers.

Home away from home for all of us was the Paramount Hotel, a club that catered to the Nova Scotian community. There were crap games at the Paramount day and night, on the sidewalk out front and behind the bar. Seasoned criminals sat there with their backs to the walls, guns loaded, even if they were simply there to visit.

If you were a stranger, you'd have thought you'd entered a den full of the most dangerous animals in the world. Although there were often fights and sometimes knifings and shootings, nobody ever called the cops.

When the Paramount was slow, or the band wasn't lively, we went to Club Jamaica on Yonge Street, south of Dundas. A man named Fitz owned it and the food – cooked by an old Jamaican woman – was as good as it could be.

Fitz was homosexual. He let girls hang around the club to act as honey for the boys. One of the girls who served drinks was a young woman named Diane. She was Nova Scotian, pretty and light-skinned.

She would eventually give birth to my three children.

Fitz had problems with pickpockets and purse stealers in the club. He liked me because I wouldn't take shit from anybody, so he asked me if I wanted to work for him, getting things cleaned up.

I wasn't old enough to drink, but if I took the job I'd be bouncing in one of the biggest clubs in the city. I agreed without giving the matter much thought.

There was an additional benefit – with the job came a key, and the key meant we could use the club late at night when no one was around.

The actual job was simple enough. I stood at the door with a hatchet under my coat and a gun in my belt. I'd tell the guys who I thought were stealing that they had better stop or I'd cut off their hands, like it says to do in the Koran. Now and then, I flashed my gun to back up my threat.

Within days, the stealing stopped. Word spread, and soon people of all colours began packing the place, listening to reggae and Motown and eating the best Jamaican food in the city.

Ten apartments were available in an old three-storey building on Euclid Avenue in the Little Italy area. The apartments came with a huge basement, shared kitchen and a shared bathroom on each floor. We rented all of the apartments, taking over the building.

Unfortunately, we were evicted because Everett was dumb enough to fire off his gun inside his room just as the landlord was collecting rent. He kicked all of us out.

Levern and I ended up taking an apartment in the east end, across the street from Regent Park, next to the Gerrard Hotel. It was not unfamiliar to me – the Gerrard was to the east end as the Paramount was to the west end.

There were good reasons for moving east. The best one being that we thought Bert Novis would hassle us less if we were outside of the boundaries of 14 Division.

At that time – although it seems peculiar now – anyone in Canada could own a rifle of any kind, as long as the weapon was thirty-two inches or longer. I'd often go to a hardware store and ask for a shotgun, a hacksaw, a pair of gloves and a ski mask, paying anywhere from twenty to fifty dollars for the kit. I'd leave without any thought of being arrested.

Of course, even then, no one could own a handgun without a licence. We carried handguns anyway, because the penalty was only a month or two in jail. The theory was that it was better to have a gun and take the risk of getting caught than to not have a gun and need one to save your life.

My father had already told me that I was old enough to run into trouble because of the colour of my skin and I ought to be prepared to defend myself properly. He never flat out said I should break the law. He simply gave me permission to do what I had to do to defend myself. His words: "Son, I'd rather visit you in jail than visit you in your grave."

No need to elaborate.

In addition to doing well in school, I was also enjoying basketball – Central Commerce went to the city finals when I was in Grade Ten. I kept trying to make sense of what I was learning in class and what I was learning on the streets. Sometimes the two worlds blurred, like when I'd pat my pocket in class only to realize I'd brought a gun.

One day Levern ran up to me during basketball practice. He was ecstatic and could hardly contain himself.

"I got some good news, brother." I thought he'd come up with an easy way to make money.

"What's up?"

"There's a Black Panther recruiter in town. He wants to meet you."

"Meet me? How does he even know I exist?"

"I told him all about you. You're just the guy to lead us in the revolution. We need a strong brother to go up against the pigs." He forced his face close to mine, eyes bulging, excited. "You got to meet this guy."

I knew about the Panthers, everyone did. Non-violent student leader Rocky Jones had started a chapter in Halifax, so there was a Nova Scotia connection. We all knew about the death of Chicago activist Fred Hampton and how the FBI had declared war on the party. Eldridge Cleaver was on the run for killing a cop. Party co-founders Bobby Seale and Huey P. Newton were in jail. I also knew about the Panthers' social programs, and their commitment to protect and help the poor. The positives outweighed the negatives.

"He wants to hook up with us tomorrow after school, at the Brunswick House bar." I turned it over once or twice more in my mind and then agreed.

Levern said, "Right on, brother, you ain't going to regret this. We have the fucking Panther Party behind us. The pigs ain't going to fuck with us anymore."

I spent the night thinking things through. Maybe the Panthers were my ticket out, away from all the problems that seemed to be weighing me down. That night I slept with my rifle close in my bed. I'm not kidding.

The next day, school dragged on. I couldn't concentrate. When the final bell rang, I raced up to Bloor Street, hailed a cab and rode over to the bar. Like in the movies, I entered to the sound of the blues – a recording of Sonny Boy Williamson on the harmonica.

Looking around the main floor of the beer hall, I spotted Levern's huge Afro. He was sitting with his back to the door. Staring at me was an older man, perhaps fifty years of age. He watched me as I scanned for cops before I approached them, seeming to approve of my caution.

Levern slapped my hand in greeting and introduced the man as Clay. I sat down next to him.

"What state you from?" I asked.

"Maryland. Been there before?"

"No. Is Clay your real name?" I asked because I didn't like using nicknames when meeting people.

"My name is Warren Hart," he replied. "Brother, I'll get to the point. We need a place for our people to hide. Lee, here, says you can get identification and apartments to rent."

ID was no problem. Most of the prostitutes we knew always seemed to have a wallet they'd stolen from some trick. Hart leaned in close.

"Brother, Lee says you can get a hold of guns and we need all the guns we can get."

It was a lot like the movies, everything steely cool; every word and gesture carefully weighed.

"What's in it for us?"

"I can teach you everything there is to know about military tactics. I can show you how to protect yourself in any situation. I'm an explosives expert and I can teach you about bombs. I can even teach both of you how to do counter-surveillance on the police."

My eyebrows rose at that.

And then he said, "I can teach you to be a man among men. But you got to measure up. Do you measure up, Ricky?"

Just then, I heard Sonny Boy singing in the background, *Don't let your right hand know what your left hand is doing.* I smiled at the coincidence.

"I can do what has to be done, nothing more, nothing less."

Hart raised his glass, and then he turned to Levern. "He's everything you said he'd be. The Party needs you two brothers."

Levern ordered another orange juice for me, while Hart finished his beer. The three of us grew quiet as some long-haired, college types took a table near us.

"I start classes tomorrow," said Hart in a whisper. "Be there, and bring some good people." With that, he got up and walked out.

When he was gone, I whispered to Levern, "Brother, we can use some of the stuff he knows." Levern jumped up, slapped my hands. "Damn right."

That meeting had consequences. I went on to become the leader of the Dirty Tricks Gang. Levern's path eventually led him to spend fifteen years in Canada's crack military unit, the Black Watch.

The next day after school, Owen the Crook, Brian, my brother Dwane, Everett, Levern, his girlfriend, Candace, and I all walked into Warren Hart's small apartment. I was carrying a small gym bag with ten handguns in it.

Sitting next to Warren was a red-haired, big-breasted white woman with a briefcase on her lap. Warren introduced her as his revolutionary front woman. Her name was Margaret Morgan. She looked like the typical suburban, middle-class adherent to radical politics.

I thought she and Hart didn't match.

Levern handed the gym bag to Hart. He zipped it open and whistled. Then he touched Morgan's arm and she opened her briefcase.

Inside there was a hand grenade, as well as a couple of small grey tubes with yellow, military-style writing on them. I took the grenade to get the feel of it and passed it to the others. Then I pointed to the grey tubes.

"What are those?"

"You know what they are, Richard."

I picked one up. "Bombs."

Hart smiled, and then he removed a large flip chart, revealing the instructions for how to make a bomb and what kinds of explosives we might use.

After demolition school that night, I asked Dwane what he thought of our Black Panther leader. My brother laughed uneasily. "I don't trust the guy. There's something up with him." He dropped out of bomb-making class that night.

As for the rest of the gang, Owen showed up drunk once and was suspended indefinitely. Everett was happy enough living off my cousin Marlene's prostitution business. He came to class one night and explained to the Black Panther that making war didn't put any money in his pocket but making love did. He dropped out, too.

The rest of us stayed in the BPP bomb school.

During the day, I was in Central Commerce math class. In the evening, I went to terrorist class. Our textbook was *The Anarchist Cookbook*. At night, I'd finish my schooling in the bars and the after-hours clubs.

I was leading a triple life.

Hart would not let us take notes. He drilled us on the need for secrecy. He told us he'd given lessons to the Weather Underground, a group of white university radicals who were actively blowing up buildings. He taught other Black Panther chapters and gave the same lessons to us.

To emphasize his credentials, he pulled out a photo taken in Vietnam. There were a few hundred white soldiers posing in a secured bunker area. In the centre of the photo was a single black face. He handed me a magnifying glass and there he was.

Captain Warren Hart.

"All those guys were under my command."

He showed me clippings from the newspapers and articles about how he'd started a Black Panther's chapter in Baltimore. He taught us police and military tactics and he showed us how to avoid traps. All of these lessons would come in useful later on in life. For homework, he gave us army manuals to read.

To build up an arsenal, Levern and I broke into an army surplus store on Queen Street and loaded a van with .30 calibre M1 rifles, along with bullets, gas masks and other assorted weaponry.

We also began to bring Hart the money we were making from cracking safes and stealing, convinced that all of it was going to the Black Panther Party.

Along the way, Hart taught us how to earn respect in the community. He told us to set an example for others.

"Don't do dope. Don't get drunk in public. Walk proudly. And never, ever back down from anyone. Know that your comrades will back you up in any situation, but don't put anyone on the spot unnecessarily, and remember that every group needs a leader."

That's smart advice in any walk of life, but on the street it was even more important. He also told the others, "Rick is my Number Two. You listen to him."

His most important advice was serious stuff for a high-school kid.

"Never show fear in front of the police, no matter the situation. Kill the pig if you have to, but never bow down to authority, or you will lose all you've worked for with one act of cowardice."

Some memories from that time come back to me like movie scenes. One Christmas, I was looking out the window at the lightly falling snow. Down below, I could see a set of footprints leading away from the building across Gerrard Street and into Regent Park, almost like a greeting card.

I checked my closet. I had ten rifles in there and I knew my brother or Levern had access to them. I had checked them previously for safety reasons, leaving only one loaded and ready if needed. The loaded one was missing. Levern was in his bedroom. I asked him where it was and he told me who took it. I smelled trouble and went downstairs. Following the footprints through the snow to a parking lot near Dundas and Sherbourne, I saw a guy with my rifle crouching behind a car. In the snowy distance a cop sat in his cruiser, writing up a report or making note of the weather or something.

As I snuck up behind him, I recognized the black teenager who was holding my rifle. He was from the neighbourhood and I knew one of his eleven siblings. I was quiet and, of course, I was armed.

"What are you doing?"

He grinned.

"I'm going to kill a pig. It's Christmas."

I looked around, no eyes on us. I looked back. Now there were two sets of footprints in the snow leading from my place.

"Gimme the rifle, now."

He handed it over without hesitation, but I thought it was strange the way he giggled. I saved a life that night. Merry Christmas, cop, whoever you are.

I was at a crossroads.

I was one of the top male athletes at Central Commerce. The school was business-oriented, and my gym teacher, Frank French, kept encouraging me to do better in everything. He could see that I was gifted, on and off the sports field. If I stuck with school and put the streets behind me, he insisted that I could get a scholarship to an American university.

He was probably right.

I was getting passing grades without putting in much effort, and I liked being the only boy in a class full of girls. But even as Mr. French was encouraging me, he sensed a change.

I liked the nightlife, and the street life, too much. I'd pay for that the rest of my life. I'm paying for it now. But Mr. French was one of the ones who tried to steer me right.

It was sometime in October 1971, and I was coming home from Grade Nine basketball practice when I found a couple of my friends smoking a joint after school. I asked for a joint to give to Levern. He loved to smoke weed. As I walked around the corner of Parliament onto Gerrard Street, bouncing my basketball, I heard Levern's voice coming from the back of an unmarked police car.

He called out: "The pigs are everywhere, it's a set-up!"

As if to underline the point of our recent activities, he stuck his fist out the window and yelled, "Black power!"

I reached into my pocket to find the joint and ditch it. Suddenly, ten plainclothes cops surrounded me. They were quick to point guns at my head. Loudly and clearly, they told me to take my hands out of my pockets and get down on the ground.

They took me to 51 Division, where I learned that someone had fired a rifle in my apartment. The woman who lived in the apartment upstairs had been sitting on her couch when the bullet tore through it, and then through her ceiling. Who knows where it went after that.

The detectives, having searched my place, passed my rifles around, trying to determine which one had been fired. Handcuffed, Levern and I watched them work. I hadn't done anything wrong, but I wondered what charges would be brought against me.

The cops couldn't tell which of the rifles had been fired without extensive testing, probably because we fired them as often as we could. Sometimes we let them off in Regent Park, not far from their division, in the heart of downtown. Rifles aside, the cops seemed more interested in the Black Panther newspapers I had, and in the stacks of Chairman Mao's *Little Red Book* that we sold on the street.

They didn't threaten us. They didn't call us names. They knew they were our principal enemies. And they knew how serious things had become.

We needed representation. Charles Roach was Toronto's most vocal black lawyer, so we called him. He rushed over to the station and advised the police to let us go, since we were in school when the gun went off.

They let us go, just like that.

We refused to spend our own money on a cab and demanded that the cops drive us home. So it was that Levern and I left the station with our arms full of rifles and boxes of bullets.

We held up the rifles for all to see, shouting black power slogans out the open police car windows.

It's hard – no, it is impossible – to imagine now.

I was still on probation and so I had to explain the situation to my parole officer, Lou Taylor. He was a positive force in the community, and was often in the Projects talking to my father and other community leaders. He helped turn many young kids around, but he had no real influence on me. Since I hadn't done anything illegal, there was little he could do.

Warren Hart was another matter. He berated me for hours for allowing a weapon to be fired unintentionally. He repeated his lessons about gun safety, noting time and again how often soldiers in the field were killed by careless gunplay.

I promised to be more careful.

He seemed more upset about the fact that I'd been caught with a joint. He told me if he ever caught me working on a bomb when I was high, he'd shoot me on the spot for the safety of the others in the room.

The promise I made about gun safety didn't last long. A week or so later, Candace came over to the apartment and stripped a .303 rifle and reassembled it, for practice. Trouble is, she left it loaded, with the safety off, leaning against a bookshelf.

While practicing his karate moves, Levern kicked the bookshelf over and the gun fell over and it went off. This time the bullet went into the apartment below.

The cops came again. They took all my weapons again. This time Charles Roach advised me to forget them. I lost hundreds of dollars' worth of rifles that night, but I knew he was right.

Just before Christmas, Owen was released from jail in Guelph. He needed some quick money to get something nice for his new girlfriend.

The easiest way to get cash was to sell off some of his guns. We headed to the Brunswick for a chat. I asked Owen to show me the gun. As it happened, he had two brand new Smith & Wesson snub nose .38s – one of which was unloaded. He handed the empty one to me while we were downing our second Black Russian.

The booze was having its desired effect and we walked joyfully to the Embassy Tavern at Bloor and Bellair to look for a buyer. I waited outside and Owen went inside to find his man. While I was killing time, a stream of pretty girls walked into the bar on the arms of bikers. I was wearing a black leather maxi-coat and my red jumpsuit with a thick black belt around my waist. My bellbottoms were tucked into my knee-high black boots. To complete the picture, I had a wide-brimmed, black leather hat, trimmed with mink and topped with a big white feather. I caught my reflection in the window of the bar, thinking how foolish a girl had to be to choose a greasy biker over someone as hip as me.

I was biding my time when a biker started to lip off at me. I let him run his mouth because he was too drunk to know what he was saying.

It got to be too much when he staggered over and pushed me, so I cocked my fist and let him have it. He was out cold before he hit the pavement. Suddenly, bikers came pouring out of the bar like angry bees, crowding around and helping their injured brother to his feet.

I made a calculation and pulled the gun out of my coat, pointing it at them and backing away slowly. Some of the bikers were liquored up enough to taunt me, daring me to pull the trigger if I had the balls.

I had plenty of balls, just not much sense. I aimed the gun at the knees of the biggest biker and pulled the trigger. The hammer clicked on an empty chamber. Oops.

"Kill the nigger!"

I started to run, pointing the gun over my shoulder at them, pulling the trigger again and again. At best, there might have been a bullet in the chamber. At worst, a gun aimed in your direction is a powerful visual.

I hit the Bay Street subway station and was stopped by a crowd coming out of the exit. The bikers caught up to me and started throwing punches. I fought back, fleeing downstairs into the subway, running as fast as I could. Without thinking, I leapt off the platform and darted down the tunnel. Trains be damned. Better to get whacked by a train than to be beaten to death by bikers.

They were stupid enough – and angry enough – to follow me. I readied myself, saw the glint of knives in the darkness. There seemed to be no way out.

"We're going to carve you up real good," said one of them.

Then another voice said, "I don't think so, boys!"

It was Owen, looking every inch The Crook, who loomed up out of nowhere. He whipped out his gun and let two rounds fly over their heads. They froze.

"I don't want any trouble," Owen said. "But I will shoot you dead if you take one more step."

They retreated.

We continued down the dark tunnel toward Yonge Street, jumping out of the way when a speeding train raced by – a close call on top of a close call.

After catching a cab, we went to Darcy's, my favourite after-hours bar in the heart of Yorkville. Owen grabbed a bottle and a girl. I traded my empty gun for his loaded one and went to the washroom to tend a busted lip.

A friend of mine, Libby, came in to check on me. He was outraged, and he wanted everyone in Darcy's to head back over to the Embassy and kick some biker ass.

I wasn't interested. All I wanted was my new girl, Sharon. I wasn't the only one; everyone in the bar – men and women – were licking their lips at the thought of her.

I had a few drinks, probably too many, because gradually Libby's idea began to make sense.

"You can't just let shit happen," I said. "There are fifty of us here. Those bikers say they're brothers, but we really are brothers. Ain't that right, Brother Libby?"

I admit I was a little drunk, but not so drunk to know I'd need an alibi. I pulled Owen aside and told him to tell the others to stick around. What was about to happen wouldn't need an army. I just wanted to shoot up the bar, so the bikers would know we could take care of business if we had to.

The plan was simple. Open the door, blast a few rounds into the ceiling and take off back to Darcy's.

No plan is ever that simple.

When Libby and I got to the Embassy, we pulled our guns out and tugged on the front door. It was locked. Everyone had gone home except for the cleaning staff. Shit.

I banged on the door with the butt of my gun until someone came over and opened up. I stuck my head inside. Nobody was there but a couple of guys mopping floors.

The guy who opened the door said, "The place is closed, mister." Well, what else could he say?

Libby and I shrugged and walked off, vowing to come by the next night. Still, Libby wanted to smell some gunpowder. There were some ornamental lights strung on poles in the lane and he asked me to shoot them out.

Bang, bang, bang.

And then I heard Libby cry out. When I turned to look, he was lying in the snow with dark red blood gushing out of his belly. My mind went blank.

What the hell had just happened?

All I could think of was that I had better get rid of my gun.

I threw it over a rooftop as hard as I could, and heard it go off again when it hit the ground.

I walked over to Libby, thinking he was dead. He was alive enough to shout, weakly, "Don't leave me here. I don't want to die."

I went back to him and slid my hands under his body. There was an exit wound in his back where the bullet had gone clean through. I picked him up, cradled him in my arms and walked down the lane back to Yorkville Avenue.

The blood was pouring from him in spurts. I was covered in it. I knew I had to get help, but it was late and there was no one around. He moaned in my arms and I saw him open his eyes.

"You shot me, man."

I have no idea how that happened. It didn't seem possible to me. I had to say something, so I blurted out, "Three white boys in a blue Chevy shot you, man."

That's when I saw Sharon.

She looked at me. I was holding Libby in my arms, both of us covered in blood. And then, miraculously, there was an ambulance at the curb.

The paramedics took Libby from my arms and stuffed him in the back. I said, "I'll follow you."

Sharon and I hailed a cab and we followed the ambulance to the hospital, but I told the cabbie to keep going. We headed for the west end to the home of a friend, where I figured we would be safe.

I was in trouble again.

Sharon and I stayed overnight, smoking weed and listening to the radio news to find out whether Libby lived or died. In the morning paper the headline read something like: "Black Youth Gunned Down In Yorkville. Racial Tension On The Rise. Police Looking For Three White Men In A Blue Chevy." Later we found out there was no bullet found in his body and nothing to match to any gun. No witnesses came forward. No cops ever interviewed anyone I knew.

My life.

Age, sixteen.

Libby had a visit while he was in the hospital from Detective Stoney Johnson, whose mother lived in the Projects. Libby stuck to his story and didn't rat me out.

He was released from the hospital two weeks later. We met at Club Jamaica. He complained that he was only going to get a few thousand dollars from the criminal compensation fund, and he thought he deserved more. He asked me for some money.

I took that as an insult. I called Dwane and told him to bring a gun. Libby looked at me as if I'd just slapped his mother and he stormed out of the club.

I never laid eyes on him again.

And I've never had another drink.

POLITICAL ACTION

Planning was underway for Toronto's first African Liberation Day parade in the spring of 1972. Warren Hart told us we were going to act as security along the route. He'd heard that various white power groups might cause trouble.

African Liberation Day was not a happy cultural celebration for the whole city the way Caribana is today. It was going to be a demonstration against white tyranny.

I was assigned to shadow any white people who didn't fit in or looked as if they might disrupt things. It was an assignment I took seriously.

Hart said he'd heard rumours that a white supremacist splinter group called the Western Guard was planning to shoot up the parade.

We pored over their pictures, as well as those of the leaders of other white radical racist groups and pictures of all the black dignitaries who were going to speak.

The main speaker was American counterculture activist Angela Davis's sister, Fania. We all had posters of Angela Davis in our apartments. Also planning to speak was the brother of civil rights militant H. Rap Brown. We'd have preferred their more famous siblings but we couldn't get them. Angela Davis was still hot, having been accused of supplying weapons to a teenaged revolutionary who kidnapped a courtroom full of judges and lawyers during the trial of the Soledad Brothers. H. Rap Brown was facing charges of armed robbery.

The Last Poets were to provide the entertainment. Their spoken-jazz performance piece "When the Revolution Comes" became the soundtrack to the Movement.

We had a war wagon filled with semi-automatic weapons of all kinds. The driver was to follow the parade from City Hall up University Avenue, past 52 Division and along Wellesley Street, eventually ending up at

Christie Pits Park, where thousands of blacks from all over North America had gathered.

Toronto had never seen anything like it, and there's been nothing like it since. It is as if it never happened. But all of the brothers and sisters my age surely know it did.

I took my place in solidarity with a huge crowd shouting hatred for racism and oppression. I wanted to be recognized, but at the same time I was trying not to be noticed.

I saw myself as a trained killer on a mission to protect my brothers and sisters, even if it meant sacrificing my life for the sake of my people.

As we walked past 52 Division we could see cops leaning out of their windows, taking pictures of the crowd while we shouted "Black Power" and "Down with the pigs." I slid my hand deep into my jacket pocket and wrapped my fingers around the butt of my Browning 9 mm itching for one of the cops to raise a hand with a gun in it so I could fire first.

Gradually, we drew near the park. Those of us on security were wearing heavy army coats and black berets with Black Panther buttons. Our mission: to protest and to protect.

I had a Browning automatic in my belt, two .38 revolvers tucked into belt holsters and a little .25 automatic in a boot holster. If that wasn't enough, I had a razor-sharp British Army knife tucked into my other boot.

What I didn't have was any kind of communication – no walkie-talkie – nothing. If trouble broke out I wasn't the only one wearing Panther gear. It would be hard to tell our guys from the marchers.

We headed for Hart's car, which was pulled over on a hill beside the community swimming pool and went over our assignments again. Then we fanned out to take our positions.

My brother, Dwane, was stationed near the south side of the pool, not far from a door leading to a room that the cops were using as headquarters. Dwane was visible to us all. His job was to alert us if he smelled anything wrong.

Brian Bush went up to the hill to the street, where he sat in a car that had a .308 sniper's rifle mounted with a scope. His job was to shoot down into the park at anyone who might be a threat to us, or to stop anyone from trapping us in the pit.

Levern's job was shadowing the organizers. He laughed when they laughed and was serious when they grew serious. Also, he was armed with handguns, ready to kill anyone who might try to harm one hair on any of their Afros.

He had one special Afro to protect. Beth Allen was a hard-working student organizer from the University of Toronto. We met when the racist Western Guard threatened to shoot up the Black Students' Association on George Street and our Panther group responded – armed to the teeth – in their defence. Not only that, Beth Allen was a dead ringer for Angela Davis. No one was going to harm a hair on her head while Levern was around.

My job was to shadow Warren Hart as if he was a head of state and I was a secret service man. I had an additional responsibility – Hart said if there was trouble, I was to shoot the Chief of Police. Or die trying.

I suppose it was hard for some people – then and now – to imagine the extent of black rage in the city. There were some 3,000 people in the park and feelings were running high.

Rosie Douglas – he of the fiery McGill University student protest – spoke, and so did the slim and elegant American, Julian Bond. There were more speeches, and then the park was renamed Henson-Garvey Park, in honour of the abolitionists, Josiah Henson and Marcus Garvey.

Nothing else happened.

The leaders went their way and people drifted off. Today, no one thinks of that park as anything but Christie Pits, except for blacks like me. At the time, and for that moment, the parade and the renaming of the park was a radical achievement.

We went back to Hart's apartment afterwards, relieved that things had gone so well, and aware that if there had been any trouble Bert Novis and his gang would have happily and mercilessly hunted us down.

Hart praised our coolness and told us that other Panther members had assessed us. Word had gone out that we were capable, and that filled our seventeen-year-old hearts with pride. Pride, that is, until Brian raised a point the next day.

"If Hart told some other Panthers about us monitoring movements in the park, then who else did he tell?" He was worried because it was known that there were informants in the Party. His paranoia got us thinking.

Brian said Hart had done wrong – no one outside our crew should have known we were there, armed and ready for action. Therefore, Hart had put us at risk, which might have made it hard for us to do our jobs when the time came. Or perhaps Hart was lying about the presence of other Panthers.

Either way, Brian aroused my suspicions.

One night Hart showed us a recruitment film for the war in Angola. The offer was $1,000 a month and ten acres of their land when the war was over. I didn't care much for the idea of blacks killing blacks in an African jungle. I was more interested in the good life – cars, clothes and girls – than I was in being a revolutionary.

He also began to talk about robberies to raise money for the defence of Huey P. Newton, one of the founders of the Panthers, who was in jail in California at the time. Then he mentioned a score he wanted us to make before he went back to Baltimore for the summer.

The bakery on Harbord was supposed to keep $30,000 in a safe, in order to cover cheques for the Portuguese population on payday. Hart said he had an inside guy.

I went to see my friend Deleo, who also had a friend who worked at the bakery. Call it additional research. The friend was there when I arrived and he explained the layout of the place.

The plan I developed was simple.

Brian would steal a car and park it near Deleo's place on Ulster Street at Brunswick. The rest of us – Benjy Gill (who we all knew through Libby or Levern), The Crook, Dwane and I – would sneak through the laneways and gather in back of the bakery. When Hart's inside guy unlocked the door we'd burst in, get the money, rush out the back, head for the car and make our escape. If any problem arose, we'd use the laneways and head for a safe house.

I made no other contingency plan. Why would I?

The next afternoon, Brian showed up with a decked-out Oldsmobile Cutlass, rumbling with power, big enough for all of us and very fast. Brian said he'd stolen it in Scarborough, meaning the downtown cops wouldn't be hunting for it.

We stopped off at Hart's place. I wanted to test him. I was familiar with his .38, and I brought two identical pistols with me. Hart's was in its holster on the table. I pulled it out and replaced it with one of mine.

"What the hell are you doing?"

"What difference does it make? I'll give you two for one, if you like, but I want to use your hollow points." From the tone of my voice, he got the idea that he'd better not say no.

"Fine, but I want it back when you're done;" he said, eyeing me carefully. "You either die with it in your hand, or you bring it back to me." I had no intention of dying.

I left Hart's place and went with our crew to a quiet part of the city near some abandoned railway tracks, where we usually went to test guns. I emptied the .38 into an old wooden shed. It worked.

We'd stolen enough cars in the past to know that we wouldn't attract attention with this one. After we gassed up, we headed back to the Projects.

I had brought nylon stockings for our faces and gloves for everyone to wear. I had another gun in a black nylon bag on the front seat. I gave Benjy a Browning automatic, and I gave a 9 mm to Dwane. He was fifteen years old.

And so we were on our way to commit armed robbery.

When we neared the bakery, The Crook and I jumped out of the car. I slapped Brian on the back and told him to leave it running. We slipped between two houses and out of sight.

The first mistake you make on any robbery is being stupid enough to attempt one. We met up behind the bakery, pulled our nylons over our faces and slipped on our gloves. I tested the back door – it was unlocked. Then I noticed Benjy's inch-thick, pop bottle eyeglasses protruding from under his facemask.

Shit. That made him conspicuous.

My second mistake was ordering him to take his glasses off. He did what he was told.

I yanked the door open and we rushed in, eyes blinking, going from darkness to light. We had rehearsed what to do at least ten times, so I didn't stop to look behind me. I just rushed past all the bakers and ran into the office.

"Freeze, this is a hold-up!"

Well, what else are you going to say? I waved Hart's gun around. The old woman who owned the bakery instinctively shut the door of the safe. In front of her, on the desk, was the day's take from the store's sales.

"Open that fucking safe."

She froze and stared at me. Hart had taught us to use as much profanity as possible during a robbery because it distances you from the people you're robbing.

He also taught us that she'd recognize her choices immediately – give us the money, or she and her employees would get hurt.

I pointed the gun at one of her bakers. "Open the fucking safe, lady, or this asshole gets a bullet." Things were already going sour. Persuasion eats up time.

She did nothing.

If I had been that baker, I'd have quit then and there, knowing my boss was cold enough to risk my life for her money. Then I heard shots, two of them at first, and then five more close together. It was the sound of Benjy's 9 mm, cracking off rounds. What the hell?

I forced everyone to face the wall, and swept what little money there was off the table and into my bag. So much for the $30,000 in Portuguese payroll money. Then I ran to the door.

"Get out of here," I shouted to our crew. "Let's move."

Benjy said, "Where's the fucking door? I can't see."

Oh, great, he was blind without his glasses.

I learned later that he'd run into a thick wooden pillar. Thinking he was being jumped by one of the bakers, he'd panicked and tried to kill him.

The others waited for me to lead the way out the back door. Waving his gun in my face, The Crook stopped me. "What the fuck is going on in there?"

I slapped the gun away and stepped outside, while the others followed. There were four of us running down the laneway now.

Dwane handed me his gun. I hit the safety and stuffed it into my bag as I ran. I had to pull Benjy's gun from him.

My third mistake was not considering the first two mistakes, because now everyone was in a panic. Lights were being turned on in houses all around the bakery. Suddenly the laneway was not so safe. We stuffed our gloves and masks into the bag and cut into the yard behind the house of Deleo's friend.

We could hear sirens coming from all directions. We had to get as far as possible away from the bakery. I ran into the street where the getaway car was waiting. Brian wasn't behind the wheel, the keys weren't in the ignition, and – shit, shit, shit – there was a cop car in the laneway twenty feet away. It got worse, as another cop car slithered around the corner of Bathurst and Ulster, headed in our direction.

Now it was every man for himself.

Dwane and I ran toward a familiar maze of lanes. He ran fast, but the bag with the guns and the money weighed me down.

The cop was on us right away. Tires screeched as he braked to a halt. He got out with a shotgun in his hands. He had it levelled at Dwane. But before he could pull off a shot, his car – still in gear – rolled forward and knocked him back.

And. Then. Time. Slowed. Down.

I reached into the bag for a gun, and as I did I locked eyes on the cop. He assumed, rightfully, that I was going to shoot him. He ran behind the open door of his vehicle and braced himself. I pulled the trigger again and again as I ran past, but I'd grabbed Benjy's gun and the damn thing was empty.

Almost before I knew it, I was fifty feet away, zigzagging behind my brother, half-expecting to take a bullet in my back.

Dwane disappeared between some houses. I ran a couple of streets further and did the same. I could hear cop cars everywhere. From experience I knew that I still had time to think, so I slowed down to a walk, breathing hard and wondering what the hell had just happened.

I had to get rid of the bag and change my appearance so that the cops would not recognize me. Taking off my coat, I stuffed it in the bag with everything else, and I hid the bag under a pile of rotten boards piled in a heap between two garages.

Now I needed a place to hide.

A heavy-duty television antenna led to the roof of a building, so I scaled it. Once I was on the roof, I crawled on my belly and peered over the edge in time to see The Crook forced to the ground at gunpoint by three detectives. I saw one yank a gun out of my friend's coat pocket. They cuffed him roughly. The Crook had tried to fit into a line of Italian worm pickers who were waiting to be driven out to the fields to collect dew worms. You might say he stood out.

The cops threw him into their car and sped away.

Now other cops were running everywhere below me, shining their flashlights into ambush spots, banging on garage doors, doing what they could to flush me out.

I knew they'd go away eventually. I just had to wait them out. All I wanted, on that cold wet roof, was to be with my girl. Not much chance of that; not for a while.

When things calmed down, I made my way back to the money and the guns. I pushed the boards aside – no bag. Damn. If Novis found it, he'd have rooted through it down at 14 Division by now.

I reached for my wallet – damn and damn again. I'd put my wallet in the pocket of my coat, and the coat was in the bag along with the gun. On the gun would be my fingerprints, from before I'd gloved up; also the nylons, and the money from the store.

I was screwed.

I couldn't think of what to do or where to go. I headed back to the Projects, where I ran into Brian. He filled me in on what had just gone wrong. Dwane had been busted a few minutes earlier, and my parents had gone to the police station to see what they could do for their son. Benjy had taken off for the safety of Regent Park.

Brian looked at me intently and said he'd heard that the cop who'd pulled up near the stolen car had recognized him. He also said, "Novis is showing your picture around. He put out the word that he's going to shoot you if you don't give yourself up."

The Projects were no longer safe, but Brian's predicament was not as serious as mine. Nobody could put him at the scene of the crime.

I called Hart from a pay phone. His ten-year-old son answered, giving me instructions relayed from Hart. I was to call him back, no matter from where, no matter what time.

I knew a girl who lived across the street from Hart's apartment. Brian and I headed there in the darkness.

Carole was glad to see us. She knew what had happened and said it would be cool if we stayed for a couple of days.

She turned on the television and there was Bert Novis, looking at the camera, talking to me. "Ricky, give yourself up. There's nowhere to hide."

I called Hart again, and this time he picked up right away. He said, "You got my thing?"

I didn't answer him directly. "Look out your window."

I flicked Carole's back porch light three times.

He laughed. "Hiding right under their noses, like I taught you. I'll be there in a second to pick it up."

"It," of course, was his gun.

But his gun was in the getaway bag, and I had a sinking feeling that bag was with the cops. He crept into Carole's backyard a minute later, and I told him what had happened. He slammed his fist into the side of the house. I'd never seen him lose his cool before. I wished I had a gun.

No, I wished I had his gun.

Hart knew some cops and ascertained that the bag had yet to be mentioned by the police in connection with the robbery. His biggest immediate worry was that Dwane might not be able to stand up to what the cops would surely put him through. That could end up linking Hart to the gun.

I tried to cool him down. I said I'd go back and search for the bag when the light was better, and I assured him that Dwane was tough enough to stand up to anything the cops might throw at him. We talked over our options. Everything depended on whether the cops had the guns, the money and my wallet.

Hart told us to sit tight. There was a contingency plan.

The Panthers had a van with a false bottom that was used to smuggle members into Canada. It would be easy enough to smuggle us into the States – the Underground Railroad in reverse. The Panthers would put us up in Boston until we could flee to Amsterdam or maybe South America. We were willing to go anywhere to get away from Bert Novis and Canadian justice.

We hid out at Carole's for two days, slipping out only at night to find safe pay phones. I called my mother to ask what she knew about Dwane. Novis told her that no one was allowed to see him until the investigation was over. I couldn't think of what to say, except to tell her that they must be working him over pretty good, and that she should put some pressure on Novis if she could.

Eventually, Hart called to say the van was ready and Boston had agreed to take us in. He also had bad news – 14 Division had his gun.

Hart said he'd send us a bucket of chicken and a bottle of wine. I knew that "bucket of chicken" was code for shotgun, but I had no idea what he meant by "bottle of wine." It had to be code for something, because he knew I didn't drink.

Brian was on edge; he wanted to bolt right away, to take his chances on the street. I lay in Carole's arms, trying to think about how we might make some money before we headed south. If Hart was really going to send a shotgun, maybe we could rob some banks.

A couple of hours later, Carole took her little dog outside to do its business. I could hear her talking softly to the puppy as I waited for her to come back to bed. Brian was on the couch, reading a book. I was on the bed reading a Panther newspaper when I heard Carole's startled laugh.

There was a strange look on Brian's face. I was about to ask him what was wrong when I saw the business end of a shotgun and a very large cop pointing it at me. Then there were more cops, and as they rushed in I heard that voice.

"You fucking move, you're dead."

Bert Novis, with his shotgun inches from my face.

"Raise your hands slowly."

I did as he said and one of the cops cuffed me. Novis never for an instant took his finger off the trigger, not until the cuffs snapped shut.

Smiling now, and looking down at me, he flicked the safety on and grabbed his walkie-talkie. "Ricky Atkinson is in custody. I repeat – Ricky Atkinson."

Brian and I were paraded outside to the glare of the media lights. There were cops all over, including snipers on rooftops. I had a pretty good idea of what I was in for, but I was smart enough to play to the cameras.

"Look, no marks on my face, no bruises."

Of course, I also knew that most people didn't much care about what happened to black men in police custody.

Novis eased behind the wheel, just as he'd done when I was ten years old and again when I was fourteen. The difference this time was that there were two big cops flanking me, and Novis was not about to hand me over to my mother.

I was curious. It wouldn't have been Carole and I doubted it was Hart who told on me. Maybe I'd been spotted making a phone call.

I had to know.

"Mr. Novis, who ratted me out?"

"Ricky, you'd go into shock if I told you."

I wasn't sure what to think. He might have been playing me.

At the station, Novis took my sneakers before I sat down and then he left the interrogation room. An hour later he came and got me and led me into another room. There on a table was all the evidence against me, tagged and smudged with fingerprint powder: a picture of footprints on the bakery floor next to my running shoes, my wallet with my identification; the guns and bullets; the money from the bakery; the nylon mask and my gloves. All of it was laid out like a buffet.

"Nice, isn't it?" said Novis. "You are truly fucked, Ricky. Do yourself a favour and we'll talk to the judge for you." Novis was bluffing. He couldn't do a thing for me.

And I was not a rat.

My instinct was to help the others.

I knew, from my training, that I was in enemy hands and my responsibility now was to give as much misinformation as I could to confuse them. The enemy was not just Novis; it was the Canadian judicial system.

I took the beef for the robbery.

Novis asked who fired the shots into the pillar. I told him it was a guy I'd met in a bar on Yonge Street, and I gave him a phoney name. I also confessed that I'd stolen the car in Scarborough, but couldn't remember where, hoping that Brian would keep his mouth shut. It might help him if I took the beef, and it wouldn't hurt me much. A stolen car was nothing compared to armed robbery.

I took another stab at misinformation.

"The guns on the table? The guy I met on Yonge Street brought them with him."

Then Novis asked me about Brian, who had been identified by the cop near the getaway car.

I told him that most cops couldn't tell one black guy from another in the dark of night, knowing that most juries would believe me.

He asked about the gloves and mask. I said they belonged to the other guy, and that he'd done many other robberies with guys from all over Ontario.

"He's the guy you're looking for," I said. "Catch him and all these robberies in the city will stop."

Novis let me stew for a while, and then I was taken downstairs to the bullpen. I knew I was headed for hard time, but I also knew I could hold my head up because I took the beef.

My brother was waiting for me in the bullpen. Something bad had happened to him.

"I died, man. They killed me." He screamed it over and over, until the cops came and threatened to beat his head in if he didn't shut up.

What they did to Dwane was put a hood over his head and then they whacked him with pillowcases filled with Toronto phone books. They kicked him and punched him until he passed out. When he came to they beat him some more.

What was the worst of it?

They sat him naked on a metal chair and attached an electrode to the leg of the chair, touching a second wire to other parts of his body, sending currents of electricity coursing through him again and again.

They wanted to know if I had a machine gun. They wanted him to rat on me. Dwane refused to say anything. He just told them all that I'd kill them.

He was fifteen years old when the torture began. The beatings and the electrocution lasted for a couple of days. Then Dwane had a birthday and turned sixteen, at which time they could charge him as an adult.

I don't know if this business of electrocution is done any more. You couldn't get a cop to admit it if they did. But I do know that what the cops did to my brother is still talked about today. Dwane has since said he'd rather die than go through what they did to him again.

It was common knowledge, back in the day, that some of the Divisions had their persuasive specialties. Fourteen Division was fond of the hood and phone books swung in the pillowcase; 32 Division had a fine selection of rubber hoses of various gauges, and 51 Division cops were fond of taking you out to a deserted section of waterfront along Cherry Beach and beating you senseless.

They took us to headquarters for fingerprints next, and then to 52 Division to wait for a ride downtown, where we would be charged at Old City Hall. I was seventeen and about to learn things most men three times my age would never know.

The cells below the courtrooms were crowded and smoky, filled with men waiting for their day in court, charged with all sorts of offences. Dwane and I were in a group of twelve. As we passed by, an old light-skinned guy in prison greens – who looked like he'd been a hippie in his day – held out his hat.

"Hey, guys, we're from down below, we could use some help."

Help? Every one of us in there needed help, but if you had a couple of bucks you might be able to get a guard to bring you coffee.

I was not only starving, I was broke. Novis had cleaned us out. "Sorry, man, I'm tapped out. Cops got our shit."

He leaned in, and the smile left his face. "Man, don't play me. You guys look like you're players; every player I know gots to have something."

We had nothing, but some of the men we came in with dropped the old guy a bit of change. He said, looking directly at me, "Man, that's what I'm talking about – one hand washes the other, brother."

I should have been able to step up to the plate and not look like a punk. So I thought I'd drop my father's name, hoping the light-skinned guy was a Nova Scotian. I hadn't spent my life hustling, just to be hustled by somebody else.

I said, "Brother, my father is Sonny Atkinson. He'll surely drop a double into the guard's account so my brother and I can grab a coffee. It would be nice if you bought us one until that happened, and then I could pay you back."

The light-skinned guy took a step back. For a second, I thought he was going to take a shot at me.

"Man, what a small fucking world. Your uncle Glen is like a brother to me; man, your father is a friend of mine. I'm Ernie Moore. If you guys need something to eat then, shit, man, it's the least I can do for all that Glen's done for me. Come on, let's get you a coffee."

He bought us honey buns and cups of coffee and said he and his partner, Duke King, had been brought down from Collins Bay penitentiary to face some old charges. He was hoping they'd get tossed.

He also told me that he and Duke had been jumped in Collins Bay by some racists, and that my uncles, Glen and Ronny, who'd been in there at the time, had come to their defence. When the guards broke up the fight, Glen was shipped to Millhaven, and Ronny to Joyceville.

Ernie said that if I got sent to the Bay, I'd better keep my eyes open in case any of those white boys wanted to beef me over my uncles. A cop slapped me around because of my uncles when I was only eleven. I took Ernie's advice seriously.

A Salvation Army guy came by and started calling names. The man of God had two messages for me: "Sharon says she loves you and misses you. Is there anything you want to say to her?" Everyone was listening carefully. I didn't want to sound like a wimp and tell her I loved her.

"Tell her to visit me as soon as I get to the Don Jail."

He wrote that down. "Your mother is asking if Dwane is okay. She also gave me $20 to give to the guards for you, for coffee, and she says she loves you. Is there anything you want to say to her?"

It's no weakness, in prison or anywhere else, to say you love your mother.

"Tell her we love her, too, and tell her they worked Dwane over, but he's okay."

Three hours later, we walked through a door made of solid steel bars, up a flight of stairs and up through a hole in the courtroom floor that led to the prisoner's box.

When I popped up, I could see cops, court clerks and a judge on an elevated dais. Sharon was there, only a few feet away. Smiling weakly, she looked scared and confused.

My sad-faced father and mother were there. In the back of the court-room I recognized two Panthers who were friends of Hart. We nodded at each other.

"Atkinson, Atkinson, Crookendale and Bush."

I hated the guard on the courtroom door. I hated the judge for hav-ing gone to school and studied law. I hated the attractive woman who read the charges because she called my name so loudly. And I hated Novis and every other detective and cop in court. The only thing that made me remotely happy was that Benjy got away clean, ironically, since he was the only one of us to actually fire a gun during the robbery.

Novis handed the Crown attorney a sheet of paper, the Crown gave it to the clerk, and the clerk handed it to the judge. The judge looked us over and asked, "Who is Richard Atkinson?"

My lawyer, David Newman, whispered in my ear, "Let me do the talking."

Newman told the judge he was acting for us. The judge said, "This matter will go over until tomorrow for a show cause hearing." Novis and his gang stood up and left. Sharon grabbed my hand but a cop pulled her away.

"No touching the prisoners."

Back down in the bullpen, Ernie and his buddy were gone. Two hours later, we took a short ride to the Don Jail.

HARD TIME

You can imagine the ride over. Or maybe you can't. There was a six-inch opening in the back of the police transport wagon. I stared out as we rode along, looking for pretty girls, trying to embed them in my memory and looking at familiar landmarks, wondering when I'd see them again.

The Don Jail, Toronto's oldest, was a landmark in its own right, familiar to me from the outside only. I'd ridden my bike past it lots of times. My aunt Flo and my grandmother lived nearby. My dad and uncles had known the last two people hung in the Don Jail, Ronald Turpin and Arthur Lucas. I knew it held people serving short sentences. I knew it held people on immigration warrants. I knew it held the city's poor.

Now it would hold me.

The wagon rolled inside and the big door rolled shut. We were thrown into a bullpen crammed with more than 100 men of all descriptions. Some, as young as sixteen, had been charged with minor thefts. Others, as old as time itself, were charged with murder.

The noise, mixed with the tobacco smoke and the smell of men in close quarters, was stifling. Some guys, entering the bullpen, tried to hustle a sandwich or a cigarette from other prisoners who had been remanded or sentenced. Most of the men around me cursed their lawyers, the prison system and their lives. Others joked. Some cried.

A few old men were there by choice. I thought it strange at the time. They had committed minor crimes, yet asked the judge for time in jail. I thought that anyone who wanted to go to the Don without a gun pointed at his head had to be crazy. I came to learn that there were men who could not cope with the choice, or the uncertainty, of life on the streets. With its lack of choice, jail was simpler.

Once inside, we were forced to strip; they poured thick, green delousing liquid over us. Then we showered. Someone threw prison blues at me;

nothing fit. On a counter, there was a pair of old socks, a well-worn pair of clean underwear, one thin white towel and two white sheets.

We were given a bail – a small pouch – of Daily Mail tobacco, a cheap toothbrush, a bag of tooth powder, and a black comb that was useless on my big Afro. I knew from working in the laundry room in training school that this was all I was going to get. I didn't smoke, and was about to hand my tobacco back when The Crook stopped me.

"You can trade that for food."

The man handing out the tobacco was someone I knew from the streets so I asked him for another and hid the extra tobacco in my towel.

Suddenly, a big guard with a thick Scottish accent hollered at us to follow him. Off we went, up a long flight of old iron stairs and onto a long range lined with cells whose bars were twice as thick as the rest.

As soon as I entered my cell, the door slammed shut and locked. I stood there, tired and perplexed. Below a nine-foot ceiling, the cell was thirty inches wide and seven feet deep – mark that off for yourself and see how small it really is.

The final touch was a small metal piss bucket on the cement floor between the cell door and my bunk.

I could hear men howling in their cells. No wonder; it was hot for June. I felt as if I was in a coffin. The previous tenant had left his sheets on the bed; they were covered with dirty footprints. I thought that was odd. Why would anyone in this little coffin stand on his bed?

At one time, this had been death row, which explained the thickness of the bars. That didn't bother me much. I called out to The Crook and told him about the footprints, and asked him what I should do about the sheets.

An unfamiliar voice replied. "He strung himself up last night. Toss the sheets out onto the range."

"You're kidding."

"I don't kid about the dead, pal."

It seems the man who'd been in the cell before me had torn his towel into strips to make a rope that he tied around his neck. He tied the other end of rope to his cell bars, stepping from the edge of his bed onto the bars about eighteen inches away. He hung on, thinking his last thoughts, and leaned back until he passed out – hanging from the space beside his piss bucket until the life ebbed out of him. The dirty footprints were from the guards, who had stepped up on the bed to cut him down.

I tore off the sheets, throwing them onto the floor of the cell and trying to make the bed with my own clean sheets. There was barely an inch between the iron bed rails and the sweaty cell walls on either side. It was all I could do not to leave footprints on my own sheets.

"For fuck's sakes!" It was Brian's voice. I stopped to listen: Apparently, the prisoner who had the cell before him left the piss bucket full. I lifted the metal lid of mine and saw the dead man's piss still there. Brian called out again.

"Ricky, toss over those sheets."

I pushed the dead man's sheets through the bars and sailed them in Brian's direction, wondering what he wanted them for. Then I saw a stream of piss.

Lesson learned: better to piss on sheets in the corridor than to overflow the bucket in your cell.

I fell asleep quickly, exhausted from a night of interrogation and a day of courtroom tension. I didn't sleep long. They woke us early. I washed my face in the sink at the back of the range, two feet away from a guy taking a crap.

For breakfast, there was toast and porridge. The coffee was weak, and the milk was watery. Then we were taken back to court.

My father was there, in case he was called to give evidence for our bail hearing. Bert Novis was also there in his brown suit. The other cops were the same as the day before, as were the clerks of the court.

My lawyer, David Newman, introduced himself. Brian and Owen had yet to get a lawyer. Dwane had Paul Tomlinson, who pointed out that his client was only fifteen when he'd been nabbed. Dwane was separated out and sent back down the hole.

My lawyer argued in favour of bail, but his argument – it was summer, there was time for us to get jobs, we could remain productive members of society – was pretty feeble.

Novis smirked. When he took the stand he pointed at me, saying, "Your Honour, that man would have shot dead all seventeen arresting officers." He went on about how many guns I had and how shots were fired, and how I had eluded capture for three days.

He said he'd known me since I was a kid, and that I had always used violence to get what I wanted.

"All seventeen officers involved in this case are afraid that Mr. Atkinson will hunt us down and kill us all if he is released."

Owen couldn't help himself. He piped up with, "Please, save the drama for the soap opera."

The judge told him to be silent in court.

Novis finished up by saying that more charges were pending and more of my crew were about to be arrested, which was news to my lawyer. It took the judge ten seconds to decide.

Bail denied.

The Don Jail has two sides to it. I was in the old side, along with people who were going to reformatories for sentences under two years. It had a reception area that you had to pass through, whether you were coming or going. It also had a small clinic, a chapel, and a library that I never missed going to. There was a small grass yard with a brick walkway. If you looked up, you could see the nurses in the hospital next door looking down on us.

The new men looked up. Convicts, who had been there the longest, simply stared at the ground as they walked around in circles. No point torturing yourself with thoughts of what you could not have.

Most of the ranges on the old side had windowless, waterless cells that were six by seven feet, with two sets of bunk beds crammed into them.

There were forty of us on our range.

I spent twelve hours sitting on the piss-stained, wooden floor or on the long benches, waiting for day to turn into night. The other twelve hours, I was in my hot, airless cell, packed up like a sardine with three other guys.

They threw everyone in together. A man who'd stolen a paper from a newsstand might be sharing a cell with a murderer who'd been on the front page of the paper he stole. Each night was the same as the last, and each day was the same as the day before. I spent as much time as I could playing chess or reading all the non-fiction books available.

I had visits from my mother. I knew that no matter what, she would find a way to visit me in the adult prison system as she had had when I was in juvie training schools. Only ten per cent of the kids in juvie had visitors because the institutions were outside of the city and inconvenient. The visitor rate for adults in the Don Jail was higher. Still, I knew guys who had family in the city, but they never came to visit. That old adage – "Out of sight, out of mind" – hit home as watched grown men suffer from loneliness. My own father rarely came into any of the jails I was in. The memory of the time he'd spent locked up was too much.

Sharon came. I always liked seeing her bright smile and pretty black face. Sometimes she would flash her perfect breasts at me through the thick glass that separated us. As the months wore on, I wondered how long she could wait for a guy who might have to spend a couple of years in jail.

That's what I thought – that I'd get a couple of years, because this was my first adult offence. In the opinion of many of the older prisoners, I was probably going to a reformatory for two years less a day.

Still, it was going to take months to get to trial. In the meantime, I'd be rotting away in a jail. The only consolation was being surrounded by my cousins and guys I knew from the Projects.

Each week, we'd go for a ride to the courthouse in Old City Hall, only to be remanded back to the Don Jail. These rides were the only times I'd get to see men from the other ranges.

Fights happened often, not unusual under the circumstances. Most of the fights were for minor reasons, and some were over things that happened outside the jail, long before the participants were arrested. Other fights were more serious and the grievances followed you, in jail or out, until the consequences turned deadly.

If you were labelled "NG" or "no good," you could get jumped and be forced to fight for your life. You were NG if you talked to the guards too often, or if you whined about your crime. You were NG if word came from the courts that you were a rat, and you were NG if you were in on a sex beef. These things raced through the prison grapevine faster than a speeding police car.

If you'd had sex with someone's girlfriend, you were a "grinder" and that was certainly NG. Many guys had girlfriends when they came in, but lost them over time. Grinding fights happened often and were usually violent.

If someone said you were NG, you'd have to fight there and then, unless you were lucky and managed to build a defence against the insinuation. If it was discovered that you had tried to ruin the reputation of someone with a false accusation, you were made to suffer the pain you had wished upon another.

I was able to survive easier than most who were new to the adult system because I understood that respect gets respect. I'd learned that lesson from reading Eldridge Cleaver while in Glendale training school.

But what I learned in the Don – and it would stay with me throughout all the years I would spend in adult prisons – is that diplomacy is the first step in quelling any problem.

That's a good lesson for any leader.

When diplomacy didn't work, you had to be prepared to go all the way to get your point across. From childhood, my father taught us to go all the way in a fight and people knew this about me, or they sensed it. I tended to get respect from bigger, tougher men. That was important, because my tender age was not going to protect me from anyone who had the balls to walk up and pull a knife.

It also helped that I had family and other gang members in there with me, at least two of us on every range. The truth is, there's never been a family like mine. I had relatives, close and distant, in every single prison I've ever been in.

It really was a family thing. My family is from Nova Scotia, going back more than 200 years. We were Loyalist slaves from Barbados, or maybe Trinidad. In the pecking order of that time, blacks were a step up from natives. Occasionally, black freemen married native women. Most blue-collar workers, thieves and pimps lived and worked near the military base and soldiers had money. Prostitution was a way to pay the rent. It wasn't personal. If a woman had balls, she told her man to make the rent and he went out and stole from – guess who – the soldiers. Not all my family were thieves and hustlers. Some worked at the docks or the railway yards, as well as in farmers' fields when work was available. Stealing and prostitution were always options when things got tough.

In modern times, two of my relatives, the Hamilton brothers, were hanged when a robbery went wrong and they killed a cabbie with a hammer. The story is that the wife of one of the men had given birth, and the hospital wouldn't let her go before the bill was paid.

The husband left the hospital, went to a prostitute, got drunk and robbed a cabbie with his brother. The robbery went wrong. They got the rope in 1949.

Also, now and then throughout the history of our family and others, white babies were born into black families, and brothers and sisters didn't always look alike. My grandmother had sixteen kids, and not all were the same color. My great-grandmother had twelve kids who didn't look alike.

No one thought anything about it.

That's who I am.

As it happens, my friends, family, and the other prisoners had been wrong – my lawyer said I was probably looking at ten years.

It would become a little clearer at my preliminary hearing, when I got my first chance to see the evidence and hear the witnesses.

I had a couple of choices.

I could choose the lower court, which is now known as the Ontario Court of Justice. That meant having a trial in front of a judge, with no jury. The trouble is that lower court judges were often new to the bench. Some of them were easily influenced by the dirty tactics of the police or by the attention of the media. Not all of them were able to deal with an incompetent Crown attorney.

Or I could choose the higher court – the Superior Court, as it is called today. In high court the judges were more experienced and were said to make fewer judicial errors. They were thought to be less subject to influence by the media or the cops.

The dilemma was that it cost the government more money to prosecute high court cases. When sentences were levied they tended to be greater, sometimes much greater, than lower court renderings.

As for the lawyers, let's just say most of them tried to work out deals beforehand. It was a bit like being on a TV game show. They were always angling to get the least amount of time for their clients, while taking the most amount of money out of their pockets.

While I waited for the legal proceedings to unfold, I spent some of my time complaining to the new provincial ombudsman about everything I thought was legitimate.

I also got into some fights, and found myself moved around the ranges in order to cool out, which is how I got to know almost everyone who was doing time.

And that's how I got to see the new side of the Don Jail. The new side was built in 1967 and was relatively luxurious. The ranges held eighteen guys, not forty, and the cells held one man, not four.

Each cell had running water and a toilet, which meant you could wash yourself down if you were sweaty. As on the old side, anyone who wanted a weekly shower was taken downstairs.

Days were broken up with visits to a cement yard with walls that loomed thirty feet high. Never seeing the outside world made the days seem to pass by quicker because there were fewer distractions. I found

I did less daydreaming as that time passed, and maybe that's a key to my character.

If the new side was cleaner, it was also more dangerous because it held guys who were in for longer sentences, anywhere from two years to life, for more serious crimes.

There was one range, 4A, where all the teenagers and the pimps wanted to go. This range was physically the same as all the others, but it was just below the range where they kept the girls and women who were awaiting trial or sentencing. If the girl above you emptied her toilet and scooped out all the water, and you did the same thing, you could talk to each other all night long. Naturally, the guards frowned on this. When they did their hourly rounds, they'd force you to flush, causing you to hang up your unique phone.

Just before my preliminary hearing, I got into a fight with my cousin, Perry, over a negative comment he made about the Black Panthers. I took offence because to me the Panthers were our revolutionary brothers and sisters, out there on the front lines, risking their lives for social equality. I told him to shut his fucking mouth or I'd fuck him up. He walked away and I hoped that was the end of it.

But he waited until I was playing chess with my back against the wall. When I was deep in contemplation of a move, he pushed the table up against my chest, trapping me. Then he picked up a cribbage board, jumped up on the table and began to whack me silly. After a minute or so, he jumped off and I jumped up, eager to take him on, but some of my cousins and The Crook intervened.

We ended up in the hole.

Wanting to teach me a lesson, the warden put me on bread and water for a week. I had read a lot of religious philosophy by then, so I chalked it up as a chance to practice fasting and meditation.

I slept on a thin mattress that I had to turn in every morning. The mattress could be taken away at any time, for any reason, so if I wasn't careful I'd have to sleep on the cold floor.

There was also a chance, in isolation, that you could be deprived of your clothes. This heightened the punishment because – by malicious design – the hole was always cold.

If the warden had really wanted to punish me, however, he'd have taken away my books. By law, he had to allow each prisoner a Bible. I read mine, over and over, in every cell I've been in.

After a week in the hole, when it was time for Warden's Court, the warden came into my cell flanked by two goons. The goons were not just there to protect him. They were there in case he wanted them to kick the shit out of me.

I'd been training myself in meditation and I was smiling when they entered. The warden asked me about the fight with Perry.

"It was a family problem," I told him. "Now it's over and forgotten."

He asked if Atkinson family members always solved problems with their fists. I rolled up my shirtsleeve to show him a long scar, the souvenir of the time when I was twelve years old, and Junior cut me with a knife.

"Sometimes we just stab each other."

He gave me another day in the hole, but he reinstated regular meals. The next morning, I was surprised to hear I was going to the most secure range in the jail, 1C, on the new side – everyone called it the "pen range." It was filled with rounders, hustlers and murderers of all types. I was the youngest rounder in that section. My reputation as a guy who would argue and fight with his fists for his rights and the rights of others had preceded me.

As strange as it sounds, I had anticipated being just where I was. Being on a range with guys who were going to or once were on death row, guys who did time in the toughest prisons in the world, guys who spent their lives perfecting crime in big cities just like I had, gave me a feeling of belonging to a select group of men, capable of anything. I wasn't afraid. I was just curious at how it all came together. By listening to others more worldly than me, I learned that I had screwed up by mixing crime and politics. Every rounder expected to take a pinch, but being an armed Panther brought more unnecessary heat and headaches with it.

That range, 1C, was loaded with black Americans. Three of them stood out – two were black revolutionaries, and one was a Black Muslim.

Edwin Hogan was a Black Panther with an excellent education. He escaped from an escorted pass while giving a lecture at the University of Ohio. He made his way to Toronto, looking for a meeting with Warren Hart. Hart did not let me in on that meeting.

Harold Barnes was the brother of Nicky Barnes, a Harlem gangster and the reigning black mob boss. He was pals with Eddie Tolan who was also in on a murder rap. Tolan, he was the last guy in Canada to be sentenced to the lash – he'd been tied to a gurney and whipped by machine, presumably because it applied punishment with consistent force

If Edwin was as serious as death, Harold was a funny guy. One day at lunch, he was making designs with his spoon in his chocolate pudding. Harold smiled and flicked a spoonful in Eddie's face.

Eddie responded by heaving his bowl, which missed the target but hit someone else. Then it was every man with pudding for himself, a full-blown food fight.

The guards panicked. It can't have been much fun for them, seeing a roomful of convicts, some of whom were on death row, flinging pudding. The fight ended when a big sergeant with a heavy and commanding English accent bellowed, "Clean up this shit!" It took us two hours and none of us missed dessert.

The third man was Richard Anderson, a tall, slim, dark-skinned man who shot a biker in a Toronto club called the Mynah Bird. The biker had called him a nigger and pushed him, so Anderson pulled a gun and shot the biker four times. He was awaiting trial for attempted murder.

What impressed me most about Anderson was his memory. I was reading my Bible after we met when he approached and asked that I open the book anywhere and tell him the page number. I did so, making sure that he couldn't see what page I'd chosen. He began to recite every word as if the Bible was open in front of him.

I fell in with him, and we paced the range together every day. It was no wonder he knew the scriptures as well as he did. He'd spent over seven years in solitary, with nothing to read but a Bible. He told me he met Malcolm X in jail, and became a follower of the Nation of Islam. He taught me to pray, and he gave me everything that Elijah Muhammad had written.

That was when I stopped eating pork and stopped arguing unnecessarily with the guards. I began praying five times a day, distancing myself from my old friends and those who weren't as disciplined as I was about religion and philosophy.

On my third day, Edwin Hogan asked me if I'd walk with him to the back of the range. The way he said it made me apprehensive. Most of the beefs took place at the back, away from where the guard sat.

Had I done something wrong?

Hogan leaned in and asked me if I was a Panther. I nodded. He grew angry, wanting to know why I hadn't said anything when we first met. I explained that my lawyer had told me not to mention my affiliation with the Panthers while he worked on my bail.

I also told him that I'd heard about him when he hit town. Hart had mentioned him, but hadn't wanted me in on their meeting.

I filled him in on what I knew about Hart.

Hogan grew angrier by the minute because he was sure Hart was the one who ratted him out. It was hard for me to believe – here was the head of the Ohio Black Panthers accusing the head of the Baltimore Black Panthers of being a rat.

From that moment forward, Edwin treated me like a brother, explaining the American prison system to me and telling me what he thought I might be up against if I was sentenced to the penitentiary.

His cell was strewn with legal briefs because he was fighting hard to stay in Canada. It turned out we had something in common – his lawyer, Charles Roach, had been my first lawyer.

Edwin, who was connected throughout the prison, once asked me for help. He'd been working on a complaint concerning the small, tin piss buckets everyone had on the old side of the jail.

In cells that held four guys the buckets filled quickly, which meant guys had to piss out their cell doors and onto the floor where we sat during the day.

Since the American government was paying the Canadian government to house inmates on immigration holds, Edwin argued they ought to provide a piss bucket big enough to fulfill an American's urinary needs.

He tried to get the American consulate and the Ontario ombudsman to look into the matter, and he needed all of the American prisoners to sign his petition. Since I had relatives or friends on every range in the jail, he asked me to distribute the petition

I did what he asked, even though it meant antagonizing the guards, who were always afraid of signs of unity among the prisoners. It turned out to be a worthy cause. Within a week, large plastic buckets with lids appeared in every cell on the old side.

That gave me an idea.

I asked Edwin if he'd help me fight for Afro-picks. Most of the players I knew had Afros and we needed to comb them before going to court and facing a judge and jury. Black prisoners usually improvised by tying four pencils together with a rubber band, but pencil-picks didn't last long. Guards tended to seize them during cell searches.

For me, it was a question of identity. I was light-skinned, mixed-race – a little black, a little native, a little white. My Afro was a sign of my sense of identity. If anyone so much as brushed against my hair, there was going to be a response.

"Mess with my 'fro, you got to go."

The realization dates very specifically for me. It begins with the James Brown anthem: "Say it loud. I'm black, and I'm proud."

It was not without personal complexity. When I was growing up, my mother always said that kinky hair was bad hair. She equated straight hair with success, and I think she felt that success was having kids who could pass for white.

The blacks of the generation before me "conked" their hair, using chemical straighteners featuring lye. My uncles, the pimpy ones, did that;

but the non-pimpy ones did not. It was a sign of who you were, and who you wanted to be. My father avoided the issue by keeping his hair military-short

Not me.

Black is beautiful, baby.

I know from my reading that most organizations, even ones full of smart people, tend toward collective stupidity. I had little hope that I'd see an Afro-pick, since the guards viewed them as weapons. I sent the second petition around, but it didn't go smoothly.

When the petition failed, I was targeted for harassment by senior administration. They started moving me around in the new side as often as I'd been moved on the old side.

There was, however, an unintended consequence that worked in my favour. Being moved around meant that I got to meet every criminal who walked in. I also I got to know all of the black guards, including a couple who saw to it that I got back onto 1C range every week or so to be with my new friends.

People come and go in prison. Like any closed society, the loss of a member hurts when the absence is unexpected. One day Edwin was called off the range. He could tell by the look on the guard's face that something wasn't right.

"Brother, give all my briefs over to my lawyer. I think the man is up to something and it ain't going to be good." Those were the last words I heard him speak.

As soon as he left the range and the steel door closed behind him, I heard the scuffle of heavy boots and fists hitting flesh.

He was taken to an immigration hearing where he lost the right to stay in Canada. Although he had the right to appeal, he was taken to the American border and turned over to the F.B.I.

Still, I did not suffer from a lack of old friends, and I made many new ones. O.J. was a big, black, street fighter with a knack for pissing people off. He hung with my cousin, Perry, and he often took on the tougher of the white guys in jail. When he got into it, the rest of us would have to back him up against any gang aggression. We backed him because he was usually right.

O.J. was a cousin of Jerry and Joe Patterson, two loan sharks in the black community who often worked for legendary mobster, Paul Volpe. By blood and proximity, O.J. was connected.

With my crew, my cousins and with people like O.J., I didn't have much to worry about, no matter what range I was on. But it was as important to be right as it was to be connected, because there were rules.

If two people were fighting and a third guy jumped in, other guys often jumped the third guy. He would be labelled a goof and a coward for not letting two men settle their differences alone. In that situation, you might find yourself facing a gang that could swell to include the entire prison population. Under that threat, you might as well check yourself into protective custody.

A guy called Barnyard, who was our safecracking teacher, walked onto the range one afternoon. His face was fresh and familiar – he had been in the news for cracking a safe in the Canadian Tire store on Yonge Street.

He was certain he wasn't going to get federal prison time, and he kept trying to get me to plead guilty to my crimes so we could go to Guelph together. Why? He had a bunch of safes he wanted to crack, and he needed a partner to plan the scores while he waited for his release.

That, alas, was not going to happen.

While summer turned to fall and then to winter, I was preparing to fight a long string of charges. Some of the guys who were not involved in the bakery job had ratted us out on other crimes we'd committed together to save their own skins on various other beefs. Notably, there were guys like Benjy – the bakery shootist – who were not in court, and I knew I could trust my life to some of the guys I was going to jail with. I hate a rat.

Ten of us were now packing the courtroom every week, fighting for remands and trying to figure out how to lessen the impact of what we were facing. Some guys tried to cut deals for less time. Others, who couldn't stand the filth of the Don Jail, opted to plead guilty, whether they were or not.

Our lawyers advised us to choose trial by judge, reasoning that with our Afros and a variety of new charges, no jury – and certainly no white jury in Toronto – would hesitate to convict us.

On December 8th, 1972, ten of us crowded into a prisoner's box meant for six. It was a crapshoot. I had no idea who was going to cut deals, or fight their cases in lower court or opt for trial by jury in higher court.

If you fought, you were looking at another year in the Don Jail. If you fought and lost, putting the Crown through an expensive trial complete with slick attorneys, suspect witnesses and lying cops, then you were surely looking at a longer sentence.

Bert Novis and his cop buddies sat behind us. When the clerks of the court entered with their stacks of paper and a dictation machine, Novis approached me.

"Listen, you schmuck," he said, leaning in to me. "Do what your lawyer says on this. Your life is on the line." He returned to his seat.

I was stunned. The other cops were stunned, too. They looked at him as if he'd betrayed the oath to serve and protect. The courtroom doors swung open and our lawyers entered, followed by family and friends, as well as the witnesses to the various crimes we had committed. Novis was right. My life was on the line.

In a whispered voice my lawyer, David Newman, offered a question. "Good news and bad news. Which do you want first?" I have always hated it when lawyers play that word game. Nothing ever sounds good when there are chains on your ankles and your wrists.

He said, "The judge who is sitting today will, without a doubt, give you the best possible deal if you plead out, right now, with no hesitation."

"What's the bad news?"

"If you go to higher court and pull everyone along with you, you could end up with a double-digit sentence." Double digits meant ten years or more.

I knew he was guessing, but he was experienced enough that I had to give his hunch some weight. Every lawyer in the room was watching to see what happened next. I was the leader of the pack, and they all wanted the best deals for their clients – at my expense. I had to think fast. The other guys looked at me as if they knew I held their lives in my hands.

I saw my father look to Novis and nod, which made me nervous. Those two never saw eye to eye on anything. In fact, Sonny once beat the shit out of Novis when he'd tried to skip paying for drinks at Sonny's bar.

Should I plead and get it over with, or should I go down swinging, fighting every individual charge? At the back of the court sat two Panthers, friends of Warren Hart. They just glared and stared.

"Order in court!"

The judge strode in and stepped lightly up to his leather chair with a smile on his face, as if he didn't have a care in the world.

"Well, it seems we have a packed house today. First case, please."

"Your Honour, this is all one case, albeit a complicated one," replied the Crown attorney. "Mr. Richard Atkinson is charged jointly with everyone in documents one through thirty, but not everyone else is charged with the others."

"Who is Mr. Richard Atkinson?"

My lawyer spoke up. "Your Honour, I have spoken to all the other lawyers here, and they have spoken to their clients, who have all agreed to plead guilty if Mr. Atkinson were to do also."

I sat there, frozen, while everyone held their breath. The judge would have been happy to have me make his day easier. He nudged me along. "Mr. Atkinson, would you like some time to consider the weight of what your lawyer has just said?"

"I need a minute."

The room exploded in a cloud of whispering coming from the other accused, from the cops, from the witnesses and from our families.

Again, my lawyer whispered, "Listen, you're going to get fucked, but this guy has a smaller dick than any other judge in the system. How hard you want to get fucked is up to you."

I've always appreciated straight talk.

I responded quietly but firmly, "I'm not pleading guilty to shit I didn't do." And listed the charges that some of the guys had implicated me in, just because they thought it would get them a break in court.

Newman sighed and made his move; or rather, he made my move: "Charges ten through eighteen, Mr. Atkinson wishes to take upstairs, Your Honour."

That caused a quick huddle between the Crown attorney and the cops. The Crown turned to the judge and said, "The Crown wishes to withdraw all those lesser charges against Mr. Atkinson, your honour."

At the end of the day, I pleaded guilty to the remaining charges and was remanded for two weeks, when I would be sentenced for the robbery, for the guns and for a safecracking charge unrelated to the bakery.

The others in the box were dispatched with quickly, a week here or a year there. Brian, Owen the Crook and my brother and I went back downstairs for the return trip to the Don.

All the scores I'd done, all of the crime I committed – I never once thought about what would happen if I got caught. Now, I was looking at as much as a decade behind bars.

In the end, Dwane got a year in the reformatory. It pays to be young. Brian and Owen got four years.

I got two four-year sentences, to run concurrently, for the robbery and the gun charges, plus another eighteen months indefinite for the safe-cracking.

The cops looked at each other in disgust, as if I'd been slapped on the wrist. My family looked at the judge as if I'd been sent up the river forever.

As they led us away in chains, Sharon rushed between the escort cops and she kissed me.

We sat in the Don for another thirty days, until our appeals ran out. I used the time to learn as much as I could about how to survive in the pen and what might be in store. Some guys taught me how to make knife-like shanks. Using basic items like rubber bands, paper clips and tinfoil from cigarette papers, I learned to make improbably lethal "zip guns."

When I learned that the guards found a fully loaded .357 magnum in the prison yard at Millhaven, I knew real weapons were a possibility.

KINGSTON PEN

"Atkinson, Crookendale, Bush – grab your stuff, you're on a load. Down below!"

The guard checked us, one by one, against the pictures on our intake cards. Some of the guys slapped my hand and wished me well as I passed by. Most didn't bother to look up from their books or papers. Guys came and went every day.

We stopped along the range, picking up more guys, a dozen in total.

"Your limos will be here shortly, gentlemen."

I love sarcasm.

They handed us paper bags with our street clothes. We dressed and moved to a holding pen.

"Let's go, boys, your limos are here."

As we walked to the loading dock in groups of four, it became apparent that the guard had not been lying – waiting for us were three black Lincoln limousines. What the hell? There was no time for curiosity. They drove us downtown to the train station. Whenever we stopped at a light people stared, wondering about the big shots in the convoy of limos.

We were led onto a train bound for Montreal, with a stop for us in Kingston. The crowd moved back to let us on first. The porter was from Nova Scotia – I could tell by his voice. I wondered if we were related. We took seats in the front of the car, with guards sprinkled all around us.

The regular passengers seemed relaxed and unperturbed as they walked through the train, passing by our chains and the unarmed guards. Some convicts even struck up conversations with folks who sat nearby. I felt embarrassed. At that time, Canadian judges viewed doing time at Kingston as harsh punishment, which they reserved for the baddest of the bad. Now I found myself fitting into that small category of Canadian misfits.

Two hours later, we pulled into Kingston, where three more limos were waiting, 1960 Chryslers. My curiosity was satisfied. So few men were sentenced to hard time that it was easier to arrange a limo ride than it was to keep a fleet of buses.

The ride to KP, as the Kingston Penitentiary was called, took ten minutes.

Across the street from KP was a similar, somewhat smaller limestone prison – the Kingston Prison for Women or P4W. I blurted out, "That's where I want to do my time."

A guard said, "No, you wouldn't, son. I worked there. It ain't a pretty place."

It took me years to understand what he meant.

As the limos pulled up to the front gates of my new home, a guard came out of a little hut, holding a Belgian-made, semi-automatic rifle. A long-barrelled revolver was strapped to his waist. Four uniformed prison guards walked out as the two, huge grey wooden doors studded with black metal bolts swung open, and we were driven in. I took one last look at the outside world before the gates swung shut.

I could see solid limestone walls and a world of bulletproof glass, gun ports and the cold stares of faces that seemed never to have known a smile. The guards, some of whom were armed, made sure the doors were shut before they gave the word to let us out of the cars.

Two guards pulled an eight-inch-thick iron bar through iron rings protruding from thick metal poles set in the floor. With a clanging sound like an old bell, the big front gates were locked. Getting out was not going to be easy. They removed our chains, and I stretched cautiously, looking around at my new home.

The administration, classification and reception building was to the east in a three-storey block made of limestone with thinly barred windows and doors.

To the south was a huge monolith of limestone with rows of two-storey windows almost hidden by thick iron bars. High above, a central dome rose seventy-five feet in the air, topped with a green copper roof.

Behind us was the north entrance, with its walls and armed guards looking down. To the west was the tallest of all the walls, with a guard tower and a guard walking along with a rifle strapped to his shoulder.

KP had been built in 1833, years before Confederation. It was a world unto itself, and I was trapped in the middle of it.

A guy I knew, Chicago, nudged me and nodded toward a double garage pressed up against the thick walls of the cellblocks. I could hear snarling dogs pacing around inside it. On top of the garage, perched on a black iron pedestal, was a lawn jockey figurine – all big eyes and thick lips, holding a metal umbrella with a light under it.

Chicago whispered, "Ain't that a bitch. You don't see those much in the States anymore."

I said, quietly, "Welcome to the Great White North."

"No talking!" ordered a guard.

We followed him to the door marked "Reception." They paraded us in front of a group of old men sitting behind an old wooden desk.

"Atkinson, you're first."

As usual, everything was alphabetical. One of the old men spat tobacco juice into a small tin can beside the desk. He got up slowly; creaking like the chair he'd just left, looking at me like his aches and pains were my fault. He walked over to a wooden counter, shiny from use, and pointed to a chair. I sat there while another tobacco juice spitter took my picture.

The old man said, "Step over here."

This time I went to a small table with a black inkpad on it. He pressed my fingers, one by one, into the pad; then rolled my inky fingertips onto a thick piece of paper.

He handed my picture and my prints to another, even older man who sat hunched over an ancient black typewriter. In his mouth, the unlit stub of an old cigar stuck to his lips.

"Sit here, please."

Then, rapid fire: "What they pinch you for? What they hit you with? Where you hang your hat? Who's your God?"

I gave it back to him the way he'd asked for it. "Robbery. Life. Toronto. Black Muslim." He looked up at me for an instant, and then typed what I'd told him on a small pink card.

I don't know why I lied about my sentence. I wasn't in for life. I just blurted it out. It sounded like the right thing to say. Maybe I was thinking that it really was my life that was being taken from me.

He tore the card out of the typewriter and handed it to me. "Don't ever forget the number on the top of this card. It is your name from now on, son."

My name was 9385Y. The "Y" stood for "Youth." I was too young to vote, but I was old enough to rot in jail. Another old man, a convict, grabbed my file and said, gruffly, "Come with me, please."

I followed him into a shower room where we were ordered to strip down. A plainclothes officer held a jug of green liquid. "Watch out for your eyes. This fucking shit will hurt like hell."

He poured the sticky green goo onto my Afro. I rubbed the burning slime all over before rinsing it off and washing myself down. The Don was full of lice and crabs, and I had come in from the Don in the company of other guys from the Don.

Someone tossed me a towel and I dried my face as quickly as I could. I'd learned the lesson long ago – shutting your eyes in prison, outside the confines of your cell, even for a second or two, is a dangerous thing to do.

Still naked, I walked out and stood there as the others were deloused. Then a stack of prison-issue clothing was dropped in front of us. We dressed without a word. That was our induction into the hall of shame.

Two uniformed guards led us away. We followed them, carrying our kit – a change of clothing and a plastic bucket stuffed with a toothbrush, some gritty pink toothpowder, a mirror, a pack of double-sided razor blades, metal safety razor, thick bar of lye soap and a shiny metal cup. As they paraded us silently into the courtyard under the main dome, I could see charred and broken furniture littering some of the cellblocks. There were twisted steel bars and broken toilets. One cellblock had holes smashed through every one of the walls, which were two feet thick. We had arrived in the aftermath of a riot.

Owen smirked and said, "Boys must have been really mad to cause that kind of destruction."

It had lasted for four days, starting with six guards being taken hostage. The guards were ultimately released unharmed, but the rioters also took fourteen sex offenders from the protective custody unit and tied them to chairs in a circle under the central dome.

Four pigeons fluttered above us and landed on an old steel girder. We looked up and they looked down, beady eyes scanning us for weakness.

Cellblocks, four of them, fanned out like tiered spokes from under the dome. Huddled around the two-storey iron grills in some of the less-damaged blocks stood knots of prisoners, watching to see what new fish were now swimming in their pool. I stood tall and squared my shoulders, staring back without blinking, straining to see the faces of relatives or friends.

To the right of us were three barber's chairs that had not been smashed in the riot. The toughest of the rioters had sat in the barber's chairs while passing judgment over the fourteen "undesirables." After the makeshift sentencing, these unfortunates had been burned, their bones broken, and their eyes gouged out while all the other prisoners hung from bars, stood on platforms or sat on floors, watching the mayhem that went on for days. Two were killed.

I heard those stories for years afterward. Eventually, I learned that the most vocal of the rioters were themselves rapists and stool pigeons whose histories were hidden from the others. They were able to seek blood and vengeance without being challenged because no one knew their dirty little secrets.

On this day, however, the chairs were manned with actual barbers. One of them nodded at me, Paddy McCarnan, a rounder from the west end of Toronto. I smiled and touched my Afro gently. He smiled back and brandished his scissors, his eyes gleaming.

"You guys, over here."

We walked over to the head keeper, who stood behind his desk with a clipboard in hand. He ran his eyes over us; no surprises here, he'd seen it all. On either side of him stood two chubby guards with cold piercing eyes. They had yellow stripes attached to their lapels, giving them an air of importance.

Behind the keeper was a blackboard with the name and number of every prisoner in the jail – where they slept and worked, who was in the hole, and who was in the hospital.

I recognized some of the names.

One of them, Big Joe DiNardo, was a guy I wanted to see. He was a well-known rounder who specialized in arm-and-leg work as a debt collector for the mob. As a professional boxer, he'd known every top thief and gangster in Toronto. Inside KP, he worked in the kitchen, but he was jail savvy. I hoped he could teach me how to survive in adult prison.

Then I saw my name on the blackboard. Owen, Chicago and Brian had been assigned the same range as me.

"Each one of you will go over there and get a haircut according to the rules and regulations of the Penitentiary Act. After that, you will be confined to your ranges until tomorrow morning, when directions will be given as to where you will go and what your assignments will be."

One of the guards handed out some pamphlets. "In those papers are all the rules of the institution. Read them. Obey the rules and everything will be fine." He gestured toward the keeper's hall, which was filled with armed guards. "Don't fuck up, boys. We don't play games here. Any questions?"

We knew enough not to ask.

I walked over to Paddy's chair, where he held up the barber's cape like a matador waiting for a bull. He gave me a big hug as he draped it over me.

"Ricky, I know you're fussy about your hair. How would you like it done?"

I didn't think I'd get a choice. "Paddy, my friend, not too much off the top, and leave the sideburns." I heard the clippers, and then I felt them running through my hair like a lawn mower. In one swift motion, my hair was parted like the Red Sea.

Paddy stood back, holding his clippers like Moses held his rod. The two guards burst out laughing. Chicago said, loud enough for everyone to hear, "Oh, shit, just like the army – bro, your 'fro is on the flo.'" That brought down the house.

I jumped out of the chair.

"What the fuck, Paddy?"

He told me what the fuck – the Penitentiary Act stated that all prisoners had to get their hair cut so that it didn't go below their collars, and sideburns could not go below the middle of the ear. Moustaches were not allowed below the lower lip without a doctor's note. I don't know what a doctor would have to say about that.

I sat back down, and he finished up. Seconds later, my carefully tended identity lay on the floor, under Paddy's feet. I looked in the mirror. Out of kindness, he'd left me a scant two inches. My mother would have loved it.

But I did not. Without thinking, I asked him to take it all off. It didn't take long – so much for saying it loud, black and proud. I'd been called, and now I was bald.

Brian, Chicago and Owen followed my lead. The other prisoners were mystified. Hair had status in that era and anyone who was bald by choice stood out. That was the point. It was a choice. More than that, it was a statement.

An old, worried-looking convict asked, in a low voice, "Son, do we all got to get our hair cut like that?"

I said, "Man, we're from Spadina Avenue."

He nodded, knowing that we were in a crew. He could keep what little hair he had.

The cell assigned to me was on the second of four tiers. When I got there, I knew instantly which cell was mine – there were four, maybe five, small paper bags in front of it.

How did I know it was my cell?

In most prisons, rounders looked after each other, leaving little canteen bags of soap, cigarettes, writing paper or junk food in front of your cell door as a greeting. It helped you to get you on your feet until the first canteen was available for you to buy things you needed. Sometimes guys left personal kites wishing you well, as a way to repay previous favours.

I had friends inside. However, I remember my father telling me not to take anything from strangers in prison, in case they might want it back in strange and unusual ways. I wasn't afraid of sexually aggressive inmates. Anyone who was homosexual had to keep himself in check or the other prisoners would kill him. The only way to lose your prison cherry was to fall for a smooth talker who moved in under the pretence of showing you the ropes. Most of the younger prisoners focussed their sexual energy on girls in porn magazines that floated all around the prison. I knew the ropes, but I studied the rule book anyway, to avoid surprises.

Basically, the cells in KP were identical to the cells in training school, except these had no hot water. I asked the guy next door to me about showering.

"Car wash once a week," he told me. I asked what he meant. He explained that the shower was a twenty-foot runway of showerheads you had to rush past. You couldn't stop for any reason or the guards would tell you to keep moving.

"You got to be quick to get clean in this shithole."

He told me how to make a "bug," an electrical device, using spoons as a resistor that could be used to heat a bucket of water.

"But if they pinch you, you're off to the digger."

Attached to the wall of my cell was a small metal box with three holes in it. You could plug in a pair of earphones and listen to prison radio. The deejays announced arrivals, sent messages to prisoners in hospital, and they were skilled enough to keep me laughing.

After supper, we were let out to socialize. Most guys settled in to watch a hockey game. They were linked together by ceramic headphones that were hooked into an electrical line that ran to the TV.

There was very little noise. Every prisoner knew to respect the space, time and privacy of everyone else. If you didn't do your time quietly, you were likely to get roughed up or your cell would be torched or worse.

I'd been given a heads-up that in the morning a guy with a hot-water jug came along. If you wanted hot water for shaving, you tapped your pencil on the cell bars as he walked by. You only got one cup, so it was either a shave or a cup of instant coffee. Shaving was mandatory, so coffee was a sometime thing.

I got another piece of advice from an old convict: "Don't ever call the water man a water boy, or you're liable to get a jug of boiling water thrown in your face. Or maybe he'll just stab you."

KP was a serious prison with serious convicts in it, and the threat of death hung in the air. In that way, it was unlike a provincial jail. Anyone could be murdered at any time. The unwritten rule was that respect got respect – that was the law of the streets – and I knew it well.

Big Joe DiNardo appeared at the main barrier to our range and called me over. He passed a small package through the bars, food he'd cooked for me in the kitchen and a chunk of cheddar cheese. But this was no Welcome Wagon social call. He looked angry.

"I hear your card says you're a life. Does it?"

I grinned, thinking I was cool for claiming I was one.

"Listen, Ricky, the last thing you want is for people to think you're a lifer. Most lifers are square johns with nothing to lose by ratting you out and everything to gain – namely, their fucking freedom. They're not rounders like us. We're crooks, inside out.

"Take that fucking card off your cell door and rip it up. Another one will be on your cell door in the morning, with your right sentence on it. Doing life is for guys too stupid to get away with murder." He pressed his face close to the bars and – if you can believe it – he got even more serious.

"You're not starting this thing out right," he told me. "You shaved your head. Why? You want to start a revolution? Other guys follow you.

Now you're marked as a leader and a troublemaker. Ricky, you don't want that shit. You want to get out as quick as possible. The good scores and the good money are all on the outside. In here, there's nothing but shit and misery."

I let that sink in.

"Tomorrow, you go for orientation. Meet me in the yard in the afternoon and I will introduce you to some good people." Before he turned away he said, "Watch out for the rats. They're as big as cats. They come up out of the toilet at night. Flush all your uneaten food and keep your cell clean."

Rats? Rats.

I thanked him, and went to share what he'd given me with Owen and Brian, but Owen would not take the piece of cheddar cheese I offered him. He had his reasons – while he was in Guelph reformatory someone told him that only rats ate cheese. This led to a fight, which led to thirty days in the hole. For fourteen of those thirty days he lived on bread and water. Then, because he'd kicked a guard in the balls when the guard called him a nigger, he spent ten days with his hands cuffed behind his back.

Cheese left a bad taste in Owen's mouth.

That night, I was unable to read as I usually did. I knew that roughly fifteen percent of the men inside were murderers. In KP, murderers were not at the top of the pecking order unless they had a reputation for being mob hit men, or if they were especially cunning and hard to catch.

I also knew that some guys did their time on the installment plan, one little sentence at a time. Prison psychologists called them "limit setters." For those guys, doing time was part of a lifelong cat-and-mouse game. Getting caught was just part of the game. I didn't want that game. I slept uneasily. In the middle of the night I heard a noise coming from my toilet, and I quickly placed a tray over it.

That was my first rat.

The next afternoon, I found Big Joe working out – pounding the heavy bag like a pro, running his punches up one side and down the other, the rhythm as fast as a drum roll. Other prisoners watched him and waited their turn, hands bound with wraps made from torn bed sheets.

When Big Joe finished we took a walk, falling in with those who were circling the yard. While others played handball, threw horseshoes or lifted weights, very few walked alone. What I noticed was that eyes were everywhere – everyone was paying attention to everything, without staring, but never missing a move or a gesture. Only fish – new prisoners – or the mentally ill were tuned out, unaware of the ever-present danger.

Big Joe pointed out the major rounders and introduced me to guys from the Montreal mob, as well as the Toronto and Hamilton mobs. I met safecrackers, bank robbers and bikers from the Satan's Choice, the Para-Dice Riders, the Vagabonds and the Black Diamond Riders.

An Italian guy stopped to shake my hand. Domenic Racco, was the son of one of Toronto's oldest mob bosses and the future heir of that organization.

"Thanks for the job you did for me," he said." It was great."

I'd blown up someone's work van for him. He wanted to make a point without hurting anyone. I got the job through Warren Hart, and I took it because I figured that a good impression might pay off somewhere down the line.

I didn't have to tell Big Joe what the mobster was alluding to. We never talked about things we'd done and gotten away with. I knew that Big Joe was both liked and respected. By showing me respect, the others in his crew would respect me.

As we circled the yard, Big Joe filled me in on the recent riot– one guy had gone off and everyone followed. There were no leaders. It was spontaneous collective mayhem.

How does that happen?

"Ricky, many of the assholes here aren't happy unless everyone around them is unhappy; misery loves company."

He worked in the kitchen, so he used a kitchen analogy. "Prison is like a big pot of stew. The lid is the guards, and their guns make sure none of the ingredients boil over or escape.

"The prison walls are the pot, big enough and thick enough to keep whatever's inside cooking peacefully. And everything inside is the stew.

"Look around; some guys are slick and colourful, full of flavour, filled with energy – others are just lumps of stupidity. Every stew needs a good roux. In here, the roux is pure hate. It's hate that brings the flavour together.

"The herbs and spices are bits of love and compassion. Every prison has its own secret collection of herbs and spices; that's why every prison seems different.

"But when the roux becomes too thick, it affects every part of the stew. When the stew begins to boil with hate, you can smell it until, boom–a riot and everything is spoiled. Once you understand this stew, you'll realize that it all tastes the same in the end – like shit."

He laughed.

We ended up in front of the heavy bag. He slid a pair of gloves on my hands.

"People are watching;" he told me. "Beat this bag like it was Bert Novis. Show them not to fuck with you." He called out punch combinations, and I did what he said the best I could until the loudspeakers blared.

"Clear the yard!!!"

As we walked back, he laid it out so that it was easy to follow. "Listen, because of your relatives – your friends, your father, your history – you don't know who your enemies are. Your friends are very few.

"In here, the drag queens have power. Stay away from them; they're nothing but trouble.

"Don't shoot your mouth off. No one likes a braggart.

"Mind your business.

"Don't do dope – the easiest way to kill you is to get you high and slit your throat.

"Don't back down from anyone, ever, but don't start any bullshit, either. You're a natural leader; you'll do okay. Getting out as quickly as you can is the real game, remember that."

Rules to live by.

The second day was easier than the first.

We were to be tested, so that the staff could make the right decision about placing us. KP was neither the best place, nor the final stop, for everyone.

We learned about options for training. Rehab was big at the time. Although no prisoner had ever earned a BA behind bars, there were no limits on the courses you could take.

As for work, Big Joe advised me to take kitchen duty.

He mentioned the Santa Claus bandit; a man who'd killed two cops during a bank robbery. He worked in the kitchen. So did another bank robber, a master baker named Joe Majestik.

According to Joe, food had its advantages in jail.

"If you give somebody a little something they can't get, you make a friend. One hand washes the other, and you never know when a friend can come in handy."

The next day I told my orientation instructor that I wanted to work in the kitchen no matter what jail I was placed in.

Five weeks later Brian, Owen, Chicago and I appeared before the transfer board. Big Joe had cautioned me to be careful. Guys who were trouble-makers could be sent to Millhaven Max, or anywhere else in the country.

They sent Chicago to Joyceville, a low-key medium security prison twenty miles away with one fence and no barbed wire. Owen went to Warkworth, a hundred miles west; our safecracker friend, Barnyard, was there. It was similar to Joyceville – medium security, one fence, no barbed wire and lots of programs.

Brian and I were classified for Collins Bay, the gladiator school. It had walls, not fences. From there, I was hoping that I might find my way to Beaver Creek Institution in cottage country, two hours north of Toronto. Beaver Creek was minimum security – no fences, no guard towers and a swimming pool. Prisoners there had access to town, and sometimes they could get to Toronto.

A few weeks before my eighteenth birthday, I was handcuffed and shackled to five other men. We were herded into a green prison van. Once inside, a guard told us what was going on. There had been a murder the day before in Collins Bay, so transferring us there was out for the moment.

Instead, he told us, "Three of you are off to Warkworth, and the other three are headed for Millhaven. Behave yourselves there and you'll be in the Bay in a couple of months."

I figured there was no way Brian and I were going into maximum security. I gave one of the guys a couple of messages to pass along; I rehearsed him over and over again until his face turned into a mask of hatred.

The van eventually pulled up to the super maximum prison, the dreaded Millhaven. A guard said, "Atkinson, Bush, Pennick – get out, you're home." I felt sick to my stomach.

The guy I'd been sitting with told me what to do with the messages I made him memorize.

We shuffled in. They took us into a room.

"Strip down," instructed the guard. We were naked in seconds. "Who's Atkinson?" I nodded. He tossed me a set of prison greens, and I dressed.

"Follow me."

We went down a hall, through a barrier, into a waiting area, past more guards, down another hall and through another barrier. I didn't like the feel of it. Something was up.

One more barrier and I stopped dead in my tracks. I was facing two lines of guards; they were in shirtsleeves, holding nightsticks. Some of them taunted me; others slapped their sticks against their palms.

I looked around. The barrel of a shotgun slid out from behind a gun port, pointing in my direction. The five guards who were behind me pushed me toward the ten guards who were waiting.

When I turned to look at the guard who pushed me, one of the others cracked my skull.

"Listen, Atkinson, we heard about you," snarled the guard who hit me. "We heard you got a big mouth on you. Millhaven knows how to shut your mouth. You got anything smart to say now?"

He raised his club, waiting.

I'd heard about the Millhaven gauntlet, but I thought it was just a story some cons made up. My head was throbbing, proof that it was no story.

"I'm fucking talking to you, boy. My name is Stringer. You got a problem with me?"

I didn't say anything. Besides, anything I might have said would be construed as an excuse.

"Then we ain't going to have any fucking problems out of you, are we, Atkinson?"

It wasn't a question.

I suppressed the urge to strike back. "I just want to chill out until I can get over to the Bay. You guys won't have any trouble from me."

One of the guards kicked open a thick steel door and I passed between the line of guards into a room with a nurse and two other guards. The nurse examined me and asked if I was okay. I was not okay, but I was okay enough. When I finally reached the cell I'd been assigned to, I sat on the bed wondering what the hell had just happened.

There was nothing to say, and it was probably safer to say nothing.

I felt humiliated, as though I'd wimped out. I should have slugged the guard who'd hit me. What did I have to lose? How much worse could it get? I was already in hell, looking all the devils in the eye.

A few minutes later I heard keys jingling, locks snapping, doors sliding and I saw Brian pass by. He, too, was rubbing his head. I wanted to call out to him but there was nothing to say, and it was probably safer to say nothing. At least my cell was spotless, with a toilet and a sink that had hot water, and a metal desk and a metal closet that wasn't bolted to the wall. There was a transistor radio on the desk. When I turned it on, I heard the voice of Wolfman Jack out of New York City. I fell asleep to the sound of soul.

Because I was on the transfer range, the other prisoners couldn't get on the range to greet me. I couldn't even go to the big yard on weekends with the rest of the prison population. I got kites from the guys I knew and that helped.

On my second day, I went to the common room to watch TV. Everyone voted on what to watch and hockey won. So there I was with nothing to watch and nothing to read.

I saw a glint of metal.

A guard, behind his protective glass bubble, drew his pistol like a gunslinger and started twirling it, pointing it at us, having his little fun. There were occasions, I knew, when guards shot into the common room or down the ranges if there was a fight, or someone was not obeying rules.

When the door opened for changeover, some prisoners gave the guard the finger, and I went back to my cell.

After a month, my mother came up with Sharon to visit me on my eighteenth birthday. I was locked behind bulletproof glass, and we talked through a small screen at the bottom of the window. I knew there was a microphone planted there to pick up everything we said.

The same day, I got a card from Margaret Morgan, Warren Hart's girlfriend. It was full of ideology, including a pep talk from Warren to keep my chin up. He wrote that he'd do what he could to help get me an early parole. I didn't know how connected he was but he knew a few people and maybe he could pull a few strings.

Shortly after that, Millhaven was on lockdown. Guards had found a fully loaded handgun, which meant every inch of the place had to be searched. The Goon Squad descended on us. I didn't give a shit about the search. What bothered me was knowing that the gun must have been brought in by one of the staff. That meant that fists or pipes or knives were no longer trumps in a range fight.

If I couldn't get a gun, I had to be smart if I was going to finish my sentence unscathed.

Four weeks later, Brian and I were sent to Collins Bay.

As we were being shackled for the ride, Officer Stringer walked over.

"Hey, Atkinson," he said. "You should be glad you kept your mouth shut. I really wanted a piece of you. Your uncle Ronny grabbed me by the throat a couple of years ago. I thought he was going to tear my head off. He was so big. We had to kick his ass real good to keep him in line. Are all the black bastards in your family so damn big?"

He was grinning when he said it.

I didn't say a word, and I didn't break my gaze. I knew, and he knew, that we'd somehow meet again. What Stringer didn't know was that at that very second I promised myself that I would kill the next guard who hit me. I'd kill him on the spot or as soon as I got out. I could match the cunning of the killers who surrounded me – those in uniform and those in prison greens. Warren Hart had trained me to kill and I had just read the story of pre-Civil War rebellion leader Nat Turner who rose up to slay his slave masters. I figured it was better to die a man than live like a prison mouse.

COLLINS BAY

The road to my next home ran along the edge Lake Ontario. I could see slabs of ice pushing onto the shore and Amherst Island, with its pretty farmhouses, floating in the distance. This place had history. Bath, Ontario was a British Loyalist town. The Loyalists had brought their slaves in chains with them. Four hundred years later, here I was – in chains.

As we neared, a guard came out of one of the little red rooftop parapets of Collins Bay and looked down on us with his binoculars. There was a rifle slung over his shoulder. He picked up his walkie-talkie, and moments later four guards walked out onto the driveway where we sat waiting.

One of them said, "They're sure filling this place up with burrheads, ain't they?"

"Sign of the times," said another. "We might have another Attica on our hands any day now."

There hadn't been much racism in Millhaven; too many other worries there. It looked as if this was going to be different.

Brian and I shuffled in. We were fingerprinted and posed for pictures. Once again, we were issued clothing, ceramic earphones, shaving kit, mirror, toilet brush and bucket. They ordered us to sit around for the count to clear before herding us to our cells in 1-Block. Guards from each of the four blocks handed slips of paper to the head keeper, who wrote the count on a board and matched it to every inmate in the prison. Some of the guards looked at us as if we were only numbers, but one of them had just come from the gym and was still in his tracksuit.

"Do you two play basketball?"

We nodded and he smiled. "I'm trying to get a team together to play teams from the community. Why don't you show up at practice tonight for a tryout?"

Collins Bay played in the top basketball league in the Kingston area, and I wanted to be in it.

As we waited for the count to end, I noticed two small boxes on the floor, marked with the name of a convict. I'd seen that name six weeks earlier. The boxes held the belongings of a man who had been murdered. His death was the reason it took so long for me to get to Collins Bay.

His body may have been gone, but the Ontario Provincial Police, who investigated all murders in federal prisons in the province, had not yet released his personal property,

I heard that a native prisoner had killed him over a five-dollar debt. That told me something about the dead man. Only a fool would borrow something he couldn't pay back.

After the count was over, we were told to go to our cells. I knew I'd know some of the people in the prison, but I had no idea who my neighbours would be.

We walked down the strip to 1-Block, passing other prisoners heading for the kitchen. There were large thick grills on each block door; each cell had a thick set of bars for a door, but none of the doors were locked.

The jail was wide open.

There were only ten blacks in Collins Bay, until a tall thin Trinidadian prisoner, known as the Bible Bandit, joined us. I knew him from Alexandra Park. He robbed four banks, armed with nothing more than a Bible. The judge, a devout Christian, gave him eighteen years.

I knew his sister – everyone wanted her and no one touched her.

"This place is about to blow up," he announced. "Maybe now that there are more of us here, we can cool it down."

Chicago said, "Fuck these peckerheads. I'll kill them in ways they never knew they could die."

Chicago hailed from the Black Stonerangers, the biggest gang in North America, and he'd done three year-long tours in Vietnam. Lots of guys in prison talk loud, bragging about women and violence. I presumed, rightly, that Chicago was the kind of man who didn't talk loud and cut real deep. We had something in common. Chicago James Edwards was in for robbing a Toronto bank. He was hunted down and arrested by none other than Bert Novis.

"Jug up!" It was time to eat.

The kitchen was divided into two sections by a brightly painted wall. There was a guard at the end of the food line. You had to pass him with your tray. The plates were ceramic, which meant they could be broken into shards, and the knives and forks were real not plastic, which meant they could be stolen and sharpened. These are things I immediately noted. However, the guard seemed more interested in how many desserts I had on my tray than the quantity of cutlery.

What caught my attention most was that there were glass bottles of HP Sauce and ketchup, as well as salt and pepper shakers on every table. Broken glass is, after all, a weapon.

The kitchen workers loaded your plate with healthy portions of fresh vegetables and meat. On the floor there were two boxes of fresh pears, donated by a local farmer. If the guard thought you had too much fruit, he'd make you put some back. Brew master inmates could make a powerful drink from a handful of fruit and some bread.

There weren't enough tables for all 400 prisoners, so the ranges were let out in staggered formation, allowing guys to chow down and move on. I looked around for a place to sit and noticed a loose pecking order.

The blacks in the joint sat at two tables by the windows. Big Joe Reddick, a neighbour from the Projects sat at a table with some white dudes. Ernie George, a black biker who became a friend, sat with a group of Satan's Choice bikers from London, Ontario. The Para-Dice Riders sat behind them, and a couple of Vagabonds sat at another table.

The Toronto crew was the biggest, followed by Hamilton and Windsor. Italians sat along a back wall and took up four whole tables. One or two natives were sprinkled here and there. The rest of the population was white and non-affiliated as far as I could tell, although most of the white guys sat with prisoners from their hometowns or neighbourhoods. In that way it was just like high school. You could sit wherever you liked, providing you gave up your seat, out of respect, to anyone who was more entrenched.

My first prison scrap happened a day after I arrived. It was unexpected. We were in the gym early, at basketball practice, at a time when most of the prison was still asleep. The basketball rolled into the weightlifting room, so I went to get it. There was one big, chunky guy in the weight room struggling to bench-press more than he could handle.

"You burrheads, keep that ball out of here."

I looked around, not sure I'd heard right. Burrheads? Are you kidding me? The guy pumping iron was the only one there; in an instant, I decided what to do.

On the floor by the basketball was a twelve-inch weight bar. I picked it up along with the basketball, and thought how foolish this guy had been to make such a racist comment. I held the bar behind my back and dribbled the ball toward him. He was groaning against the weight and was about to say something else when I brought the bar down on the meaty part of his leg.

He dropped the barbell and it crashed into his chest, pinning him to the bench. I raised the bar over my head and looked down on him. "You ever call me burrhead again and I'll smash your head in."

"Okay, okay," said the fool.

I dropped the bar on the floor and went to leave. He cried, "Man, help me with this weight."

"Fuck you."

Many guys whine about how bored they were, but I always thought the opposite. Like many of the smarter prisoners, I learned to forget what was beyond the walls and concentrate on my routine. I began to think of prison the way a monk might think of his monastery, as a place to learn and grow.

No matter how busy I kept myself, I knew I was rotting. I thought of my father with a couple of drinks in him turning our house into party central, with relatives laughing, dancing and eating soul food until all hours of the night. Everyone I knew on the street was living a different life.

I read, studied and pounded the heavy bag. Also, I started a chess club and played every day. White guys would fight over card games, brothers fought harder, but chess was more contemplative and didn't lead to such aggression because it ended with "Checkmate." In the Don Jail, most of the blacks I met who had done some time on death row played chess. At Collins Bay we played in the kitchen. You could play chess anywhere, even in lockdown just by having a tapping code to send moves to a player in another cell.

Having a formal chess club in the prison had an added benefit. Students from Queens' University in Kingston were allowed in to play with us and that meant I got to socialize with them.

On Friday and Saturday nights, the gym turned into a movie theatre, and the entire inmate population could attend. I was surprised when Chicago walked up to me one evening and showed me a very sharp knife.

"These peckerheads can get real dangerous in a group, in the dark," he told me, putting the knife in his waistband.

Off we went to the movies. If he'd been frisked by one of the guards, he'd have landed in the hole. I felt a little better knowing one of us was armed with more than fists.

The brothers usually sat on the stage but Big Joe from the Projects sat on the gym floor with the white boys, and Ernie George sat in the front two rows with his biker buddies.

Ernie Moore, my honey-bun-and-coffee saviour from the cells at the Old City Hall jail, had failed in his bid to have old charges dropped. Here he was the Bay's ultimate hustler, sitting with his hippie friends, smoking weed and having a good time. Ernie was the guy you went to for a radio, a coveted job or information on the prison grapevine – anything from a smoke to a sip. He also worked outside of the institution on a work release program, providing information to the world about the Canadian prison system.

I came to learn that if the movie was good, every prisoner in the joint crowded in. Cigarettes and joints were passed, and sometimes there were small containers of moonshine or hard liquor. A boring movie sent the guys drifting back to their cells. If the movie was really shitty and only a few guys remained, those guys would be asked to allow the gym to be used for sports. But it was rare for anyone to leave the gym on movie night.

The movie that evening was *100 Rifles* with Jim Brown and Raquel Welch. As soon as Jim Brown appeared, there was grumbling. Somebody yelled, "Get the nigger out of the movie!" I couldn't tell who said it. A couple of guys stood up and left. You couldn't tell if they didn't like westerns or if they couldn't stand black men in westerns.

"Lynch the black buck!"

The men on the floor laughed nervously, but the brothers were dead silent. In the middle of the movie, Jim Brown took Raquel Welch into his big arms and kissed her. She seemed to melt into him. Ten more men stood up to leave.

Chicago said, "Get her, Jim! She's gonna love that black stick!" Down on the floor, someone shouted, "Fuck you!" A few more guards came in and took positions in the gym. Things settled down, albeit nervously.

Suddenly, in the darkness, I noticed a glint of metal – a knife, flashing in our direction. I froze as it sailed over everyone's head and caught in the curtain behind us. I picked it up and slid off the stage, making my way down onto the gym floor.

Chicago and the Bible Bandit followed me. Within a few minutes, the rest of the brothers joined us. I showed them the knife. None of them saw it flying through the air.

"Listen, if someone sticks me I can stick them back," I told them. "But sitting up there like ducks in a shooting gallery is just fucking stupid."

So, in effect, we desegregated movie night. The stage actually had the best view and from then on it was first come, first served. Idiots still yelled out in the darkness when there was a black actor, but from then on, people seemed to accept that we were going to sit where we wanted. Short of a riot, there was little they could do about it.

Eventually, our ranks swelled to twenty, some of them Vietnam veterans, the most blacks in any prison in Canadian history. How times change. We didn't all like each other but if a beef began over racism, we were all in it together.

Joe DiNardo was eventually transferred in from Joyceville to work in the kitchen. He promised Chicago a kitchen job, and within a couple of weeks there was Chicago, dressed in whites, grinning as he handed out plates.

Contrary to the concerns of the administration, there wasn't a single episode or snide remark. The guys in the kitchen took pride in their work; many of them earning certificates that would be useful on the street.

DiNardo and Chicago took care of me, slipping me treats when they could. Sometimes we cooked for ourselves, which was easier than you might think. The trick was to turn an iron upside down, and to use a tin ashtray as a frying pan. We stole spices from the kitchen, now and then bribing a guard.

In a way, we were in the vanguard of the slow-food movement. Most of our food came fresh from prison farms to prison tables. We got it within minutes from its picking or plucking, thanks to the work of convicts in the farm camps.

During the summer, all the guys made little metal devices to keep their cold-water taps running, so they could chill their pop and prevent food from spoiling. I wrote a letter to the warden asking that we be allowed to order a small fridge to keep our pop cool, rather than running the taps and running up his water bill.

My plan was sensible but it backfired. He ordered his guards to be more aggressive about taking our water tap devices away from us.

Our reaction was to clean our toilets spotlessly, so that we could fill the bowl with cans of pop, jars of milk or plastic bags full of meat. Some guys never pissed in their toilets, disciplining themselves to use the one in the first cell on the range, which was usually left open for those locked out of their cells during the day. Some guys wouldn't let anyone sit down on the toilet for a second, even if the cell was crowded. Others covered the bowl with cardboard, draped it with a towel and used it as an end table.

There were occasional attempts at escape. Amusingly, while on his way to Kingston General Hospital for some minor treatment, Richard Anderson persuaded his guards to pull over so he could throw up. He bolted, jumping into Lake Ontario so that he could swim across to freedom. Poor Richard thought that Amherst Island, a mile offshore, was American territory. He thought wrong. In any case, he only made it ten yards in the water before they reeled him in.

We were allowed to paint our cells any colour we wanted, so I painted mine black, including the sink and the toilet. I painted colourful stars all over the walls with fluorescent paint. With newspapers and glue I created planets and hung them from the ceiling using thread. At night, I'd turn on my black light and my cell would become a three-dimensional universe.

I also used my metal shaving cup as a candleholder, concentrating on the candle while I meditated, creating a world within a world while I did my time.

The days flickered by, one by one. I was bothering no one and letting no one and nothing bother me. People came and went. Some left without a word, their empty cells instantly occupied by someone else. Others had farewell parties. Soon, Big Joe and my cousin, Wade, left the institution for the street.

My books about Buddhism taught me that nothing was forever – not my friends, not the prison, not even me.

Sharon was coming up regularly – it was always nice to snuggle up to her and do the touchy-feely thing – but in a world without women sometimes it was easier to do without. Also, our visits were becoming more and more strained.

From the first months I spent in the Don Jail, I heard rumours that she was unfaithful to me. I worked hard to push those thoughts aside, reasoning that she was a teenager like me and, in her place, I would probably be doing the same thing.

The snuggling came to an abrupt end when Everett came up to visit me. He said Sharon had told him that she and I weren't a couple anymore, so he figured that, since everyone else was taking a shot at her, he might as well make his move. He didn't think it would be an affront to our friendship, but he'd also heard from someone that I wanted to whack him.

I was hurt by the news, but in my world you had to respect a brother who manned up and went face to face with someone over a woman.

Really, I couldn't blame him.

The next time Sharon came up, I confronted her. She swore Everett was lying, but the damage was done; it was officially over.

Brian had the same problems with his girlfriend Cathy, who had just given birth to his daughter. He showed us pictures of the little girl every chance he got. Unfortunately, his girlfriend was into drugs, and she was messing around with many of the people in our old crew.

I began to understand that if your woman is young, good-looking and on drugs, expecting her to be faithful was a fantasy. This was especially true around the guys in our crew who were trained from childhood to be players and manipulators.

The old-school convicts always said, "Get rid of your bitches when you take a pinch. It's better for both of you that way. When you get out, the girls aren't burdened by years of guilt. You aren't burdened by jealousy, and getting back together is easier to do."

That old-school attitude changed a few years later when private visits were allowed and couples could spend a weekend alone, once every few months, in a trailer sitting in the corner of the prison yard.

My problem was finding a way to meet women in a world where there were very few. I picked up a couple of pen pal magazines and spent all my canteen money on stamps, writing to something like a hundred women all over the world. I included pictures, of course.

I was tall, handsome and athletic, dressed in prison greens with a big smile on my face, willing to write anything to get a response. Within a week, I began to get letters and pictures in return, restoring my ego and building back my confidence.

I became bolder and bolder, sending some of the women erotic letters ten pages long. I got the responses I wanted from women who wanted to have fun and who didn't mind that I was in jail for robbery.

One woman, ten years older than me, came to visit from New York State. She wanted sex, and she made no bones about it, grabbing me in a quiet corner of the visiting room. The guard on duty had to tell us to be more discreet or he would cancel the visit.

At a social event in the prison that allowed family participation, I saw an opportunity. I gave the chairman of the inmate committee a carton of smokes in return for his office keys, and the American woman and I had a chance to bump and grind for a few minutes. Lucky me.

She wrote a few more times but ended the relationship, telling me that she was only interested in using me for sex. Since I couldn't provide that more often, there wasn't much point in visiting.

Her rejection didn't slow me down. As long as I had a few stamps and the nerve to reach out to strange women in strange countries, I'd never be lonely again.

After a time, I came to the realization that most people resist change of any kind. They wanted to get up at the same time, eat the same food, watch the same shit over and over on TV, play the same sports or games, and return to their cells each night the same way they had the night before. Any unwanted change in the rhythm of prison life just pissed people off. But there was a rogue element among the staff that relished tension, because tension meant unrest and unrest meant overtime.

In a way, the society of guards was parallel to that of inmates – the more seasoned ones would sometimes intimidate the newer ones into giving up their overtime. Now and then there were fights in the prison parking lot and it wasn't unusual to see a guard with a black eye or a split lip.

I never had to stab anyone in the joint but I had my share of fistfights, usually with people who made racial comments or with idiots who thought I wouldn't fight because I was so young. I was never afraid to fight because a sharp knife cuts a muscled man as easily as it cuts a skinny little addict. It was your willingness to face death that earned you the respect of others.

As for conflict with the guards, there were good ones and bad ones. At times, it was like gladiator school. Bad guards had to fear razor blades stuck to the levers used to open the cell doors. They also had to be aware that sometimes those levers were smeared with shit.

If a guard spotted a narrow hole dug into a prison wall, he or she had to stick a finger in the hole to check for contraband. There were occasions when the hole held a needle and sometimes the resulting finger prick was from a needle tainted with HIV positive blood.

A prisoner who had been making noise in solitary confinement bothered one female guard –a rarity at the time. She tried to shut him up, but whatever she said or threatened didn't work so she maced his dick.

I don't imagine that you've ever had your dick maced, and mine never was, but I can tell you that it burns so much that it is a medical emergency. Her payback? Everyone pissed or shit into a bucket, and the slop was stirred and kept on hand until the right moment. When she walked by she was doused with five sticky gallons. Yes, it was her turn to scream.

I was still a teenager. The tension was getting to me, and I missed Owen, so I put in for a transfer to Warkworth. It came through quickly and easily.

WARKWORTH:
FROM BARBED WIRE TO BARRELS

The drill was familiar. I was strip-searched, handcuffed, shackled and put in a station wagon headed for Campbellford, followed by the medium security prison in Warkworth. On the way, one of the two guards asked me if I was glad to get out of Collins Bay and away from all its problems.

Friendly banter with guards was more than alien to me. I told them I'd have liked to stay with my brothers, but I needed to think about my future on the street, not jail. That opened the door to more conversation.

They told me that Collins Bay was about to explode, and that I was on the list for trouble from the guards, because I seemed to draw the black inmates around me.

That's the guard mentality. I was a problem, not a solution. They also told me about rumours that I was going to be stabbed by one inmate or another. Apparently, there was a kite circulating suggesting that I'd been dealing dope. That was just plain stupid, since I didn't touch the stuff and didn't like anyone who did. Another kite suggested that I was about to kill Big Joe DiNardo after an argument we supposedly had over him serving me pork in a stew. As a Muslim, I didn't eat pork, but there was no way I'd ever attack Joe over that.

Soon the wagon rolled over the crest of a hill and there it was, a sprawling prison nestled in a valley, surrounded by farms. Warkworth had only one fence. Instead of the usual barbed wire, it was topped with colourful plastic barrels that aimed to prevent anyone from climbing over. A prison vehicle patrolled the fence, carrying a guard armed with a rifle and a handgun, just in case.

Already, the whole jail felt like that glass cube I was interred in as punishment at training school. This is going to be interesting, I thought. We stopped at the front entrance and began the usual shuffle into the institution. I was fingerprinted, photographed and issued clothing, shaving kit, bucket, toilet brush and a mirror. Then I was told to report to the office, where I stood in front of an open door, looking at all the secretaries typing and filing papers.

Fred Sisson, a senior security administrator, curled his finger for me to come in. He was a soft-looking, blond man in his early thirties. I followed him into his office, closed the door and turned to face him.

"Mr. Atkinson, this place runs unlike any other prison in Canada, but we have a lot of leeway to do things differently here," he began. "Your file says you have a racial sensitivity problem. We don't have a problem with the coloureds here. Any problems, we ship them to Millhaven, and that's where you'll be going if I hear a single negative thing about you. Got it?"

He had already made his mind up that he was going to treat me like a piece of shit.

I gathered my things and walked to the cellblock. The unit head gave a lecture about how the prison ran, and I was handed a copy of the rule book – always a useful read.

I was allowed to roam, so I stepped out into a little courtyard where Owen was waiting. He looked as happy to see me as I was to see him.

"Let me buy you a pop," he said, leading me to a vending machine. As I began to talk, Owen pulled out a little harmonica, put it to his mouth and used it to answer me. At first I thought he was joking, but he kept answering in harmonica talk. There was something wrong with him.

"Take that fucking thing out of your mouth, man, we got to talk."

I filled him in on the politics of Collins Bay, but he seemed to be in another world. In a moment of awareness, he confided that he was losing his marbles – all he did was stay in his cell, not talking to anyone, studying music and playing the blues on his harp.

He reached into his pocket and gave me one.

He said he'd be going to the Frontenac prison farm camp in ninety days, and asked me to hang out with him until then. I put the harmonica to my mouth and answered him with musical notes.

"Maybe by then, I'll be as crazy as you."

We both laughed and it seemed as if the old Owen – Owen the Crook – was standing in front of me. I gave him back his little harmonica. I wanted to wait to visit the Warkworth music room and sign out a more kick-ass instrument like a guitar or saxophone to help pass the time.

I settled easily enough into the routine.

Warkworth had more organized activities and more freedom than Collins Bay. Perhaps because of this, violence was rare, even during the floor hockey games.

Also, Warkworth only had seven black prisoners at one time under a quota system. It figured. Historically, the Ku Klux Klan had held huge gatherings in nearby Picton. Some of the guards spoke openly of their love for the Klan.

In Collins Bay, I had enrolled in a University of Toronto correspondence course in chemistry. I brought my study materials with me. I was assigned to the prison school and given the extra duty of tutoring other students in science and chemistry.

The guard who ran the school was a former British soldier who had been stationed in Indo-China. He loved to tell war stories and we loved hearing about the blood and gore of combat.

Eventually, I was told that the chemicals sent in to be used for my courses were too much of a security risk, so I stopped working on chemistry studies.

My classification officer asked why I didn't complete the theoretical aspects of the course.

"I don't need the white man's certificates to survive in the world," I told him.

That comment would haunt me for years. Every time I went before the parole board, it was quoted back to me as proof of my bad attitude.

After Owen left for the Frontenac Institution, my days grew lonelier. Then I broke my leg playing soccer, holding up my own transfer, since only the able-bodied were allowed to work at the farm camps.

As time went by, I let my hair grow out into an Afro. Officer Sisson told me to cut it or he'd throw me in the hole. I refused, citing a loophole I found in the prison law books. Some loophole. True to his word, Sisson threw me in the hole.

When I went to the Warden's Court the next day, I pointed out that my hair did not conflict with prison policy, and that I was being illegally detained in solitary confinement. He let me go until he could get clarification from the prison's legal counsel. As a result, the black prisoners looked up to me, and the guards hated me because I had contradicted authority.

Finally, the simmering racial tension at Collins Bay blew up and ten black men were transferred into Warkworth, disrupting the seven-blacks policy forever.

With the status quo upset, the warden sought to maintain control by ordering all black prisoners to get haircuts. The brothers asked me what to do.

I showed them the rule book and explained that our hair didn't conflict with the rules, but they should make up their own minds about what to do. Summing up, I added, "I'm not getting my hair cut, and that's final."

Sisson called Brian up to the office. Brian came back with his hair cut. Later that day, the rest of the black prisoners were handed a photograph of a guy with a ruler superimposed across his forehead. The face was blacked out, but I knew recognized Brian's "before" Afro. In return for his compliance, Brian got a three-day pass to Toronto to see his baby daughter, Dana. He failed to return and was officially a fugitive on the run. I wished him well, hoping we'd never see him inside again.

For the rest of us, the limit of tolerance was nine inches – all in – measuring across the forehead. A huge, mentally challenged brother came up to me with the picture, asking what to do. I held a ruler up to his head. Even with his head shaved to his scalp the way it was, he exceeded the limit. I said, "Man, they going to cut your head off – your whole head is over nine inches."

He went off on the guards, cursing and screaming, "No one's going to cut me up." It took ten guards to take him off to the hole. I was called by security and asked if I'd go to the hole and cool him off. "Tell him we won't cut his hair, he ain't got any, anyways." They let him out a couple of days later.

I wrote to Warren Hart and told him what was going on in the joint. He advised me to stop causing trouble and get my hair cut.

"We need you out here on the streets as soon as possible," Hart responded. "What does your hair have to do with anything?"

He didn't realize how much my Afro meant to me.

Days later, I was called into Sisson's office. He ordered me to shut the door behind me. I did so – noisily. He was sitting behind his desk, fists clenched, eyes bulging.

"You have put in a transfer request. Let me tell you right now – the only way you're going to get out of here is to punch me in the face. That will get you two more years on your sentence, and a transfer to Millhaven. I'm not afraid of you," he said, leaning forward with a hiss. "I can kick your ass any day."

He was goading me. I could have beaten him easily. I was nineteen years old and combat-fit. He was well over thirty, soft and privileged. I didn't think he could beat his wife, let alone me.

He put me on "OP" – off privileges – for one month. The reason stated was: "For agitating the coloured inmates over their hair." Before I could say a word about the rules, he tossed a piece of paper at me.

"Read this, smartass."

It was a policy change, allowing any warden to order a haircut for any prisoner, if that prisoner's appearance disrupted the good order of the institution. Force could be used to affect the policy.

"You have until tomorrow morning to comply, or you can go to the hole. Show that to your brothers, man," he laughed, mocking me.

The policy change was signed by the Commissioner of Penitentiaries. I showed it to all the brothers and they all agreed to cut their hair, but I had a decision to make. I went to my cell to think. I was only a couple of months away from a parole hearing. Also, I had ace cards. I could easily pass any entrance exam to get into university. I had family support; and I had a job waiting for me. Stacked against me: I had breached security once, when I retrieved a soccer ball from the perimeter fence.

I knew I had a shot at freedom, so I got my hair cut the next day.

I spent many of my days on the mason gang, working with a Jamaican guy who had laid bricks his whole life. He taught me everything he knew.

At night, I generally stayed in my cell painting, working with clay in the pottery room or studying. When I was in the yard, I spent time with a Greek guy, talking about organized crime and playing sports.

Outside of prison, the air had changed.

On February 4, 1974, the Symbionese Liberation Army, a revolutionary group, kidnapped American heiress Patty Hearst. One of the founders was Donald DeFreeze; a black informant who had escaped from Soledad Prison. Word was that maybe he was allowed to escape. There were no groups in Canada capable of doing what the SLA did during their run, but Canadians watched American television, and the fear of armed radicals was in the air.

This was the climate, the first time I was up for parole. One board member asked me why I didn't finish my chemistry degree. She chastised me for wasting her tax dollars on a course I didn't finish. I explained to her that I couldn't finish because the prison wouldn't let me.

Another tore into me about my hair, and for having an anti-authority attitude because I refused an order. I explained that the order wasn't lawful, noting that when the rules changed I got my hair cut.

It wasn't looking good, but it got worse when the third member of the board dropped a bomb. He wanted to know about my involvement with the Black Panthers.

I couldn't say much. The Panthers were still active. It was a hot issue for me to acknowledge or discuss, and he wasn't letting me off the hook.

"We have confidential information you have been in touch with the leader of the Symbionese Liberation Army, and that if we let you out you'll run off to the States to join up."

I thought for a minute and told the truth.

"Donald DeFreeze is a rat and a rapist. There are no blacks in his group except him. I wouldn't have anything to do with him, and your information is false."

They sent me outside to await their decision. It came quickly and was no surprise. It would be another year before I could see the parole board again.

If you looked at this as me being punished for something I didn't do, you would not be entirely wrong. Donald DeFreeze, on the other hand, died in a two-hour shootout with police at the terror group's hideout in South Central Los Angeles in May 1974.

After the hearing, I became less sociable, staying in my cell, doing my hobbies, reading and playing the harp, a musical habit that has stuck with me.

The route I took to harp music was indirect. I had a beef with a French Canadian guy. Initially, I snagged a trumpet mouthpiece from the music room, brought it to my cell and I began making duck noises with it.

He snapped after a couple of days. Knife in hand, he ripped open my cell door and he threatened to kill me if I kept it up. I told Owen the Crook I needed a knife.

The Crook surprised me by siding with the French Canadian and telling me that that he was not alone. Apparently, other inmates objected to what Owen called my "incessant quacking with that piece of shit trumpet." He was the only one who had the balls to say anything.

"Don't stick him," Owen said, reaching into his waistband, where I hoped he had a knife. "Drive him crazy with this."

In his hand was a huge, shiny, chromatic harmonica 64.

"Ricky, learning to play jazz on this ain't easy, but there's nothing anyone can say to stop you." He was right, because the rules allowed you to have an actual musical instrument in your cell.

I took the harmonica and started making hee-haw noises.

I might have started using it for less than musical purposes, but in time I learned to play for real. To this day, I play, and by now I can give you Sonny Boy Williamson just as easily as I can give you Toots Thielemans.

After awhile, I had to get out of Warkworth. It was a soft joint geared to guys who were headed to lower security institutions. As a progressive jail, it also had many extra advantages that many prisoners across Canada didn't have access to. Being labelled a failure at Warkworth would set me up for longer prison stays in other prisons and that's what I wanted to try to quell the anger inside of me.

I also hoped that I could transform myself and present a new "me" to other wardens who might cut me the kind of break I was never going to get in Warkworth. There were too many protective custody inmates trying to fit back into the general population, causing tension and drama. The place was racist and I was unnerved seeing solid rounders, who once stood up to the man, reduced to bowing down.

So I worked up a plan. Somebody owed me money for cigarettes. I called him on the debt. He worked in the machine shop and I asked him to make me a knife, but not just any blade – I wanted a real knife made for a king, a foot long and curved like those carried by Arab princes.

A couple of days later, he handed me a towel wrapped around my ticket out. Then I wrote a carefully worded anonymous kite and dropped it in the mailbox, knowing that the knife was under my pillow, waiting for Sisson and the guards to find.

The next day, at work with the mason gang, ten guards approached our detail, with Sisson in the lead. The guards ordered everyone to step away from me. The head of security said, "Atkinson, turn around and put your hands behind your back." They found the knife, as I knew they would, and I was chained hand and foot and led off to the hole.

No one said a word.

The next morning a key in the lock awakened me. I jumped up, instantly alert. Four guards stood there, looking in. One of them had a food tray with two pieces of toast and a glass of water, the usual diet for someone who's in real trouble. I ate the dry toast piece by piece, wondering what was coming next.

An hour or two later, the door swung open again. This time there were two guards, plus Sisson, plus the warden. Sisson said, "You're in big trouble." I didn't care what he said. The warden was the one who held the power.

"Richard, it seems we have a problem," the warden told me. "One of your friends dropped a kite on you, concerned for your safety and the safety of others in the population. I spoke to this individual this morning, and he's worried about you."

"Bullshit," I said.

The warden looked stunned by my insolence. Sisson clenched his teeth, his eyes bulging. The two guards stepped forward. I stepped back.

This time, I spoke respectfully. "Listen, sir, I wrote that kite. It's in my handwriting. I just want out of here. I want to go to Millhaven or Collins Bay. I don't care which. This is non-negotiable."

The warden went cold. He raised his hand and pointed a finger at me. Lowering his hand, there was silence. And then, "Richard, as you wish. Fred, gather his stuff, put him in a car and ship him to Collins Bay immediately."

When he turned to leave, I thanked him.

He stopped. "Richard, I hope you know what you're getting into."

An hour later, there was a white sheet on the floor in front of me with all my belongings wrapped in it – minus the things that had been stolen from my cell while I was in the hole.

Nobody liked a box thief – someone who stole from your cell – but that was just part of doing time. I had no control over anything, including my possessions.

BACK IN THE BAY

Ten minutes down the highway, one of the guards turned and said, "Ricky, I don't want to sound like I'm in your business, but this ain't a good time for you to go back to Collins Bay."

"Really? When is it ever a good time to go to prison?"

He laughed. "No, no, I'm serious. Word is that you're going to get killed. You know, because of all those racial problems that went down a while back."

I didn't react. I hated to hear guards talk prison shit. You could never tell whether they knew something, or if they were just starting trouble. He might have wanted me to check into protective custody, or maybe he just wanted to rattle my cage.

I just smiled. "Your grapevine is different from mine. I heard that the head of security is going to welcome me with open arms so that I can run the inmate committee."

The driver laughed at the thought of security officers embracing me. His partner said, "No fucking way any coloured person is ever going to be on the inmate committee in Collins Bay."

I stared out the window at the farmhouses and the rolling hills in the distance, wondering what I was going to face. The fair-fight rule of one-on-one was out the window if fifty whites tried to stab ten black people. And I want you to imagine the headlines had all ten men been killed.

But I was not going to punk down. If I had to kill to defend myself, I was ready. And if I was killed, so what? All those who wait to die have waited long enough.

Halfway to Kingston, the driver asked if I was hungry. I said nothing. The trip from Warkworth to Collins Bay wasn't long enough to merit lunch.

"We can go to a little restaurant I know," he said. I still said nothing. "Think of it as your last meal."

Now I knew he was messing with my head, so I sent him some sarcasm. "Yeah, I could use a nice thick steak."

He said, "I'm not shitting you. We'll stop. You'll eat. I live near the restaurant. There's nowhere to run. But if you take off, I'll hunt you down and kill you."

He sounded like he meant it.

We left the highway. There was not a house in sight for miles. I hadn't a clue as to where I was but there, nestled in a wall of forest, was a little restaurant. We pulled into the parking lot. They took off my handcuffs and shackles and I walked in like a free man.

The place was small, only six tables, four of them empty. The driver seemed to know everyone, and the waitress handed me a menu. I couldn't even afford a glass of water, but the driver said, "Get what you want, it's on us."

His partner leaned in: "Last meal, eat up." I was happy and nervous at the same time. They were risking their jobs for me. Did they know something I didn't? Was I about to be murdered?

I ordered a steak with two eggs and French fries, along with a slice of apple pie and some strawberry ice cream. I'd have ordered the same thing if I was on death row.

When I finished eating, they took me back to the car and chained me up again. A short while later, as we pulled into Collins Bay, the driver turned to me. "Don't say a word to anyone about the grub."

That was nearly forty years ago. I have never mentioned that meal to anyone until this moment. I want to thank those guards now. Thanking them then was not part of my mental makeup.

Two preventive security officers – "Keepers" Street and Frankovitch – were waiting for me. One of the guards dropped the bedsheet filled with my personal belongings. Somebody said, "They must have wanted you out in a hurry."

The inmate helping them sorted through my stuff, removing items that were allowed in a medium security jail but not in the Bay.

Officer Street called me into his office. "Listen," he said. "Since all that racial shit, this place has quieted down. We don't need you stirring up trouble. I'm going to put you in 2-Block, upstairs, to save you all the noise in 1-Block. But if I hear one word about you, you're off to Millhaven. You got me?"

I got him.

I was still sitting there when the noon count was called. It seemed odd; I thought I'd been set up, because 2-Block did not have a guard station. If you wanted to kill someone, it was the best place for it. People had been beaten to within an inch of their lives on 2-Block and no one downstairs heard a scream.

I knew I had to get a knife.

Chicago came in shortly after and we shook hands. I grabbed my belongings and followed him onto the strip. Once we were out of earshot, I asked him what was going down.

"Brother, this is a different jail," he told me. "All that nigger shit has stopped. Maybe not a hundred percent but it ain't like it used to be."

I said, "Be nice to have a shank."

"I'll get you one tomorrow," Chicago promised. "But you ain't gonna need it."

I tossed my stuff into cell nine on 2-Block, and hurried back downstairs, following Chicago to the kitchen.

I was waiting for someone to say something negative so I could go off, but no one did. A few people I knew approached and shook my hand. The Italian mob nodded when I went past their table, including Domenic Racco. Two or three brothers raised their fists in a black power salute, welcoming me home.

As we inched towards the chow trays, one of the members of the inmate committee approached. "The committee would like to talk to you."

The air in the room smelled of food, not fear. There was laughter coming from some tables. Maybe things had changed.

Before I could take my seat, Big Joe DiNardo brought me a specially prepared meal. Prison food can be as bland as hospital food, and kitchen workers were not supposed to feed the prison population any deviation from the menu. However, Joe and his kitchen colleagues had ways of spicing up whatever was served on the regular cafeteria-style prison line. It was a special treat.

Joe served me with a hug. After the steak the guards had given me for lunch, I wasn't hungry, but out of respect I ate what Big Joe brought.

By the time I walked over to the committee table, I was feeling bloated. The chairman reached into his pocket and handed me a joint. "Here, Rick, get this into you."

I put it in my pocket; there was no refusing.

He said, "Man, all that shit in the past is in the past."

Putting one hand on the committee chairman's shoulder, I thought about the death threats and kites left on my bed, the name calling in the middle of the night, the stabbing of friends and family, the beatings and the murders of guys whose only fault was they weren't white.

I leaned forward and whispered, "If so, then so be it."

My cousin Mad Dog, and his friend Andy came over, slapping hands and grinning. Mad Dog had a huge red Afro.

"Man, the pigs just leave me alone," he told me. "No one bothers you about your hair here anymore."

Hmm, maybe my last meal was not my last meal.

I took a job in the wood shop, building pallets for the Canadian Mint. I found myself working beside Darcy, the owner of my old after-hours haunt, Darcy's Bar. During slow periods in the shop I sat with this older rounder, playing chess and listening to stories about people I knew who were still going to his bar.

Eventually, I was put on 4-Block, where I could play my harmonica. Before long they told me that, since I was behaving myself and because my transfer had been voluntary, they would write me up for farm camp.

I knew that would take a couple of months.

I had kites from Millhaven saying that the prison population there hated The Man too much to be racially divided. The black gangsters there wanted to know what we could do in the Bay so that beefs didn't carry over. I decided to start a group to unify the black and white populations. I had help from Chicago and a guy named Greenwich, who was educated but who normally kept to himself.

We laid out the basis for the Black Inmates Friends Assembly or BIFA. We approached the administration; they thought it was a good idea. Then Officer Street called me into his office and dumped ten kites on his desk.

"'If that nigger starts a nigger group, he is a dead nigger,'" he said, reading aloud.

No surprise. Some of those notes had already been slipped under my cell door.

"Mr. Street, nobody likes change, but this is a good thing for everyone," I offered. "It can't be looked at as any different from the native brotherhood group or the Jewish groups, or the chess club."

He batted that back at me. "The native brotherhood and the Jewish groups are religious groups, and you can hardly call a chess club similar to a black revolutionary group."

I showed him our logo – a black hand shaking a white one. "Black and white together, how can that be construed as a revolutionary group?"

He looked at the logo for a long time. "Your life is on the line with this one. You never know when one of those kite-writers will step out and stab you. But I think I'll allow this to happen, if you'll agree to let our social development people to sit in during your meetings."

I had to weigh that one carefully.

Everyone hated The Man, but everyone liked the social development and recreation officer, Bernie Aucoin. He didn't even have to wear a uniform. After some thought, I agreed with Street but I made one demand. "During the voting-in of members, and the reasons why they can or can't be members, Bernie can't be there." He agreed.

BIFA was now a reality.

Inmate Greenwich wrote to the Black Students' Union at Queen's University. We also sent a draft of our constitution to Charles Roach, my first lawyer and a leader in the black community.

I got in touch with Al Hamilton, founder of *Contrast*, the black newspaper in Toronto, and Leonard Johnston, owner of the Third World Books and Craft Store, asking for book donations. In no time, we received a box of used black history books.

I also wrote an article about what we doing for *Contrast*. Edwin Hogan, the Black Panther leader who mentored me while I was awaiting sentencing in the Don Jail, had been returned to jail in Ohio. *Contrast* often printed letters from him and I knew he'd read what I wrote.

Our first social event was a dance attended by some of the girls from the Black Students' Union at Queen's. They came in miniskirts, smelling so sweet and smiling so invitingly that even the hardest criminals were grinning by the end of the night. There was even soul food for supper.

We brought the leftovers back to the cellblock and passed them around to our friends. I got a kick out of Ernie George's Satan's Choice biker buddies leaning over the plates of colourful food, licking their lips and giving me the thumbs up. Bernie Aucoin said he hadn't seen anything like it.

BIFA has now taken root in prisons throughout Canada, the United States and England.

RATS AND COWS

A month or so later, still riding high on our success, I came back to my cell and saw a newspaper on my bed. On the front page was a picture of Warren Hart with a story about the Toronto Black Panther cell.

According to the paper, Hart had been a government informant. There were details about the guns we'd given him from the army surplus store break-in, and how those guns had been used in western Canada to set up and imprison some of the revolutionary natives there.

My stomach churned. I remembered what Bert Novis had said to me in the cop car, after my arrest, about how surprised I'd be if I knew who ratted me out.

I had a very short list of those who I thought could have dropped a dime on. It was clear now. Hart was the rat.

The reason he'd given up his undercover status and gone public? Warren Allmand, the Attorney General, had stiffed him out of a $60,000 payment for having set people up. People like me.

Nobody seemed to care that a group of teenaged kids were made dupes of the government, or that I'd been given a loaded gun by an under-cover rat and then persuaded to commit a robbery. Not that I'd needed a lot of persuasion.

I kept my hatred of Hart and the government to myself. I was smart to do so – within six months I was transferred to the Frontenac farm camp.

My mind was still reeling. It reels to this day. If I am a criminal I was created, in large part, by that double-crossing rat Warren Hart. By exten-sion, I was criminalized by the government of Canada that was so eager to have Hart's secret reports.

When I finally graduated to farm camp, I was put in a car with my belong-ings and driven, unshackled, 200 yards outside the prison walls. We pulled up to a long, two-storey brick building with no bars on the windows. The bottom floor was the visiting area, with an administration office, a kitchen and admission and discharge areas, where I took my box of personal belongings. After the usual admittance processing, I ran upstairs. There were two huge dormitory-style rooms with sixty beds lined up in rows, punctuated by four banks of chest-high, metal military lockers. Showers and a washroom were at the end of each dorm. I asked where Owen slept.

I found his neatly made bed and an expensive-looking bathrobe hanging from a metal closet door. At the foot of the bed was a television. No prisoner, in any of the prisons I'd been in, had their own TV.

On the bed was a book of blues sheet music.

I smiled at the set-up; Owen the Crook always went first-class. I turned the TV on. I hadn't seen a colour television since my arrest. I kicked off my shoes and put my head on the pillows. Next to me was a dirty bed with a pair of old work boots on the floor. The boots were covered in straw and cow shit. I wondered how Owen could live next to someone like that.

After half an hour or so, a short, soft man of about fifty walked up to the foot of Owen's bed. From the look of him, I took him for a fraud artist, or someone who had killed his wife, or maybe a rounder. When he reached across and turned off the TV, I knew he was a rounder.

"Who are you?"

"My name is Richard Atkinson."

We were the souls of politeness as we shook hands. "You're Owen's friend. He's told me a lot about you and your crew. By the way, this is my bed. Owen sleeps over there."

I jumped up.

He was gracious. "No, stay there, you can watch my TV any time you want." But I stayed on my feet, wanting to respect his space. Just then Owen came in, fresh from the shower, with a big grin on his face. Well, he wasn't exactly "fresh." He still smelled faintly like a barn. We shook hands.

"Owen, you smell like cow shit."

"No shit; get used to it. You'll be working there tomorrow. All the new guys hit the barn before any other jobs come up."

I had been looking forward to farm work, but I didn't want to smell like shit. I thought Owen had set something up for me, like driving a tractor or doing clerical work. He said, "It's cows for you, pal. Maybe a tractor job might come up, but you'll still be hauling shit. This is a dairy farm."

"I'll try to get you a job in the stores if I can," said Owen's cellmate. "That's where I work."

I looked at Owen's friend. He was a mobbed-up rounder with a slight French accent. Rounders knew how to get things done. "One hand always washes the other" is our creed. Working in a prison warehouse that has supplies of any kind of useful stuff is a job that's coveted by inmates and guards. The farm camp was the primary storage area for all goods used in Ontario's nine prisons. Working there was at the top of any prisoner's preferred soft-job list. Owen's friend had just become my best new friend.

"Smell you later," I said, slapping Owen's hand. Off I went to make my bed and put my stuff in my locker.

As predicted, the next day I was assigned to the dairy barn. I reported in work boots and coveralls. The first thing I did was pick up a piece of straw and put it in my mouth.

"Don't put straw or grass in your mouth around a cow barn," Owen scolded. "You can get tapeworms from their shit. I read it in a book." The Crook was schooling me.

He handed me a bucket of hot soapy water. "We wash their udders and, then put the milking tubes on their teats. You've got to squeeze them first, to make sure they don't have mastitis."

He washed an udder with a warm, wet paper towel, grabbed a teat and squeezed it. White milk squirted out. He did the same to all the teats on the udder.

"Once you do that, you put these tubes on each teat and that's it. Next cow and then the next, until the whole line of a hundred cows is done."

I'm from the Projects. I had never been this close to a cow in my life. All of my assumptions about how soft and cuddly cows were went right out the window when I stepped up behind one, grabbed its shitty tail and got a hard kick in the shins.

I made my way down the line, hating every minute. They kicked me. They crushed me against the stall railings. They shit all over. If you weren't quick to grab them, they slapped you in the face with their shitty tails. I suddenly had new respect for farmers.

The good side of it was that camp was laid back. There was no tension, rarely a fight and nobody with a shank. After thirty days, if you behaved, you could go off property to a movie or a skating rink, or to the mall across the street on what was called a socialization pass. It was supposed to help us get used to being around normal people before we hit the streets for good.

One thing that was missing was a gym, so outside of the hard labour offered in the barns, there was little else to do. Winter was coming and it was starting to get dark in the afternoons. The nights were cold.

I settled in like a slave, making ten cents an hour, but I was happier putting in a full day's work here than I had been doing anything in Collins Bay.

It wasn't easy to adjust to being around cows. I'd been on milking duty a couple of weeks when one of the cows stepped on my foot. I began to hit it with punches like a professional boxer. I don't know why I did it but for some reason I needed to let off some steam. The next day, another cow crushed me against a railing and I rolled a series of punches on its side and on its head.

After a few days of this, the cows would moo and prance around nervously when I came into the barn, making it harder to milk them.

One day, a cow coughed when I was behind it. Green shit flew out of her ass and all over my face. I tore into that cow with my fists. Next thing I knew, the camp boss, Mr. Kirby, was standing beside me.

"Atkinson, I knew something was up. Milk production is down. You hit a cow again, I'll kick your ass."

Kirby was the epitome of what I thought all farmers were – short and stupid-looking. He had a dairy farm of his own in the real world. He may have looked stupid, but he was well-schooled in animal husbandry. He was also made of solid muscle from years of hard work. But he was in his forties, and there was no way I thought he could kick my ass.

I asked Owen if I could fight him without getting shipped out. We both knew that if he took a swing at me first, it was licence for me to fight back. Owen said he'd never seen Kirby mad. I kept pushing his buttons every chance I got.

After a week of him muttering about how stupid city guys were and me muttering about how stupid farmers were, I pushed a cow out of my way and he exploded.

He came at me with a pitchfork. I grabbed a rake. We circled each other until Owen and another prisoner grabbed me and pinned my arms.

"Get the fuck off me, the man's trying to kill me," I cried. Owen let me go. I raised the rake above my head. "You want to fuck with me, old man? Let's do it."

Kirby said, "Make your move, asshole."

Then he dropped his pitchfork and hurried over to his office on the other side of the barn.

"You saw that, Owen. He tried to kill me."

I figured Kirby would call the goon squad and I'd be shipped off to Millhaven, but I had two witnesses to the assault against me. One of them went to the office to see Kirby. Owen and I waited for the guards to come running in. The other inmate came back with weird news. "Man, he's in his office crying like a baby. I think you drove him crazy, Ricky."

When he settled down, Kirby called me on the speaker system, and the three of us went to the office. Kirby said, "Atkinson, I don't want you in my barn any more. You don't say anything, neither will I. Just get the fuck out of my face before I do something really crazy."

I left the barn and walked back to camp. A guard asked me why I wasn't at work.

"Ask Kirby."

And that was the end of it.

A couple of days later, I was assigned to work in the storage area with Owen's mob friend. My job was to load and unload trucks in a warehouse that held canteen items – clothes, toiletries and cleaning supplies – for every federal prison in Ontario. It wasn't long before I figured out that the Montreal rounder was stealing skid-loads of stuff.

One day he asked me to unload a trailer, but to leave one skid on it. I asked the driver several times, "Are you sure you want me to leave that skid?" He seemed nervous.

When I checked the invoices, they reflected that the truck had been totally emptied. Damn. I was stealing, yet I wasn't getting paid. I brought it up with Owen, but he was up for parole in a week and didn't want to rock the boat.

I was furious. "Listen, man, he's using me to make a buck, and I'm not getting a penny for it. I can't be his bitch. I've got to do something." The next day, I stuffed five cartons of smokes in a bag, in front of the mob man.

"This is my end for today's work."

Just in case he didn't get the point, I said, "I don't steal for anyone unless I get paid."

He said, "You know who I am?"

"Yeah, I know who you are, and you're not a made guy so I got no fucking worries, my friend. You can't use me like a bitch and not pay me. If your ship sinks, don't I go down with it?"

"I got you this job after the barn incident," he said. "At least you could be grateful for that."

"I am grateful, but this job pays ten cents an hour and you're stealing thousands. That makes it a different ball game."

I walked out with the smokes and sold them in two minutes for the equivalent of a month's pay. The next morning I was called to the warden's office. The rounder had dropped a dime on me.

The warden said, "Ricky, you're a young, good-looking guy; how would you like an easier job, cleaning the finance office, working around all those ladies?"

I was about to get screwed out of a vast revenue stream, and there was nothing I could do about it. Still, but I tried.

"Warden, I kind of like driving a forklift. It gives me something to look forward to when I get out."

"Well, we need a cleaner in the office," said the warden firmly. "And we don't need another forklift driver."

There was nothing I could do but make the best of it.

"Warden, I'd kind of like to just kick back until my parole hearing, without any headaches. I think I'll take that cleaning job."

He smiled and patted me on the back. The next day I walked past the rounder on my way to the office. I nodded at him. His game was stronger than mine. I had no reason to hold a grudge. Besides, it was no hardship to go to work in an office surrounded by delicious young women. But to this day I wonder if he and the warden were in cahoots, splitting the take, with no one the wiser. Over the years, other wardens have been charged with misappropriating government funds.

Owen the Crook made parole. He didn't have an address to give me, but we both knew it wouldn't be hard to find each other in the "hood." Then Dwane sent word that he was getting married. He wanted me to be his best man.

I asked my classification officer about going on my first UTA, an Unescorted Temporary Absence. I got three days and nights. All I needed was a ride.

Dwane promised to pick me up the day before the wedding. I remember waiting for him with my duffle bag. When he was an hour late, I knew something was up. Dwane was never late. I managed to call my mother, who was surprised to hear from me. When I told her Dwane hadn't shown up, she started crying.

It seems that halfway between Toronto and Kingston, Dwane got into a race with another car on the highway and blew his engine. It took three hours for the tow truck to arrive, and another three hours to ditch his old car and find a new one. He called my uncle Joe in Montreal, asking him to stop at the prison and pick me up. When Joe pulled up in front of the church there was a cheer.

"He's here! Dwane's here!"

At least that's what everyone thought. Estelle, my brother's bride-to-be, rushed over with my mother by her side. Their faces turned from relief to despair when they saw me. Dwane hadn't called to tell them what was happening.

My mother looked me in the eye and said, "If you would have stayed in that fucking prison, none of this would have happened."

Yeah, it's my fault. I thought she might be right. Welcome home.

The only one who seemed happy to see me was Uncle Glen. We slapped hands and he slipped me a couple of joints on the assumption that I needed something to relax me. We all needed some relaxing.

My mother asked me to stand-in for my brother during the rehearsal, causing another flood of tears from Estelle. Just as the rehearsal was ending, Dwane stormed into the church with a guilty grin on his face.

"Thought I wasn't coming?"

He grabbed Estelle and hugged her. That didn't stop her tears. He said, "Check out my new car," as if that was going to make everything better.

I sparked up one of the joints and zeroed in on a former girlfriend, a pretty, light-skinned girl I'd known since I was a kid. After the rehearsal, we wasted little time on small talk. I didn't get much sleep.

The bus ride back to prison was long and I had plenty of time to think about freedom and those venomous words from my mother. I began to think that Montreal might be best for me when I got out.

I was up before the parole board in October and again I argued hard for freedom. My formal plan was to move to Montreal and work for my uncle Joe in his dry cleaning business, while also pursuing my dream of becoming a boxer.

None of this sat well with the board.

One of them, a woman, looked over my file and suggested I should try to find work in the arts. She knew of my interest in pottery and she must have found it novel – the big tough kid with the delicate hands and an interest in throwing pots.

But the two men on the board came at me from different angles. One said that he'd trained boxers, and he stressed the dangers of the sport. The other was fixated on the past, my crimes and my hatred for the government.

I knew neither of them had ever been called "nigger" or "half-breed" or "burrhead" nor had they been treated like a second-class citizen by cops or anyone else.

I concentrated my sales pitch on the woman, moving into "sell or die" mode. I stood my ground, believing that if I changed my mind, the board might get the idea that I didn't really know what I wanted.

My ace in the hole was Joe, who had promised to take me in until I got back on my feet. The woman finally relented. The others followed. I still think of her. She was far wiser than I gave her credit for. I now see her as someone who was genuinely concerned for my well-being.

And she was right.

I still play my harp and I'm drawing, painting and working clay at the wheel. I'd have been better off if I'd taken her advice sooner and more seriously.

BIENVENUE À MONTRÉAL

Before leaving the farm camp, I picked up the wages the government owed me, not that it was much. While I was in the accounting office, one of the pretty girls bent over to get something from her purse. I don't know if she did it to tease me or if she simply didn't know that I was behind her. It's been thirty years and the memory of her bending over still brings a smile to my face. That day, I smiled all the way to the bus station and all the way to Montreal.

As soon as I arrived, I picked up the city's European pulse and was happy to be among people who openly enjoyed their freedom. It was the festive winter of 1976. All around Montreal, work crews were busy putting final touches on everything to do with the Summer Olympics, which were scheduled to open on July 17. Uncle Joe lived in a predominantly Jewish neighbourhood, with a mixture of blacks and whites that reminded me of my childhood. I walked into his shop and was enveloped by the sounds of machines washing clothes, steam presses hissing and pipes knocking out a rhythm that sounded like music.

Uncle Joe sat before a steam press iron, hidden in a cloud of steam. Aunt Gail held a blouse in one hand and a button in the other, with a needle and thread in her mouth.

Gail was tall and thin, in her early forties, with long brown hair. Her smile was not inviting. She barked an order at me, to take a load of clothes out of one of the huge washers, and she went back to sewing the button on the blouse.

Collins Bay served as the prison laundry for the entire Ontario penitentiary system. In comparison, my uncle's shop was small and crowded. He and my aunt were far too busy to stop working.

As soon as Joe caught a break, he shook my hand and bought me a coffee in the shop next door. He was a smaller, skinnier version of my father. He happily shared essential information with me – like how the Montreal girls were easier and more carefree than the girls in Toronto.

After the second coffee, he got straight to the point.

"Ricky, I really need your help. My wife and I are behind the eight ball. We're working our asses off putting in twelve-hour days just to catch up on the bills. We can't pay you a lot for working, but we can feed and house you. As soon as I get back on my feet, I'll take care of you with a proper wage and shit."

Yes, well, I was a thief, a robber and a safecracker and maybe I was still young, but I knew when someone was pitching a hustle my way. Uncle Joe was on the mound throwing fastballs.

In the end, my instinct was to help my family, no matter what. So now I was in his game, playing by his rules. He slapped me on the back and said he'd take me out after work the next day and show me the town.

My uncle took me out all right, usually on Saturday nights to the seedy country music bars on the main drag in Montreal's Chinatown. I wasn't much of a fan, but I went anyway to bond with my father's brother.

Boxing was big in Montreal and I signed up at a gym on Avenue du Parc under the tutelage of manager Roger Larrivée, While I was training, I met a cute little girl named Chantal, who had younger brother who also was into boxing. Within a month I was the heavyweight champ of Montreal and within four months the Quebec heavyweight champ. I put a lot of energy into staying clean, enjoying my freedom and helping my uncle keep his struggling business afloat. I loved exploring the beautiful city of Montreal with my new girlfriend.

One day in the late spring, I found myself exhausted after a late night with Chantal, followed by an early morning emergency involving a leaky boiler flooding the basement of my uncle's shop. I hadn't had much sleep, but I put in a full workday. After hitting the gym, I was driving back in my uncle's car when I dozed off at a stoplight. My foot slipped off the brake, causing the car to slide forward, hitting the car in front of me.

The owner was reasonable. He agreed not to call the cops if I paid for the repairs. The estimate – for a thousand bucks – arrived a day or so later.

It might as well have been for a million. When I mentioned it to Chantal, she offered to turn herself out. I declined. That would have taken an investment in clothes and a trip to Toronto to get her trained. I also knew that her father had a gun.

The only solution was a bank.

At least, I thought the only solution was a bank. I was young, smart, fast and tough. I already had one in mind. It wasn't far from the Olympic Village and there was a mattress factory nearby. My plan was to set off a bomb in the mattress factory and plant a few fake ones here and there as a diversion – just – just enough to keep the cops busy while I made my getaway.

First, I tried a dry run with the explosives.

There was a construction site near the Cavendish Mall in Côte Saint Luc. I dug a hole, covered it with a grate and blew it up as I was walking back to my car. *Boom*. Within seconds, the balconies of the surrounding apartment buildings were filled with people staring at the rising smoke.

That's when it dawned on me: I was in a Jewish neighbourhood, on the Sabbath, four years after the Munich Olympics and a few weeks away from the opening of the 1976 Olympics. Plus this was Montreal and thanks to the radical violence by the *Front de libération du Quebéc* (FLQ), bombs were always on people's minds.

I got out of there in a hurry, hoping no one had noticed me. Montreal clearly was not a place where I could do this kind of work.

The following Friday I got on a bus to Toronto. I packed a gun, gloves and a two-dollar Halloween ghost mask I painted so it was flesh-coloured.

Life is strange, or maybe it's just my life. The bus stopped in Kingston, and a woman in her fifties got on. She was tall, attractive and businesslike. She asked if she could sit next to me. I put the gym bag with the gun and the disguise under my seat. She started chatting, the way some people do with strangers on the bus, as a way to kill time on the road.

She was a former nun who spent her time working in chapels in prisons in southern Ontario. She pulled out a photo album and began showing me pictures of guys she called "her boys." Page after page of them, all guys I knew. On and on she talked about how "her boys" wouldn't have gotten into trouble if there had been someone in their lives like her and so forth.

I kept my mouth shut until we hit the Don Valley Parkway about fifteen minutes from downtown Toronto. Then I asked to see the album again and I pointed to the guys I knew, filling her in on what they were in for. She took her album and found herself another seat.

As we neared the bus station on Bay Street, she came up to me and was about to say something but I cut her off.

"Screw you, you're a hypocrite."

She slunk back to her seat as if I'd shot her. She may have been wounded, but there was no quit in her. She started in on me again and I cut her off again.

"You abandoned me in my time of need. That's not very Christian of you."

Undeterred, she sat down beside me again, chatting a mile a minute, apologizing, offering to make it up to me, offering to buy me something to eat. I was about to brush her off for good when we pulled into the station.

There were cops milling about. I still had her album, so I asked her to carry my bag. She held it to her chest as we shuffled off the bus and past the cops.

When she offered me a place to stay, I took her up on it. She had a large bachelor apartment in a three-storey brownstone building near Harbord and Bathurst Street. It was sparse and simple, filled with lot of books about religion. She made me a sandwich and a cup of tea. Then she pulled out a prison-style mattress and set it beside her bed.

"You sleep here for the night."

I sat down on the bed instead.

"If you want to know what it's like to be a convict, you sleep on the floor." And I lay back and closed my eyes. In the middle of the night, I felt her – naked – snuggling up to me. Some church lady.

In the morning, I got up first. I had things to do. She started chatting as soon as I woke her up. She made tea and offered to take me to her bank and get me a couple of bucks.

I hadn't considered this. Could I be a gigolo?

Nope to that, but I found myself wondering about her bank. We took a streetcar. She chatted all the way. If you like coincidences here's a good one – her bank was familiar. I'd knocked it over for Warren Hart.

I took a deep breath as we entered, taking care not to leave any fingerprints. The place was fat with customers, but no one paid any attention to me. I was with the woman they all knew as a one-time handmaiden of Christ.

I stood in line with her all the way to the wicket. The head teller came over for some small talk. When she looked at me, I smiled. Normally, the head teller was the keeper of the keys and, therefore, the main target.

In this case, it became apparent that all of the tellers kept their drawers open during rush hour. I got lucky when I heard one of them ask another for a $1,000 bill. She would be my target. The one with the big bills rendered the most profit in the least amount of time. No point being greedy, not when every second counts.

I had my getaway planned before we left.

The talking nun gave me a fifty-dollar bill and the key to her apartment. She said she would be home just after 4 p.m.

"Maybe you can spend another night."

Yeah, maybe I could.

I took the fifty and went to Malabar, a huge costume store, where I spent some money rounding out my disguise with some theatrical makeup for the mask, plus fake eyebrows and a beard.

Then I went to my parents' house. They were surprised to see me and wanted to know about Montreal and Uncle Joe. I told them that everything was fine. No sense worrying them.

Dwane was at the Paramount Tavern, so I borrowed my sister's bike and rode over to see him. I also I peddled past the bank, performing a mental run-through and timing myself. All I needed now was someone I could trust to watch the bike while I was busy.

Having satisfied myself about the plan, I headed for the bar, where I was immediately at home among the pimps, players, drunks and working stiffs having an afternoon drink. I knew all the black faces and I knew they'd be my witnesses if the cops came snooping around.

My brother jumped up, rushed over with a smile. We slapped hands and hugged. The smile left his face as soon as he felt the gun in my waistband. Pulling him aside, I told him my plan. He agreed to watch the bike.

After buying a round of drinks, we went back to the nun's apartment. I changed into a cheap suit that I had found at the Salvation Army. By the time I was done with the makeup and the trimmings, I looked like an average white businessman in his forties.

My brother's clothes were bright, and quite distinct from mine. After the robbery he could walk away without worrying about the cops mistaking him for me. We made our way to the bank without saying much. I was unafraid and committed to the job, in spite of the risks. My need for cash was eating me like a cancer.

Pulling on my clown mask, I entered the bank and took a couple of strides. Leaping over the counter, I landed beside a startled teller. It happened so fast that no one realized what was going on.

Easing the teller out of the way, I yanked the drawer open and began pulling out wads of money, focussing on big bills, shoving as much as I could into my trusty gym bag.

Brave girl, she reached for my arm. I pushed her away and waved my gun in the air.

"This is a fucking robbery. Don't anybody move or I'll blow your fucking heads off."

The place went dead silent.

An instant later, I had what I had come to get and I made my way out the back door. The whole thing had taken maybe fifteen seconds. I ran like a track star across the street and into the laneway. No one followed me or shouted at me to stop.

Cutting between two houses, I ran through the backyards, crossed another lane and then went between two more houses, where my brother was waiting with the bike. Elapsed time? Maybe a minute.

I dashed away on the bike, only slowing down when I reached the laneway behind the nun's apartment building. I was safe, and I knew it.

It was a good job. I had a bag of money and no one got hurt. All I had to do now was change and get back to the bar. Before my brother arrived, I had stacks of bills laid out. Not a lot of money, perhaps, but it amounted to $300 a second.

I knew then that there was no future for me in Montreal. I didn't have enough friends there. My old gang was in Toronto, the home of easy money.

At the bar, I told Dwane I'd be home for good in a month or so. We were relaxing with our drinks when two, big black gangsters walked in. Big Joe and Jerry Patterson.

I hadn't seen them since the Don Jail. Jerry hugged me right away, feeling for a gun.

"Montreal that dangerous? Or you in town on a mission?"

"You know how much I like my little friends with me all the time," I told him. Jerry laughed.

"Nigger, you don't have little friends," said Big Joe. "We're all heavy-weights here, man."

I dislike the word "nigger," no matter who uses it but I got his point.

I also knew he was paranoid, maybe with reason. He'd done time for breaking the back of a hit man who'd been sent to get him. I knew he didn't trust anyone much, so I said as little as possible, but I showed some manners.

"Thanks for the comfort bag in the 'haven."

Some haven, Millhaven.

"Man, ten dollars' worth of chips and chocolate bars is nothing. Shouldn't we always look out for each other in those shitholes?"

I responded correctly. "We should always look out for each other, wherever we find ourselves."

Jerry laughed again and looked at Joe. "That's what I'm talking about, Joe; with this brother on our side, we can take this motherfucker over, man."

Joe shot him a look. They got quiet.

I left them and went to play chess with a friend. My mind wasn't entirely on the game. I'd already figured out that Joe and Jerry were muscling in on the card games and the dope action. Now they wanted to take over. The local mafia boss, Paul "The Fox" Volpe, would help plant the flag.

By the time I called "Checkmate," I had thought it through and was reconciled to the notion that a union with Big Joe and Jerry could be profitable. However, I was not about to let them stand in my way if I decided to work without them.

I took the Sunday night bus back to Montreal and got in as the sun was coming up. Back at the dry-cleaning shop, Chantal was waiting for me. She said she wanted the nightlife. She thought she was ready to be turned out.

She had no idea what she was talking about. I had relatives who had been raped by stepfathers, uncles and brothers. Some of them started tricking before they were ten years old. Some were still in the game. None of them bragged about being hookers and none of them wanted their daughters on the street.

She didn't know it then, but our relationship was over.

I called my parole officer and told her my father had been in an accident. I was needed at home. She gave me a travel permit, assuring me that she would do the paperwork to have me transferred.

I took the bus back to Toronto and called Chantal with the news. I never heard her voice again.

HOME AGAIN

I was on parole, but I was on familiar ground. Nothing could stop me except Bert Novis, and I didn't think outsmarting him would be hard because I'd picked up a few things in prison.

I walked from the bus station straight to my mother's house, surprising her. After filling her in on in what had happened in Montreal, I asked if I could stay for a couple of days until I got settled.

She said I'd have to ask my father.

That night I hit the bars to make my presence known. Before the night was over, I was travelling with ten of the old gang, going from bar to bar, gathering steam as we went, making noise, punking people and moving on.

Most of us had known each other for years, in and out of prison. We feared no one. I could smell the money in the air. With the boys around me, I knew it wouldn't be long before we started filling our pockets.

I worked it so that I reported to the John Howard Society for parole. They were less restrictive than the Salvation Army, and I needed all the leeway I could get if I was going to put the gang together. One day after reporting, I headed over to a boxing gym that was about to open – a new gym, for a new me. The owner was Tray Travis, who had trained Eddie Melo and Nicky Furlano since they were kids. Both of them became Canadian champions under his guidance.

The gym was under construction in an old bowling alley. I pitched in, helping to tear up the old floor. Two weeks later, the Queen City Boxing Club opened for business.

I began sparring with other heavyweights like Horst Geisler, Paul "The Investment" Nielson and Bobby "Pretty Boy" Feldstein.

The first card I appeared on was a professional/amateur affair. Travis asked me to fight, and I couldn't have been happier. Working in my corner was Ira Hussey, an old friend from Collins Bay. He knew what he was doing. After the first round, I sat down in my corner.

"Ricky, do you believe I can see what you can't?" I nodded. He could see both of us, and all I could see was the man in front of me.

"Then walk out there and throw a jab. He's going to counter with a hard right. Duck that and tap him to the body; come up and drop him with a right hook to the head, then walk back to the corner, because the fight's going to be over." I nodded that I understood just as the bell rang.

I had no fear of the fight itself, but I feared the embarrassment of losing. I had never been knocked down, let alone knocked out. I never considered the possibility of hitting the canvas. Even so, it isn't easy to walk toward a guy who wants to rip your head off. I was big and strong and fast. Ira had given me a plan.

I jabbed and the other man countered, as predicted. So I did what I'd been told to do, and the fight was over. Ira was ecstatic. It was rare for a trainer to predict and call such an accurate combination of punches. He reminisced about that for years.

Harry the Greek grabbed my arm as I left the ring and slipped me a $100 bill, along with his phone number. Big Joe DiNardo patted me on the back. I felt like a champ.

After I showered, I watched Nicky Furlano and Eddie Melo win their fights by knockouts. Travis, at my side, nodded toward Junior Jones, who was the Canadian amateur champion. "You'll fight him in a couple fights, but let's build the crowd first, so we can make some money," Travis said.

Junior saw us talking and he smiled. We had no hate for each other, but we both knew what was coming. He could street fight and he could box. Beating him wasn't going to be easy. He knew I wanted his title.

That's when Jerry Bates stepped in and asked to train me. His step had a bit of a hitch, because he was from a place called Cut and Shoot, Texas. It was a rough town. Fifty years earlier, Jerry refused to take a dive in a KKK-sponsored match and they blew his leg off with a shotgun. He was lucky; he might have ended up as strange fruit hanging from a tree.

Before too long, I called the number the Greek had given me and we met at one of his haunts. He'd made a thousand bucks on my pro-am fight. He offered me two jobs.

One was collecting used oil from gas stations. Those rusty barrels of old oil sitting in gas stations everywhere were a gold mine for someone slick enough to get them cheap from the station owners and sell it to refiners. Sometimes those owners had to be persuaded that doing business with Harry would be in their best interest. He needed someone with muscle to move in on the other refiners.

The other job was a kind of double-dip – he wanted me to rob a few of his card games.

He was offering $100 a day for the oil job, and 100 percent of what I took from the card games, minus his investment in the game.

The oil job was a little too blue collar for me at the time, but robbing a card game was attractive because it was not exactly against the law. Running a game was illegal in the first place, so the owner of the game could not call the cops. My crew had experience at this sort of thing, and The Crook was my choice. He agreed, because he needed some money to see a girl he was banging.

The game was in the basement below a store on the Danforth in Greektown. We parked a stolen van out back and waited for the Greek to give us the signal.

His role in the plan was to play loose and bet large, loading the table with cash. We were to wait for him to come up for some air and give us the cue – he would light a cigar, shake hands with one of his pals and drive off in his Cadillac.

That's when we put on our ski masks.

When Harry's inside man came out, our job was to jump him, kick the door open, knock Harry's guy down and rush in, screaming for everyone to freeze. That is exactly what we did.

There were two rooms and the scene was busy. In one room there were fifteen guys at the poker table. In another side room a hooker was plying her trade. She immediately knew what was going on.

"Time's up," she said to the guy on top of her. He wanted to finish, but I put my gun to his head and got off a line for the ages.

"*Coitus interruptus*, friend."

The hooker happened to be the wife of a friend of mine. She gathered her robe around her for the sake of modesty. I didn't take her trick money. She'd earned it.

Owen kept his gun on the crowd while I scooped the money off the card table. Next, I made my way down the line, collecting watches and gold chains.

It sounds easy enough, but the truth is these robberies were a lot riskier than banks. The guys at the table could be robbers themselves or hit men or cops.

Elapsed time: two minutes.

We dumped the van where I'd left my car and went to see Harry. He was as happy as if he'd won the Queen's Plate. He got more than his investment back. We made ten grand apiece, more or less.

I drove Owen home. The next day he was leaving to see his girlfriend, who knows for how long. I got a room in a hotel, and then went to the Four Brothers Club on Spadina, looking for a girl to party with.

The scene was familiar: players, hookers, pimps, weed smokers, coke snorters and craps shooters. I made my way around the room, greeting friends and family.

"Buy me a drink," she cooed.

The sweet-talking Glenda ran her tongue over her lips and batted her lashes. We hit the dance floor during a slow song; I could feel the warmth rising.

"Why don't you take me home?"

I knew Glenda. She had pulled her first trick at fourteen, encouraged by her boyfriend to make some extra money for them both. I also knew that I wanted her more than she wanted me. I've always been attracted to women who know what they want, and make no bones about it.

I took her back to the hotel. As we settled in, she took out a bag of white powder and a needle. I didn't do dope, but I didn't mind if she shot up. By the time morning came, the room looked like it had been hit by a tornado, only now she was out of dope and aching for more.

There was something I needed to know.

"Girl, if you want to play with me, you have to play a little less with that. Can you do that?"

"Why do men always want to control my life?"

"I care about your health. I also know that one day the party's going to be over, whether you like it or not. Face the reality, and you'll see what I see."

I saw a pretty black girl in the grip.

"Now you're a fucking philosopher with a crystal ball," she said, with a pause. "I'll give it a shot, and we'll see how long it lasts, but take me over to your cousin's one last time so I don't lose my mind trying to fit into your way of living life."

If she was willing to wean herself, I was willing to help.

I left her with my cousin, took some of my cash and bought a yellow Ford Marquis from a lot on Queen Street.

The gang – me, The Crook, Everett, and Dwane – began to do steady work, adding Bobby Marsh, blond, blue-eyed, half-black kid to our group.

Meanwhile, Levern and his brothers were running an after-hours playground for pimps and hustlers. They were also busy travelling around Ontario and Quebec selling phoney dope to small-time pushers. It always surprised me that they found repeat customers.

They hung with us, but they were not down for the gunplay that seemed to follow me wherever I went. The risks were serious. I was always armed. By choice, I never hung out with anyone I didn't know well because I was always aware that someone might want to set me up.

Money was rolling in, raising the question of how to handle it. I couldn't very well open a bank account. In fact, I didn't need a bank. All I had to do was rent a garage, steal a car, park the car in the garage, put the cash in a small safe and lock the safe in the trunk – along with a cache of guns.

Nothing to it and no fees.

In addition to stealing anything that wasn't tied down, we cultivated fences who were ready to buy whatever we stole.

Then there was the side action.

I had heard about a Chinese guy whose parents owned a dry-cleaning shop on Queen at Spadina. He wasn't affiliated with any of the Chinese gangs, but he was selling hash in quantity, making him an easy target. I talked it over with Dwane and we decided to rip him off.

The plan was simple. We waited outside his apartment on the twenty-first floor while one of our friends outside of the building called and asked him to make a delivery. We jumped him as he came out.

He was just a little guy. I snatched him up and headed for the balcony with him scratching and clawing and doing everything he could to slow me down. It was like the movies. I held him by the ankles and dangled him over the side, a little trick that I'd learned the hard way from the cops. I knew it worked to concentrate the mind.

"Tell me where your stash is or learn to fly."

To make my point a little more seriously, I let go of one ankle. That's all it took. He said he had another apartment in the building and gave me all of the details. I grabbed his keys. My brother handcuffed him and sat him on the floor.

I took the elevator down to the dummy apartment and let myself in. I found a screwdriver exactly where he said it would be and removed a panel from the inside of his bedroom closet, helping myself to a stash of hash and cash.

Once I was out of the building, I signalled up to my brother to come down. We split the money and gave the dope to some of the guys to sell in the after-hours clubs.

The next day, I went over to my mother's house. My father looked at me over his coffee and said, "Bob Ellis was here, looking nervous. I don't know what you boys are up to, but you better take care of it."

St. Christopher House social worker Bob Ellis feared no one. He was genuinely concerned about helping kids in any way he could. I was beyond any of his anti-gang preaching, but I figured he must have something important to tell me. He had an ear where many couldn't hear.

The meeting didn't last long.

The Chinese pusher who had been robbed had approached him and asked for help.

"Mr. Ellis, the Chinese guy doesn't get anything back," I told him. "If he gets out of the game, he's cool with us. No further reprisals. If he stays in the game, well, shit happens and it could be out of my control."

"Ricky, I can assure you he's out of the game, but don't play me," said Mr. Ellis. "I've known you since you were a baby. It's always under your control."

I turned to walk away and he reached out to touch my arm.

"Ricky, there are so many games to play, and you're so gifted in so many ways. When are you going to get out of this?"

That was the key question, but nobody leaves when the going is good. I was as deep in the game as the game was deep in me.

Before I could answer, an unmarked police car rolled past. The driver smiled at Bob, and then he looked at me and drew his fingers across his throat, an obvious threat. It was my old pal.

"How you doing, Mr. Novis?" I asked.

"Soon, Ricky."

When he drove off, Mr. Ellis asked me if I wasn't tired of having Novis on my case. I shrugged. "He's just one of many." I thought I could outsmart them all. The test came minutes later.

I left Bob Ellis and spotted a knot of guys shooting dice in an alley. One of them was a punk who owed me money. I eased my way over but someone spotted me. My guy stood up, ready to run. I pulled out my gun.

"You can't outrun a bullet, asshole." The others stuffed their money in their pockets, full of fear, but I wasn't after them.

I walked over to the guy who owed me money and stripped him of his winnings. I might have taught him a larger lesson but somebody hollered, "Cops!"

Three police cruisers and an unmarked cop car skidded to a stop a hundred yards away. The doors flew open, cops fanned out. Shit. If I got caught with a gun while on parole, it meant a trip back to the slammer. It was Novis.

He got out of his unmarked car, scanning the scene, obviously looking for someone special. The gamblers fled as one. I took off with them, running down Vanauley Walk, passing Bob Ellis as I did, holding my gun under my coat, running for my life and looking for sanctuary.

I saw a doorway and ran inside as if the place was mine. Closing the door behind me, I and turned to find a family staring open-mouthed at me, in the middle of their dinner.

The man of the house didn't bat an eye. His wife jumped up to look out the window. The kids stared at me, as their food got cold.

Outside, the cops were shouting orders, rounding up anyone who looked suspicious. The thing about the gun is that it was dangerous for me to be carrying it, but it would have been suicide for me not to carry it. From my perspective, there was no point in letting the guy who owed me money off the hook. It would have sent the wrong signal.

The cops cleared off fifteen minutes later, during which time no one in the house said a word. I took the money I'd taken from the gambler and dropped it on the table.

The husband sucked the last morsel of meat off his pork chop bone and nodded. His wife counted the cash, which had gone from the gambler to me to them in a matter of minutes. They would eat better tomorrow.

I left without a word, as if all of this had been normal. Everyone in the Projects survived to live another day.

IN THIS CORNER

In addition to everything else, I was keeping in shape with roadwork. It served a dual purpose – I was running from the cops, and I was running toward a career in the boxing ring.

When the fight was set with Junior Jones, Jerry Bates had me sparring regularly with Pretty Boy Feldstein and with Paul "The Investment" Neilson. Both of them were in line for a shot at the Champ – George Chuvalo. The sparring sessions were vicious and I was learning to box like a pro.

The evening of the match with Jones had layers of intrigue. One of the fighters dropped out at the last minute, so the card wasn't sanctioned by the Canadian Amateur Boxing Association. Even if I beat Junior, I wouldn't take his title.

The boxing commissioner was my cousin, Clyde Gray. For my money, he was the best welterweight in Canadian history. He shrugged. "Rules are rules, Rick. I don't make them."

Junior approached me before the fight with a suggestion.

"Since we're not fighting for my title, there's no point trying to kill each other. We're not getting paid a penny for this."

I agreed, until Bobby Marsh came up to me and told me that there were a couple of big-money American promoters in the crowd. Bobby was the son of one of my father's friends and the Marsh's were a boxing family. Two of Bobby's brothers became champs, including Leo who I sparred with every day.

"Ricky, Junior told them that he was going to knock you out tonight. You better kick his butt," Bobby said, and I figured he was in the know. "There might be some opportunities down the road with these guys."

It looked like Junior had been setting me up for a fall, with all his talk about taking it easy. When the bell rang, we walked out to the middle of the ring and Junior reached out to touch gloves. I responded with a right hand that would have stopped rush-hour traffic.

He reeled back, shocked. From the look on his face I knew immediately that it was Bobby Marsh who had set me up. Nevertheless, the tenor of the fight was set and we fought like rabid dogs for three rounds. His strategy was to dance, while trying to take my head off. Mine was to counter, while trying to rip out his liver.

Each time I went back to my corner, I stood rather than listen to Bobby's instructions. Lying to me about Americans with money being in the crowd was one thing. A lie like that can put more fight in the ring and that's what everyone wants. What bothered me was that Bobby's lie ended whatever friendship Junior Jones and I could ever have.

At the end of the fight, the crowd stood and cheered us for a full minute. The referee was Sammy Luftspring, a former welterweight champion and future boxing Hall of Famer.

"Boys, that was the best three-rounder I've ever seen," he told us. "You should be proud of yourselves." Maybe so, but the outcome was unsatisfactory. I took the decision but had no title to show for it.

When I went home, I planned to take Glenda out to celebrate. She was pacing up and down, almost hysterical, in need of a fix. I tried to talk her out of it.

"Listen, you're an athlete and a gangster, that's the life you chose," she told me. "This is the life I chose. If you don't want all of me, you can't have any of me."

I took her back to my cousin's house and broke up with her a week later. There were no tears. We both knew I'd been good to her. She died a couple of years later, when someone gave her a hot shot – a needle filled with poison instead of dope.

I began sparring with Pretty Boy Feldstein who was preparing for a fight with George Chuvalo. He didn't take it easy, knowing that Chuvalo would be tough.

Things got off to a bumpy start at the weigh-in. George was mad for some reason and he attacked Pretty Boy. It took a couple of us to break them up. After the weigh-in, I walked Pretty Boy to his car in the parking lot. Chuvalo followed us, cursing and calling out Pretty Boy to fight him on the spot.

There was no point fighting for nothing in a parking lot, so we drove off. Chuvalo managed to punch the side of the car a couple of times. He left fist-sized dents in the metal.

I don't know if he spooked Pretty Boy but he sure spooked me, and I knew then that Pretty Boy didn't stand a chance.

On the night of the fight, I was approached by a Canadian-born hustler from Detroit, a former Golden Gloves champion, a singer and a gangster named Charles "Spider" Jones. He earned the "Spider" because of the way he sidled around in the ring.

He swung his coat over his shoulders loosely, with his right hand clenched. I figured he was going to sucker punch me but I didn't know why. I patted my side, to indicate I was carrying. I wasn't, but the ruse worked.

He said, "We got to talk."

"Talk, then."

"I was told you were going to take a shot at me as soon as you saw me; take your shot." He'd been misinformed.

"Whoever told you that is going to bite a bullet. Who was it?" I asked.

He nodded to a young fighter, a kid called Popeye from the Queen City Boxing Club. I called Popeye over and confronted him. He acted as if it was no big deal.

"Yeah, I said that. I thought it would be really cool to see you two get it on."

Popeye was seventeen years old and he boxed under various names, ready at all times to fill out a card. Sometimes he wouldn't even fight for money but for the pussy promised by the promoters. He still lived with his mother.

Spider warned him to leave the promoting to others. We laughed it off, no point hurting the kid. It was much better to laugh because if Spider and I had got it on, it would have been ugly.

As for ugly, Feldstein dropped and kissed the canvas in the ninth round, ending his boxing career. After the fight, Junior Jones came over and wanted to know why I'd tried to kill him during our three-rounder. I told him I'd have hurt the Queen of England if she came at me with gloves on.

"I'm quitting for good," he said. "I don't want to fight for my life against guys like you and not get paid for it."

I knew where he was coming from. I was good in the ring, but I was uneasy being somebody's whore, stepping almost naked into the ring for the amusement of the crowd.

One night I was listening to the radio in bed when there was a news report that a man had been killed in a shooting at the Wellington Hotel. The police were on the lookout for Everett Crosby.

Shit.

I jumped up, got dressed and gathered the crew at an after-hours bar. The story was stupid and fatal. My cousin Dewey had been dancing with his woman, Debbie. The two of them were practicing foreplay by arguing drunkenly with each other. The usual mixed-race crap.

Everett cut in on them. He danced with Debbie for a while until Dewey walked up and slapped her in the face. More of their kind of "abuse-me-I-love-you" foreplay.

Some white guy, who had no idea what was going on, jumped up, shouting, "No nigger hits a white girl while I'm around!"

He and Dewey started fighting, taking it into the street. Everett and some others were in on the action. When an Italian guy came at Everett with a beer bottle, Everett shot him dead. The story sounded plausible. I was pissed at Everett for bringing heat on all of us.

"Where is he?"

No one said anything; the question didn't need an answer. I said, "Get him some money, and new identification."

My guys were already on it. I went back home to wait for the morning news.

The story on TV was that an Italian square john from Sudbury had been jumped by a gang of rowdy blacks and killed for no reason. He left behind a wife and three kids. The story ended with a clip of police cars carrying away people for questioning, including several of my crew.

Cops were tearing up the city, hunting for the killer. The dead man's wife pleaded for justice. I was stopped at gunpoint by cops wanting to know where Everett was. I had no idea, but I knew that if he wasn't long gone he was in trouble.

It was harder to spot homicide dicks than it was to spot the hold-up squad, which meant my gang's usual counter-surveillance techniques weren't much good. We had to scale back and slow down our operations, all of which meant we were losing money. And life on the street is all about money.

One night, the usual happened in an unusual way. An unmarked car skidded to a halt in front of me. Bert Novis stepped out, carrying a sawed-off carbine.

"Put your fucking hands up."

I put my fucking hands up. That was the usual.

He cuffed me and pushed me into the back seat, and off we sped, not stopping until we came to a deserted parking lot.

"Ricky, we got to talk. This is serious, man."

This was the unusual. I held up my hands, rattling my chains. When he freed me, I asked, "What's up, Mr. Novis?"

"Everett's been calling the police station every day, threatening to shoot me on sight. I know he doesn't have the balls to go toe-to-toe with me but I'll kill the punk, Rick. I can't take any chances. I got a wife and kid to think about."

"Mr. Novis, what do you want from me?"

"We know what went down in that bar. You get him a message. Tell him if he gives himself up, we'll be looking at manslaughter – four to five years tops, in the pen. But if he doesn't give himself up, it's second-degree murder with a life sentence and, I swear to God, if I see him first, he's dead."

It was a pleasure for me to see this big bad cop so badly rattled.

"Mr. Novis, I don't know where he is."

"Don't you shit me, don't you fuck around. I'm not playing games this time." He waved his rifle in my face. "You think I like sleeping with this under my pillow?"

I held up my hands in defence. "Okay, take it easy. I'll find a way to get word to him." There was nothing else to say.

Everett was hanging low, far away from the scene of the crime. He evaded capture for two years and was working as a bus driver in Cleveland when he was ratted out by his woman because he'd slapped her around.

He got life with no parole for twelve years, although he did a lot less time than that. Then he went straight. Later, I did time with his son in a British Columbia prison.

A few weeks later after Novis's blowout, an old girlfriend told me that a friend of hers was looking for someone to extract a belligerent boyfriend from an apartment she had rented. The girlfriend was willing to pay for the service. I had no interest in the domestic problems of a stranger, until she showed me a picture.

I had to work to keep my cool. The woman in the picture was really pretty. She had been at ringside the night I fought Junior Jones. Her name was Diane. I remembered her from years ago when she was a teenager waiting tables at Club Jamaica.

I agreed to help, but I wasn't going to take any chances. I showed up with Bobby. He showed up with a gun. As expected, the boyfriend was mouthy and aggressive, and I had to slap him around to shut him up. Then I took Diane to a hotel for the night, to give her boyfriend time to clear out his stuff.

Diane and I talked. She had a gorgeous redheaded girlfriend. They later asked if I'd share a house with them in Scarborough. It seemed like a good deal, sort of like the TV show *Three's Company*, but with a sweetener. It was rent-free for me.

Diane became my girlfriend. She was working as a model. The redhead was working for an escort service. I made them feel safe.

Safety is relative.

Me and Bobby and others from the gang once robbed a card game in the Hollywood Hotel. Our inside man was someone we'd grown up with. His relatives were in charge of the game. What we didn't know is that there was a big mob wedding in the city that day and half the Ontario Mafia was on hand.

One of the guards on the door was a guy I'd met in jail. I knew he'd have to show face and make a move, so I spun and kicked him in the chest, sending him crashing into a table filled with booze. Before he could recover, I pressed my gun into his chest and snatched his from its holster. I sneered at him, but really I was just doing him a favour in front of his bosses.

"You thought I didn't see you reaching for this?"

I was in full makeup. No one recognized me, but I knew I was in over my head. Oh well, in for a dime, in for a dollar. One of the mobsters had a huge ring on his finger. I pointed to it.

"I'm not giving you this," he said defiantly. "It can't come off. It's too tight. Besides, it has flaws. It's not worth what you think."

"I'll be the judge of that."

I reached behind my back and pulled out the small hatchet that I carried with me at times like this. You never know what you're going to need. I grabbed his hand and pressed it down on the table. He yanked his hand back, sliding the ring off his fat finger and looking at me like I'd just made the biggest mistake of my life. Maybe I had, but now was not the time to show it. I told Bobby to grab his wallet.

"Mister, if what you say is true, we'll mail the ring back to you. We're all honest crooks, aren't we?"

I tossed the ring into my briefcase. Bobby extracted the man's driver's licence and put it in his pocket. We completed our search and took off.

As we sped away I said, "Bobby, if those guys find out who we are, heads will roll." Bobby nodded – ours were the heads that would roll.

The money was divvied up four ways. Our inside man got his end. Our guy in the getaway car, the one who carried the walkie-talkie and kept his eye out for the cops, also got a cut. Bobby got what he'd earned.

I kept all the jewellery in my briefcase. It would be a long-term investment. I knew word would go out immediately to the fences to be on the lookout. Any one of them would willingly rat me out for a reward.

I took the ring to an appraiser I trusted. He confirmed the flaws in the stone, which knocked the value down by seventy percent. It was now worth my while to be as good as my word. I put the ring in an envelope and mailed it back, along with the driver's licence.

A few days later, my uncle Ronny the Bear told my father that there was a hit on me as a result of the robbery. Sonny called me right away. My father didn't have to tell me I'd screwed up. I already knew it. We shook hands when we parted, knowing it might be the last time we'd see each other.

I called a meeting. Our choices were limited, and dangerous. We decided to strike first and see what would happen. We grabbed the guy who set up the game and persuaded him to open up – with the help of some applied pain. He confessed that he'd ratted us out after the mob had threatened to kill him. He gave us the name of the man who wanted us dead. I knew who it was.

I'd just mailed him his ring.

Here's the spot we were in: the Mafia had hundreds of years' worth of experience with warfare and vendetta. They knew what to do and how to do it. They were also willing to do it.

If we had an edge it was that we knew the city, and we had a honeycomb of safe houses, rented garages, stolen cars and improvised safety-deposit boxes filled with guns.

Other than that, we were on our own.

Black gangsters couldn't help me, in part because I had nothing to offer in return. The Panthers were a shadowy remnant of their former glory. They'd become more political. It would be virtually impossible to persuade them to help in a criminal matter, particularly after the debacle with Warren Hart. The Black Muslims from the Nation of Islam were powerful enough to wipe out the Italians – I'm betting you had no idea they were that strong in those days, in Toronto the Good – but I'd become something of an infidel. I knew they would not step up for me.

None of the biker clubs were strong enough at this time to be of any help. I wasn't about to trust them. It was too easy for them to rat me out and gather a risk-free reward.

There were no Jamaican posse groups at the time, and gangs like the Bloods and Crips had not yet moved into the city.

I had one hope.

The Irish mob.

I set up a meeting. I knew that the skilled and capable Irish safecrackers in Toronto and in the west end of Montreal would benefit from a connection with members of my family living in Montreal who had some of the best safecracking skills in Canada. After a long negotiation involving a lot of give and take, with me doing most of the giving, the Irish boss said, "Fuck those Italian bastards."

I reached out to shake on it.

The Irish boss said, "We'll work this out. You do what you said you'd do, and we'll wait for the phone calls."

In the world of business, taking on a partner can save your enterprise. In my world, taking on a partner can save your life.

I had a flickering thought that my life would be a lot easier if my business was legit.

It was just a flicker.

The Irish mob gave me what I asked for – a rundown of the activities of the man who wanted me dead. Armed with that knowledge, and with an arsenal of guns, we drove to Guelph, where he was based.

My plan was to reason with him, and if that didn't work, I'd shoot him dead and we'd go to all-out war.

His girlfriend ran a store. We parked nearby one night and waited. After a time, a big black limo pulled up and parked behind the store. The mobster was alone. Owen the Crook sensed an easy victory.

"Holy shit, let's get him right now."

I held him back. "Let's see if he is locked into his routine. He underestimated us. We can always catch him going home if he's this relaxed."

We tailed him back to his girlfriend's apartment and watched him get out and open her door. He seemed eager enough as they walked into her building arm in arm. "What do you think?" I wondered aloud. "An hour, maybe more?"

The Crook said, "He's too horny to last that long. Fifty bucks says the trick is in and out in less than thirty minutes."

He lasted twenty-five.

I paid Owen his fifty, pocketed my Browning pistol, and we stepped from the car and walked slowly over to the mob boss. I approached from the front, while Owen circled around, to come up on him from behind.

Nearing the man, I stuck out my hand and said, "It's a pleasure to meet you." He looked around nervously, not remembering who I was or what I wanted, but he shook my hand, not wanting to offend.

He was wearing the big stone.

"I see your ring arrived safely."

He blanched, and his grip grew limp. For a second I thought he might run, until The Crook stepped up from behind, holding a big .44, cutting him off.

Of course the Italian knew that if this really was a hit he would have been dead by now. I patted him down. He was clean. I motioned to a little trail between a row of trees leading to another apartment building.

Owen followed us, looking for cops.

After a few steps the mob boss, who was a little out of shape and perhaps tired from his amorous labours, pointed to a park bench.

"Let's sit. My legs are tired."

"I should have let my friend blow your head off," I told him. "Then he could have gone up to that apartment to enjoy that whore you're screwing."

He was cool and, more calmly than another man might have, he said, "That won't make your problems go away, and whores come and go. Why would I give a shit about her if I'm dead?" He added, "You stepped on some big toes, robbing my game."

"I'm an honest crook," I said. "I was working for the Irish in the east end. I have to pay my dues, and when an opportunity arises I take advantage. Nobody told me you were behind the game."

At the mention of the Irish, his eyebrows rose slightly and the corners of his mouth tightened. I'm guessing he'd have been easy to read at the poker table.

"When somebody embarrasses me in front of my friends and relatives, then fuck the Irish."

I stepped back. "Respect was extended to you when your ring came back in the mail, as promised. What thief would have done that? There are others who thought I should have sent you a bomb."

"Don't threaten me," he growled.

Owen tightened his grip on the gun. And I laid it on the line for my Italian friend.

"You listen to me. I have no kids, no job, no business to look after, but I have ten guys just out of Millhaven, ready to blow your whole fucking family away, and I have another ten inside who will take care of your cousin in Collins Bay tomorrow. I really don't give a fuck about how you conduct your business but if you've got a bone to pick with me, then you're going to have to finish it with the Irish. Talk to them, not to me."

I had more to say, but I was startled by an explosion. My head snapped around; there was smoke coming from the barrel of Owen's gun. He nodded towards some bushes. "Fucking squirrels. Rats with bushy tails. I hate rats."

The old man's nerve was shaken.

He got up and we headed for his car. I was waiting to hear him say the words that would save his life, and maybe mine.

He said, "You gave my late wife's ring back to me. That goes a long way. Tell the Irish I will call him tomorrow." He drove off, and so did we. What a relief.

I knew Owen loved animals. He'd never have shot an innocent thing just for the hell of it.

"Nice touch with that squirrel thing," I noted.

He said, "I think this guy is too much a pussy for us to back off. I think we should step on his toes a few more times. I'd still like to go fuck his girlfriend."

I cut that line of thinking off quickly.

"We don't have the money for war. If we start robbing banks to get it, the heat from Novis will make it impossible to move around."

I turned the car toward Toronto, but I didn't go home. I spent the night in a motel in the east end, sleeping with my automatic rifle and a couple of handguns.

A day later, Harry the Greek called. He was a natural go-between, because the Italians didn't trust the Irish. The meeting was set for a Greek restaurant, neutral ground. We cased it out beforehand. I got walkie-talkies and found locations for my lookouts.

The Mafia boss pulled up in a black Cadillac Fleetwood. He had muscle with him, a man I knew well from Collins Bay. The Irish mobster arrived wearing most of the jewellery I'd taken in the robbery, a dramatic touch.

I entered the restaurant in full disguise. How confident was I? Earlier in the day, I'd walked past my parents and they hadn't noticed me. The Italian bodyguard stepped in my path. "Restaurant's closed, mister."

I played him, looking around like I was hungry. The other doorman said, "Look, mister, read the fucking sign; this joint is closed." I took a deep breath, as if it hurt me to be turned away. And then I said, "Johnny, nothing is closed to those who know how to pick a lock."

"Shit, Ricky, is that you?"

Owen stood nearby. I had dyed the end of a bucket mop black and set it on his head, then covered it with a gold, red and black wool cap. He looked like a proper Rastafarian. To set off the dreadlocks, I'd given him a scar on his cheek and covered a couple of his teeth in gold foil. No one saw that his hand, inside his pocket, was gripping a cold hard .44 magnum.

I winked and the first bodyguard said, "Fuck, man, you guys should be in the movies. I'd never have known it was you two." The second one said, "Yeah, Ricky Two-hats; never know who he is."

The meeting took an hour.

The Italians complained about their crosses and medals and sentimental heirlooms. We gave it all back. In return, we were given a list of card games, dope pushers and loan sharks who were, from that moment, off limits to us.

The war was over.

We shook hands, although the mobster declined to shake with Owen. Maybe he was upset about the squirrel.

Just because the war was over didn't mean the end of business, and in the crime business rules are broken all the time. We all had mouths to feed, so the following weekend I dressed two guys up as Rastas and sent them to rob one of the Italian drug runners.

THE PLAYERS' BALL HEIST

In 1977 I found a perfect opportunity to make my ambitions known: someone had organized a party for all the black criminals in town. The Players' Ball was a chance to show up and strut, with the men in gold and furs and the women in gowns and jewels.

If I was going to get in the game, I needed tickets, so I drove over to a club on Avenue Road. My knock was answered by Dwight Gabriel, who I'd known since we were kids. He was from the neighbourhood, and he played trumpet in a band called Crack of Dawn. We slapped hands. I needed ten tickets.

"Ricky, we're all sold out; not a ticket anywhere."

"Brother, don't shit me. There's got to be a ticket here or there. Money ain't the object."

"Man, if I'm lying, I'm dying. There's not a ticket to be had, and nobody's giving up a ticket, no matter how much you got. Lots of niggers coming from out of town, just hoping against hope to get in. But you snooze, you lose, brother, that's just the way it is."

I wanted to bust him in his trumpet-playing chops.

"You telling me that I can't come through that door if I don't have a ticket?" I sounded serious now, as if I was willing to kill to get in.

"No one in without a ticket, brother. That's the way it's got to be."

I smiled and walked away.

Before I got back to my car, I knew exactly what was going to happen, and it wasn't going to be pretty. After all, I had jacked up the Italian mob and I was still alive. The difference was, I had never stepped on any toes in my own community. But no one slaps me in the face without getting slapped a little harder in return.

I figured that if I crashed the Players' Ball and robbed everyone in sight, it would put me on top of the world. Or it would get me killed.

I called a meeting and laid down a plan.

My needs were clear. I had to have people who were not known to anyone at the ball. Bobby Marsh said he knew some Italians from the west end. I had to make sure none of them was connected to the mob guys we'd robbed or they might be setting me up to get whacked.

Dwane and I worked out an escape route, and we rehearsed it to make sure it was to our liking.

The Italians were going to need disguises to avoid attention. One of them, in particular, needed to look black enough to get the doorman to open the door.

I was going to have to walk a razor's edge. Some of my relatives would be at the ball, and I'd need to be able to return what I took from them without drawing suspicion, while protecting them from strangers who were sticking loaded guns in their faces.

The gunmen I needed had to be the best in the city – fearless and cool. The Italians were expensive and their leader was aware that if found out, he'd be killed by black gangsters. We rehearsed the score over and over.

My instructions were cold as ice: "Fuck up and you sleep with the fishes." I got that from the movies. I figured it was a phrase he'd understand.

I gave him the makeup kits and Afro wigs and showed him how to apply it to his guys. Then I left to make sure everything was in place.

I had stolen cars parked here and there around the venue. The Italian crew leader had a walkie-talkie to keep in touch with my brother. I had one as well. I drove around the back of the club, looking for a place to observe in safety, while my brother took the front door.

Cadillacs and Lincolns began pulling up, with players of all shades and nationalities spilling out, strutting their stuff and flashing their tickets. The scene was as flamboyant as opening night at the Toronto International Film Festival.

For a moment I thought about calling off the score. I had reservations about spoiling what would be a fine and historic night for many of the gangsters I knew well.

What changed my mind?

A brown Caddy pulled up and I saw two pimps get out. One of them, a player named Charles, had insulted me when I was younger; I'd wanted to touch his diamond brooch and he brushed me off, saying, "Nigger, it will be years before your hustle is good enough for shit like this."

The other guy was pimping one of my close cousins. I'd thought about gunning him down more than once. On the other hand, if I gunned down every pimp who turned a cousin, I'd have had a lot of killing to do.

The robbery seemed the best way to settle that score.

The Italians pulled up in their disguises and went in. As soon as the robbery was under way my brother's voice crackled over the walkie-talkie.

"Something's not right. We're being set up. Undercover are all over the place. I think we should abort now."

I have never ever questioned my brother's ability to spot a cop, and I had no reason to doubt him now.

I got on my walkie-talkie.

"Call it off."

Most of the people inside would already have been taken down, but there hadn't been enough time to finish the job, meaning there would be problems cutting up the take. Still, it was time to cut and run. Better to live and have those kinds of problems than to be dead or in jail.

Before I could start my car, all hell broke loose. Several brightly dressed pimps and lavishly dressed whores jumped the fence behind the building, landing on my car.

I waved them off with my gun.

A carful of players pulled up behind me and the driver leaned frantically on his horn. It was every man for himself now. I gunned my engine and was peeling away into the night when one of the Italians ran past, waving his shotgun and carrying a bag of loot. I opened my door, he jumped in and we disappeared.

I took the Italian to my house, and poured the loot on the table. In among the cash and the jewellery I spotted a small diamond butterfly that belonged to my cousin Crystal. I set the butterfly aside, along with a small diamond heart inset with rubies that formed the letter "J." It belonged to one of Joe Patterson's whores.

I sent the Italian away with a fistful of hundreds, and soon my brother was knocking at my door. He said there had been undercover cops all over the place, ready to take down everyone in the club. Before the uniform cops arrived to give them a hand, everyone came bursting out of the club. Some of the partygoers were naked and carrying their clothes. My robbers were nothing if not thorough.

"Man, it was a set-up" Dwane said. "Those cops were in position before the score started." I wondered if they hadn't been placed there just to keep tabs on the players. My brother shook his head.

"They had specific targets; when the Italian crew leader came out, they were onto him. He got away through the crowd. If they were just there to watch, all they'd have done was take notes and file reports. Something wasn't right. It just didn't smell good."

An hour later, the phone rang. The crew leader's wife, and she was frantic. "The cops just hit my house and grabbed my husband and two of his guys, along with all your shit. Someone close to us must have ratted us out, because no one knows where we live. We just moved in yesterday."

I drove over to find out just how it had gone down. She wanted to know if her husband was going to be killed in jail if they put him on a range with black guys. I assured her no one was going to be killed.

When things settled a bit, I met with Joe Patterson and gave him his whore's diamond heart. He said that if he'd been there, my robbers would all be dead.

"Brother, why you do that?"

I told him about Dwight denying me tickets.

"Man, that pussy don't control no shit. I could have gotten you in, no problem."

I had to fire back.

"If an Eaton's employee stops you from going in to Eaton's, do you call Mr. Eaton to whine like a bitch, or do you just bust in to get your shit?"

Big Joe knew that I'd taken down the Italian card game, so I told him that some of the people from that game were sleeping with the fishes. Yeah, yeah, I know it's a cliché. But I could see he believed me, so I dropped a bomb on him.

"If anyone wants to meet me before sundown and go toe to toe, I'm more than ready, because I'm back in town."

That seemed to do the trick.

If I was really back in town, there were things to take care of. Some of the Italians had been identified. We got a list of those who would be appearing in court.

The Italians were contract players who worked for me. I knew I'd have to protect them if I wanted to be taken seriously. Bobby and I went around talking to people, trying to get a fix on what we were up against. In the end, all but two witnesses backed down.

Derek Mercury, who I had known since First Grade, had a woman at the party. She lost a necklace, a valuable family heirloom that had been recovered in the possession of one of the robbers. The only way she could get it back was by taking the stand and testifying. We couldn't budge her with bribery or threats. It must have been some precious heirloom, or else she was some kind of stupid, because it would have been easy enough to kill her by setting her up with a bad trick.

Even so, I suppose that might not have freed the Italians. We'd just have to play it out, and see if she showed up in court.

The other one who wouldn't budge was a street fighter, a guy named Rocky who bounced at the Colonial Tavern. He'd lost his watch. But he was more afraid of what the cops had on him than he was afraid of us.

I sent the Italians a quote on what it would cost to eliminate these two judicial threats. It was a job that could involve intimidation to force them not show up for trial; kidnapping until after trial or murder – the ultimate silencer. I could easily subcontract it and make a profit at the same time. Most likely, it could be accomplished without lifting a finger against Rocky – who I liked, or Derek's woman – who I did not. They couldn't afford it.

Several months passed. On the day of the preliminary hearing, I showed up at court with Bobby Marsh. Wheeling and dealing was in the air, with cops trying to get convictions at all costs, and lawyers hustling for lighter sentences for some clients while selling others out. Crown attorneys were doing what they could to keep the wheels of justice running smoothly.

In the midst of it all, I saw the Italians and their friends standing by the staircase, with Bobby caught up in the middle. More to the point, I saw a brown-skinned girl, who was louder and more vocal than anyone else. She drew stares from the cops. I heard her shout.

"You're a fucking rat." She was looking right at Bobby.

Before I could fully understand what she'd just said, he punched her in the chest, knocking her back. Before she could recover, he pointed at her and snarled, "You ever say that again, I'll kill you, bitch."

She stood up and walked away, followed by the Italian wives, all of them shooting looks at Bobby. What the hell?

Rocky and Derek were off to one side, looking trapped and worried. Derek's woman didn't have a care in the world. All she had on her mind was her mother's necklace, and how she was going to get it back, even if it killed her.

The Italians hadn't accepted my proposal, so there was nothing to do now but wait and see how it played out. They had lawyers. One of them approached me.

"Ricky, there are two witnesses here, both of them are unsavoury. Is there any way you can talk to them before we walk this into court? If not, it will be too late. These boys are going to do time."

I walked over to Rocky and Derek and gave it my best shot. Without actually saying I'd have to kill them both, I made it clear what they'd be facing in the wrath of the Italians.

Nothing doing.

The Italians got three years for robbery.

As I was leaving court, the brown-skinned girl stopped me, confronted me.

"Ricky, listen. You didn't know where the Italian lived, but Bobby did. And think of this; he punched a girl in a courtroom full of cops, and nobody did a thing about it."

The implication was clear. I had to weigh that information. In my world when in doubt, wipe them out has always been a life-saving strategy.

ONE THING
LEADS TO ANOTHER

Jerry Bates, my trainer, figured I was ready and wanted me to turn pro. "There's no use in staying amateur. You can beat most of the pros already. Besides, there ain't no money in amateur fights or even the Olympics, where anything can happen to stop you from getting a gold medal." He was right, but the 1980 Olympics were two years away, and by now you know the pattern of my life – there was going to be a detour.

Bobby and I got invited to a biker party in Peterborough. It seemed like a good way to make connections. I didn't want to take my car – there was heat on it. Bobby's brother Leo had a van and I borrowed it for a few bucks.

My uncle Ronny the Bear heard we were heading out of town, so he jumped in. It's bad etiquette to show up at a party empty-handed, so we picked up some hash oil and headed out.

The party was at a farmhouse on the outskirts of Peterborough. As we approached, we ran into some full-patch bikers riding in the other direction in a hurry. We stopped one of them and asked what was going on.

"Man, some dude from out west accidentally shot one of our guys in the head with a shotgun." Okay, then.

We beat it out of there in a hurry and headed into Peterborough for a drink and a look at the strippers in a biker bar. Then we headed back to Toronto.

I stopped behind a darkened gas station in Omemee for a piss and a leg stretch. When I got back to the van, Bobby was eating a chocolate bar and carrying a carton of smokes under his arm.

"Hey, is there a store open?"

He just grinned and then Bear showed up, chewing on a piece of deli meat; there was a little IGA market across the road closed for the night.

Bobby said it would be easy enough to go back in and crack the safe.

I said, "We don't have any tools, and there can't be more than a few bucks in there."

The Bear stepped back and kicked in the door of the gas station. "We've got tools now. At least take a look at the safe, Rick. If you don't want to open it, cool; we'll leave."

I wasn't happy but I couldn't say no.

The safe was in the back office. Bobby played to my vanity – if I could open the safe in ten minutes I could keep his share of the take.

It took an hour to get it away from the wall, and then Bobby started to time me as I went to work. I beat ten minutes. Inside the safe, a few thousand dollars – more than I'd expected – and a stamp and coin collection. I let them gather it up and went to start the van.

Bobby came back and promptly went to sleep in the back. The Bear rode shotgun, smoking hash oil.

An hour later, as we were about to hit the 401 for home, a cop car passed us. The cop nodded at me, but when he saw Bear's black face his eyes widened and he flashed us over.

I gave him my driver's licence and my insurance card, and also my parole card, as required by law.

He asked me to sit in his car. I knew he was going to call for help and take the car apart.

The Bear and Bobby approached and asked to take a piss. The officer pointed to a place behind a gas station. I figured they'd toss the dope and it would be easy enough to explain away the money we had from the burglary.

A few minutes later we were surrounded by other cars and I saw the cops cuff Bobby and my uncle. The cop who'd stopped us turned to me and said, "Richard, you're under arrest."

"For what?"

"Possession of burglary tools."

"What tools?"

"You'll see."

He drove us to the Newcastle OPP station, and there was the evidence displayed on the floor next to a sergeant's desk: a box of change and candies from the IGA, the tools from the gas station that I'd used to crack the safe and, on the desk, some vials of hash oil. We were screwed.

No, I was screwed.

The tools, which should have been cleaned and left behind, had my fingerprints all over them. If I was stupid for not taking care of business I was stupider for having partners who couldn't think straight. Stupidest of all was leaving Toronto in the first place.

Too late for that now.

We talked in the holding cells. I was feeling angry and grim at the same time, as well as sorry for myself. I played the sympathy card.

"I've got a match coming up and you guys don't know this, but today's my birthday."

Being family, Bear spoke up right away. "If Bobby takes the B&E, I'll take the dope beef and you won't have to go down." We looked to Bobby.

"Nobody knows about the B&E, and the burglary tools alone can't stand up in court," said Bobby. "Why roll over on something they don't know about?"

The trouble with that is that it was both short-sighted and stupid: the cops would find out about the B&E as soon as the supermarket opened.

The sergeant called me out. He was a boxing fan and knew I had a fight coming up, my first as a pro. He also knew that Bobby's brother, Leo, was a boxer. Since it was Leo's van that held the tools and the dope; one of us was going to have to take the beef or Leo could also be charged.

"Richard, if you tell us about the break-in, and if one of the others takes the dope beef, this being your birthday and all, then we'll let you go," the sergeant offered.

Back in the holding cells, I explained what the sergeant had said. Bear was fine with it but Bobby wanted to fight the charges and he thought he could win. That's when it dawned on me – all he cared about was Bobby.

An hour later, the IGA store called in the robbery. The charges now included safecracking, possession of hash oil for the purposes of trafficking and theft. The sergeant, bless his heart, repeated the offer, but Bobby wouldn't budge.

After a brief stay in Whitby, I was shipped to the jail in Lindsay, a neglected fortress in an upscale small town; or maybe it was just a turn-of-the-century bucket made of brick and stone in the boondocks.

The walls around the exercise yard were fifteen feet high and had no barbed wire. Standing outside the OPP car, cuffed and waiting, I made mental notes in case I had a chance to scale those walls. The windows were large enough, with old thick bars set in what looked like loose and crumbling bricks, making escape a real possibility.

I hoped that would not be necessary because being in a gang meant you followed the rules, and one of the rules was standing up for your buddies.

What was I facing?

According to the criminal code, the max was fourteen years for a break-and-enter into a place where no one lived, life if the place was occupied. I figured I might get a couple of years if Bobby refused to take the beef.

As we were led inside, one of the guards – six feet of solid muscle – smiled and said, "You boys won't give us any problems, will you?" He was smiling when he said it, so I answered, "We're here for a good time, not a long time."

The second guard who was older, shorter and wore sergeant's stripes, was not so cordial. He smacked a little leather club against his open palm and said flatly, "I hope I won't have to use this."

Bobby replied, "If you do, can you put a little Vaseline on it first so it won't hurt so much going up my ass."

His attempt at charm backfired.

"Watch your mouth, there's a lady in the room," Bear said, referring to a lone secretary typing at her desk.

She blushed and the short guard slapped the club into his old hand harder than before.

"Don't worry, sergeant. I can handle all these guys," said the big brave guard.

"I'm going on break," announced the secretary as she walked to the front door.

We watched her ass wiggle. The Bear grinned like a wolf but there was no time to enjoy pleasant thoughts. When the sergeant opened the cage door, he motioned me to follow the big guard.

I was led up a flight of stairs to a storage room. Down one of the ranges I caught a glimpse out a window into the yard. There was a bench against the wall that would be helpful if I was going to try and go over.

The big guard told me to call him Officer John and ordered me to strip. After searching my clothes he waved his fingers in circles. "Turn around. Run your fingers through your hair. Open your mouth." And then, "Bend over."

That's part of the search protocol: a prisoner with contraband might shove it deep inside his ass, but only an idiot would risk wedge something between his cheeks and risk having it fall out when walking.

Of course, there are idiots in prison.

"Spread your cheeks."

I tested him. "Officer, my file will state that I'm a federal prisoner on parole. We don't have to spread our cheeks. We won that one in court a few years ago."

"I'll have to look that one up," he said, shuffling through my file. "If you're lying you're going to spread 'em, whether you like it or not."

"No problem. I just want to do my time and get out." He smiled, and I knew right away that, like a lot of big men, he didn't have a lot of heart. And this is how it works, in prison as in life: you use a little psychology to read people, to look for weakness, to find an edge. All I had to work with was conversation. Sometimes that's enough.

He surprised me with a casual admission as I was getting dressed. "I'm from the east coast. I don't like coloured people. I hope that darky downstairs doesn't give me any problems." Apparently I wasn't black enough to frighten him.

I said, "Ronny may be called The Bear, but he's just a big old teddy bear." A useful little lie.

We walked back down to the little cage, and Officer John ordered Bear to follow him. I kept my eyes on the guard, and as my uncle walked past I knew that his racism was based on fear – I suspected that, as a boy in Nova Scotia, he'd run into more than one big, Afro-Metis willing to fight him at the drop of a hat.

After we were processed, they took us to the range on the second floor. Three cells, each with two box spring beds, a single, bare light bulb screwed into the ceiling and a metal piss pot. I paced for an hour or so, then called Officer John and asked for something to read.

He brought me a handful of cheap western novels. I read until I slept, just one more night in the thousands I'd spent in jail, wondering how many more there would be.

Officer John was on duty in the morning, along with the old sergeant. Breakfast was the usual cereal with watery milk and dry toast. Officer John seemed nervous for some reason. I knew why when an unmarked police car pulled up and four detectives got out, chief among them Bert Novis. I wondered why such heavy heat had descended on sleepy Lindsay for something as minor as a B&E.

I understood when Officer John handed me a copy of the local paper. The headline, boldly declared: "Gangsters From Big City Terrorize Small Town." The story contained a sketch of our criminal histories and an outline of our alleged crimes. Of course, it also it mentioned the heightened security needed to escort us to the local courthouse.

We were shackled, cuffed and led away, surrounded by the four detectives armed with shotguns who paraded us between a double row of OPP officers.

The streets of Lindsay were crowded for the show. I spotted Diane and Levern, both looking downcast.

Our case was quickly put over for a bail hearing, and a date set for trial a couple of months down the road. I was puzzled by Novis's presence and unhappy to find him involved in my life once again.

I had no one to blame but myself. And that might have been the second time in my life that I'd come to the realization that I was responsible for what was happening to me.

I marked the moment.

Diane arranged to visit. I wondered why. She was bright and attractive, but we had only lived together a short time. I wondered how I could have made a big enough impression on her that she would chose the lonely life of a convict's girlfriend.

Maybe she loved me.

A few weeks later, three guys from British Columbia walked onto the range. They were facing a variety of drug offences, as well as the more serious charge of attempted murder, resulting from the shooting of the biker we'd been on our way to meet the night of our arrest. These guys filled us in on what had happened at the farmhouse.

It occurred to me that there was something different about criminals from the west coast. The westerners didn't seem to mind killing for dope. It could have been me getting shot in the head for hash oil.

One of the guys took a dislike to Bobby. The tension festered until Bobby knocked him out and they separated us, putting me and Bear on one range, Bobby on another, and the Vancouver boys off by themselves.

Within days Bobby had two visits from Novis. Something wasn't right. The first chance I got, I asked for an explanation. It seems Bobby's girlfriend, who had just given birth to a daughter, had been caught with a handgun she kept at home. To get her charges dropped, Bobby told Novis about a cache of guns that we had hidden.

Deals like that are not unusual. I didn't mind the loss of the guns in return for Bobby's girlfriend's freedom. It did make me wonder what else Bobby would give away to beat his charges.

I decided I had better get away from him and do my time in the Kingston Pen Transfer unit, so I called my Montreal parole officer, Beverly Boyd, and filled her in on what had happened to me since I'd left. I liked her, and I had disappointed her. She was the first parole officer who had a genuine interest in my success. She even showed up at the nightclub in Montreal where I celebrated my first night of freedom after I got out of Collins Bay.

She actually cared for me.

My eyes were moist when I hung up the phone.

Just before my transfer to Kingston came through, Officer John told me that Bobby had been talking to Novis more than I knew. Shit. Nine months later, I went to court and my lawyer explained my options.

It didn't look good. Some kind of cop miracle had transpired. There was a torn dollar bill mixed in with the money we'd taken from the IGA. In one of those great coincidences, when Novis reinvestigated the crime scene, he found the matching half of the bill in the corner of the safe I'd cracked.

Gee, I wonder how that happened.

Novis had just sealed my fate tighter than a coffin unless I could get the link tossed between the torn bill and me. We fought hard but the bill was admitted into evidence.

Bear pleaded guilty to the drugs charge and got a year. Bobby went down for the B&E on the gas station and the IGA. He also got a year.

My option was to take the least punitive route: plead guilty and take two years in the Pen, on top of what I had remaining on my robbery charges. Instead of walking away free as a bird – which would have happened to me if Bobby had done right – I took the lion's share of the time.

COLLINS BAY REDUX

I fit right back in, and was immediately elected to head the Black Inmates Friends Association (BIFA) group I'd founded. They really needed my help.

My friend Chicago had helped me form the group originally. He carried on with the group after my transfer to the Frontenac farm camp. He also carried on with a good-looking woman who was head of the Queen's University Black Students' Union. She came to see him often and a relationship developed.

Somehow, Chicago managed to persuade her to sell everything she had and give him the money, on the pretence that they'd both go to the States when he got out. That didn't happen. He left her in the limestone dust of old Kingston town.

She was so mad that she gathered her friends and they walked up to the prison wall, and started throwing rocks over the top and calling the black prisoners all the names they could think of. The cops forced them off the property.

BIFA was falling apart.

Diane was coming up to see me regularly, so I kept my nose clean. The only real trouble I had was when I tried to protect some of the newer black inmates from their own stupidity. Case in point: one of the newer guys owed the Italians drug money and when the Italian tried to collect, the black prisoner sliced him with a knife.

Mob-boss son, Domenic Racco, called me into the yard for a walk and talk. He wanted to know if we'd retaliate if the Italians moved on the brother.

He was feeling me out because war made time hard for everyone. Mediation was the preferred route.

I hated getting involved in drug or money problems inside prison, primarily because I didn't do drugs, and I made it a point never to owe anyone for anything. But I had to be careful with Racco. I was talking to someone who was a friend first, future Toronto mob boss second, and the head of the jail's Italian crew third. I was pretty sure he wanted to avoid trouble, but I also knew he needed to save face.

I had a high card, and I played it.

"Dominic, we match your guys man for man, but we have some of your white friends on our side because your guy fucked up, major."

"How did he fuck up? He is owed money. He has the right to be paid."

"No shit. If it were that simple, I'd wash my hands of it. But I'm head of the BIFA, and when one of your guys calls one of us a 'nigger' and gets stabbed for it, all the brothers say, 'Right on.'"

He turned to one of his confederates and they spoke in Italian for a moment, then the confederate walked over to the Italians who were watching us.

Racco's man came back and they conferred again.

Domenic said, "Listen, I'm sorry our guy wasn't more sensitive, but money is the bottom line."

I leaned close to him and spoke so no one else could hear: "Our guy will pay the money he owes. And when your guy gets out of the hospital, if he wants to go one on one then, hey, life is a bitch in the big house."

He stroked his chin.

"Pay the money this week and the day our guy gets out, their beef is on. Agreed?"

Maybe I should have worked at the U.N.

I filled in the brothers. Most of them were packing shanks, and all of us were risking getting rounded up and sent off to various prisons all around the country, just for backing a guy we didn't know but who was one of us by virtue of his skin colour.

The guy who did the stabbing wanted a guarantee that no one would jump him before the Italian got out of the hospital. Nobody could give him that kind of guarantee. The money was paid out the next day, and we all waited for the Italian to heal and get out of hospital.

Then I got word that the Italian had put up some money to for another crew to have the brother stabbed. So I did the right thing and warned the brother that his time was up.

His choices were limited, He could end the animosity by killing the guy he had originally stabbed, or he could check into protective custody. He disappeared from the prison population the next day. The atmosphere cooled down considerably.

Or rather, things changed.

Johnny Papalia, known as Johnny Pops, entered prison. He was one of the most feared and respected men in Canada, and the highest-ranking Italian mobster in prison at that time. We often walked the range together after he moved next door to me on 4-Block.

Johnny Pops was based in Hamilton, but he knew the streets I grew up on. He knew most of the people of my father's generation, and he knew that I had relatives in almost every prison in Ontario.

He also knew the power of cocaine.

He warned me cocaine would destroy the old ways, and a new generation would take over. He said if I were smart, I would get into it in a big way. If I wanted help, he told me I should call on him. I held that thought.

My sights were set on loan sharking with Big Joe Patterson, who already controlled the black neighbourhood. I believed that the two of us working together could rule the Spadina area.

In 1997, Johnny Pops was shot in the back of the head at close range by a hit man who was paid $3,000 and a couple of ounces of cocaine. I never did call him.

Eventually, I was transferred to Beaver Creek, the "Club Fed" in the heart of cottage country. There was a swimming pool in the centre of the compound, a golf course in an open field.

Inmates on work release were allowed to drive, and they parked their cars in the lot. Some of those cars were Caddies and Lincolns.

On my arrival, somebody tapped me on the shoulder. I looked around to see a brown-haired white guy. "Andy Ferguson. How are you doing?" We shook hands and I waved at the surroundings.

"Not bad."

He said, "Don't think this place is so great. You'll be out in the swamp tomorrow, cutting down trees like a slave. And you better watch out for the guys here. Most of them are out-and-out rats." Good to know.

"I'm working on the carpentry gang. I'll try to get you in with me. Guys like us don't get any breaks; one screw-up and you're back behind the wall before you can say 'What the fuck?'"

Andy filled me in on how the place ran. If he was right, it was not exactly a country club.

An older, dignified inmate introduced himself and said he was there to show me around and help me get acquainted.

He painted a different picture, praising the warden and telling me it was easy to do time in the beauty of the surroundings. He was doing a life bit and seemed to get along with everyone. I was surprised to learn he had a pilot's licence. He said the government paid for his course at the nearby airport, and his room was filled with manuals and books about flying.

After a few days, I was called to the warden's office. He looked like Colonel Sanders – white hair, white spade beard, and a formal white suit. He must have seen the look on my face because he took the time to explain that he had an important function in town later on.

He'd heard I was an up-and-coming boxer. He was interested so I told him about my past, the fights I'd had, and my intention to turn professional when I got out. Also, I wanted to take a cinematography course.

As we chatted, I heard my name called out for work so I excused myself and left. I sort of liked him, and I guess he liked me because he gave me permission to do roadwork whenever I wanted.

Here's how good we had it: prisoners could bring anything into camp, within reason. Some guys used the relative freedom to make runs into town for booze or weed, which was sort of risky, since if you were caught you'd be sent back behind the wall. You just had to be careful or someone would rat you out.

There were other freedoms, too. When Diane came to visit, we could slip out behind the trees and enjoy ourselves; as long as there were no kids or older visitors. The guards were not overly concerned.

I settled in nicely. Things picked up when Andy got me assigned to the carpentry gang. He managed to convince the warden to build a mini-golf course and said he needed me as a helper. We took our time and made the course as intricate as we could.

My skills were good enough that occasionally the warden rented me out for small jobs in the community; I'd perform some minor chore for some old person and get a semblance of freedom and a home-cooked meal. The warden got money for his church.

My time at Beaver Creek went by without a hitch. As my parole hearing drew near, my classification officer began talking about a new, all-black halfway house that was opening in Toronto.

There was a feeling that if I was among the first residents, and I served as committee chairman, the new venture might stand a better chance of success.

The Smith brothers ran the halfway house. I knew one of them from the neighbourhood. The other was a former provincial prison guard.

I agreed to be part of the experiment.

My parole hearing took place in Peterborough. I was pleasantly surprised to see my juvenile probation officer, Lou Taylor, on the board. The other two members were white. In front of them, I reiterated my past misdeeds, in some detail, and told them my plans for the future.

They had different points of view, and I had to think quickly about how best to answer their questions. It was a bit like a boxing match, stick and jab and, counter, duck and punch.

One of the board members concluded that, since there was nothing negative on my file, I must have been so manipulative that I got others to do my dirty work for me.

That's the system – you're damned if you do, and damned if you don't. It invites manipulation. Thing is, I really had lived clean in prison – I didn't smoke, I didn't drink, I kept away from drugs. I only fought when threatened, and I stayed clear of troublemakers.

Another member asked why I hated cops so much.

That question really got to me. I didn't hate cops. In a civilized society they have a function to perform. And I didn't hate my mother's brother, who was a cop in Sudbury. I liked him.

But I knew getting busted, for me, was part of the same old racist game. If you ain't white, you ain't right.

At least in this regard I was a bit like my dad. Sonny never gave me many father-and-son moments, but once, when we were sitting outside on the porch, a cop drove by and he said suddenly, "I hate white people to the core."

I wondered if my white mother could hear him.

I also wondered how he could hate white people and still love me, considering that I was the product of a white mother. But I have come to learn he didn't hate white people as much as he hated white authority.

I often thought of my mom electing to marry a black man ten years before America gave blacks the right for mixed marriages, and wondered what she endured in those early days, before I could remember.

So I let the board have it.

I told them about Warren Hart and government entrapment. I told them about the police brutality I had seen. I told them about the alienation I felt during the height of the civil rights movement. I didn't stop telling them. I told them what it was like to be called "nigger." I told them about what it was like for my father to be pulled over and harassed because he had a white woman in his car. I told them about the stores and restaurants that refused to serve me because of the colour of my skin. And I ended my rant by telling them how the cops had beaten up my aunt Babes and my uncle Frankie.

One of the board members called me a liar.

He said no cop would ever beat up a woman. I answered him with seething silence. Lou Taylor came to my defence, telling them he'd been there that night and had seen what happened. The other members looked at him as if he was mentally ill.

I was asked to leave the room.

Lou winked as I left.

I knew I had one vote of three, so I sweated as I waited. That's what happens when you fail as a criminal – others take control of your life, and there is no worse feeling than helplessness. Half an hour later, I was denied full parole. But I was instructed to attend the Josiah Henson Halfway House.

BACK OUTSIDE

Kenny Cleveland picked me up and drove me to the halfway house. I'd known him for years. He was a good trainer, although not the best, and he was a hustler who might make a good manager. He promised me a fair deal and he worked on me all the way back to Toronto. I thanked him for the ride, but made no commitment.

The Josiah Henson House was on Springhurst Avenue in Parkdale, a tough west-end neighbourhood filled with pimps, whores, pushers and hustlers. I knew most of them, and felt at home. As a bonus, Diane lived a ten-minute walk away, through a neighbourhood that was filled with people who were crazy, or marginalized and hanging on the fringes of the social order.

I was reminded that prison is a microcosm of society. The only difference was that the prison I was now in had no fences, and the yard was the size of the city.

I was the first parolee to enter Henson House, followed by my cousins Shakey and Mad Dog, and then Eugene Payton, who had grown up with us. There were others I did not know, including a black biker from Montreal. He was the first full-patch black in Canada.

The Smith brothers wasted no time telling me how hard it had been to convince the government to set up the house. I knew the brother who'd done the convincing. I'd met him at Warren Hart's house, when he came in with Rosie Douglas. I didn't much like him; he'd made a snide remark to Hart about my age. "Underestimate Ricky at your peril," Hart told him.

Here I was, with my freedom in his hands.

It was a freedom that required a certain kind of protection. We all armed up, hiding guns within the walls and anywhere else we could think of. Why? Because in a halfway house you're vulnerable – your comings and goings are regular and predictable. It's easy to take a guy out if he's on a schedule.

The Smith brothers never found the guns because we weren't searched. The reason we weren't searched is because, in the halfway house, we were low security.

Settling into a routine was easy. I jogged to Diane's in the morning and jogged home again before the 11 p.m. curfew.

At the Lansdowne Boxing Gym, I received instruction from George Chuvalo's trainer, Teddy McWhirter. Teddy was from Detroit, and he was the best inside trainer of them all – an opinion shared by boxers from around the world who came to work with him.

The gym was owned by a bookie named Birdie. Cops, gangsters, and professional and amateur boxers frequented it, each tolerating the other out of respect for the sweet science.

This meant Birdie had access to hard men who found it easy to collect debts. Since I was broke and needed money, Birdie gave me plenty of lucrative work, much of which I contracted out to members of my gang.

The gym was also a place of work for Bill Lehman, Sr., who was an independent trainer. His son, Bill Jr., was big and fast; so was I. He floated in the ring; so did I.

We were a good match. As sparring partners we gave as good as we got with any of the professional heavyweights who came to work out.

Bill Sr. also had a daughter, Dawn. She was young and attractive, and was training to be the first professional woman boxer in the country. We all sparred with the Blonde Bomber.

My cousin Clyde Gray had the distinction of pulling her licence before her first pro fight because he didn't want women in the ring until there were more controls established to protect them.

Dawn cried softly at the press conference when the announcement was made. I didn't understand why gender stopped her from fulfilling her dream of turning pro; all of us who worked with her in the gym saw her as a professional.

She was just ahead of her time.

Billy Lehman, "Razor" Ruddock and I all had our first pro fights around the same time at St. Lawrence Market. George Chuvalo was the promoter of those evenings of entertainment. None of us tasted defeat that night.

I was in the ring with the U.S. Navy heavyweight champ, a guy named Jack "Attack" Watson. I won, as far as I'm concerned, but it was declared a technical draw because one of the scorers had some sort of stomach upset and kept leaving for the washroom. In actual fact, he missed too much of the action to be of any use.

The vagaries of circumstance?

Billy quit the ring to raise a child. Razor fought Mike Tyson twice, and he earned twelve million in the ring. I went on to more fights.

And more prisons.

My cousins kept pushing me to set up scores for them. I resisted because I didn't want Bert Novis breathing down my neck. Part of me really wanted to go straight and not just for myself. Diane had been faithful for so long that I felt I owed her my best.

The black biker was the house cook. He worked out daily, keeping to himself at night. He slept on a thin mat on the floor, with a big knife laid out beside him. It took him a while to relax and put the knife away. He, too, made his way to the Lansdowne gym, and we began to spar with each other and with others who would eventually become champions.

After a month or so, Eugene Payton missed curfew. The Smith brothers gave me a couple of hours to track him down; if I couldn't find him and get him back, they'd have to call the cops. I hunted for him over the phone. It took an hour to find him with one of his whores in an apartment only a block away.

He refused to come back, and a warrant was issued for his arrest. That was the beginning of the end of the halfway house experiment.

A month later, I was having supper with Diane when a handful of detectives barged in on us, guns drawn. One of them slapped a warrant on the table. They heard I was armed and were looking for guns.

They were right and wrong – I needed a gun when I was collecting gambling debts, but I wasn't stupid enough to keep one anywhere obvious. They tore the place apart, and they seemed angry to come up empty-handed.

Then one of them spotted a pair of Nunchakus hanging on the wall. Brian had given them to me to give to my brother, who was studying martial arts.

One of the cops said, "We got you, Ricky."

The others took Diane to another room.

The cop pulled out his notepad and pencil and asked, "What are those sticks?"

I felt like I was in high school, knowing that I'd fail if I gave the wrong answer on a test. "They're sticks used in ancient China for threshing wheat." He wrote that down.

"Bring the woman in."

He asked Diane the same question and she answered truthfully, that they were Nunchakus. The cops seemed proud of their cleverness.

"You're both under arrest for the possession of prohibited weapons."

They threw me back in the Don Jail.

I was denied bail because I was on parole. Lou Taylor came to visit me, and gave me the name of a lawyer friend of his. In the meantime, I asked for a copy of the Criminal Code. Try as I might, I found no reference to Nunchaku.

Diane decided to use my old lawyer, David Newman, for her case. He told her the law prohibiting Nunchakus was so new it had yet to be added to the Criminal Code but, if convicted, I could be looking at five years. My suspension hearing was set for two weeks later.

Diane told me I'd be a fool to use the lawyer Lou recommended. Why? She said that when she approached him about my case, he asked her to do something personal to pay my bill.

Just so you know, lawyers ask for pussy or blow jobs all the time. Some of my peers accept this, but I was insulted. I dumped him right away.

Truth is, I had enough money to hire any lawyer I wanted; truth also is, this lowlife scum went on to become a judge.

I hired another lawyer, Michael Morse, and we made a successful argument for bail, without surety. I was beginning to look forward to my day in court. This whole thing was harassment, in my view. Just another example of how things were rigged against me.

In fact, this was a watershed event, one which set me firmly on my path: if I was going to be harassed and arrested without cause, then it didn't much matter if I stayed clean or not.

TIME TO GET SERIOUS

Once again I called my crew together and, just like that, I was back in the game. We met in an abandoned factory, a place I knew wasn't bugged, and I outlined my plan to get back into the robbery business. Everyone seemed happy. We rolled joints and toasted our renewed partnership. One of the boys raised a pistol in the air and let off a clip, shattering an overhead skylight.

My friend Jerry was about to get married; an occasion that gave me an opportunity to save a little time and do some business with the black crime elite.

Jerry and I sat down with O.J. and Big Joe Patterson to work out how to share power and divide up our areas of interest. It took a couple of hours.

I gave up my leadership position to Joe. With leadership comes responsibility, and with crime leadership comes fear of arrest, concerns about power, and worry about getting killed by other gangs. He was welcome to it.

Instead, I went back to planning the things I was good at: robbing card games, jewellery stores and banks, as well as loan sharks and drug pushers. Oh yes, and break-ins – I was fond of furs and cigarettes.

My crew, as before, was multi-racial.

That requires a bit of explanation. In the hierarchy of the time, black Nova Scotians were suspicious of Jamaicans. That dated back to 1796, when a shipload of legendary fighters of mixed Indian and African race called Maroons were deported from Jamaica after rising up against their colonial masters. They ended up in Halifax, where they were set to work building the city's defences. They swaggered around town. They were arrogant and received better pay. None of that sat well with Scotian blacks.

Even now, when a Jamaican walks into a Scotian function they are not exactly made welcome, and that's 400 years of living history right there. We respected American blacks more in my day, but I was pragmatic, and I was an equal-opportunity leader. We tolerated West Indians in my crew.

Owen introduced me to a friend of his named Carrie Burke, and asked that he be included. I'd have to devise a test for him. I don't trust anyone without making certain.

Not even you.

When my hearing on the weapons charge came up it became apparent that there was no established case law concerning Nunchakus. An entire morning was wasted with legal wrangling.

After lunch, my lawyers, David Newman and Michael Morse, invoked a bit of theatre, walking into the courtroom with a couple of unconventional exhibits. Newman had two fence pickets joined by a chain, and Morse had two toothpicks held together by a piece of string; both were Nunchakus, according to the written definition of the law.

They demanded to be arrested and put in the box with Diane and me. Everyone burst out laughing until the judge asked if I was on Legal Aid. I was not.

"These arguments are costing Mr. Atkinson a considerable amount of money," observed His Honour. "Between the four of us, we have well over one hundred years' experience in the law. Why don't I remand this case over until tomorrow, while we go over to the law library and find a solution to this problem?"

He said the law library, but I have a hunch he meant a bar across the street where they could kick around jurisprudence, toss back some Scotch and decide my fate.

The next morning the judge said – and even though it was more than thirty years ago, my recollection of what he said is clear – "Mr. Atkinson, since you had just gotten out of prison, and since this law is new, then we can assume you may not have had access to any news articles or information that would have kept you abreast of the law concerning the possession of Nunchakus. In this case, ignorance of the law is an excuse I can accept."

My charges were tossed but Diane had not been in prison when the law was made so she could have had access to the information; as a result, he fined her $100 and discharged her, upon which the Crown attorney argued that a probation order be attached to the fine in case she didn't pay.

I guess this stuff counts as legal cleverness.

I handed Newman a $100 bill. He paid the fine. We were free. I went back to work.

I began to case a bank. I had noticed a hole in the security at one branch that I felt we could exploit. Whenever a Brink's van delivered bags of money, the guards left the bag on the floor of the open vault, in plain view. It happened like that more than once, a habit born of complacency.

I sent Owen the Crook. He simply jumped the counter, snatched the bag and ran right out the back door. Carrie, who was waiting for him in the alley, took the money and walked off between some houses.

I was the one setting out the goals and objectives. To carry out the action plans, I picked men who had both the skills and the motivation to do what needed to be done. By making sure everyone knew their roles and their responsibilities, I became a CEO of crime.

Guys who needed money were asking me to set things up for them. Hey, you're getting married. Need some money for a wedding ring? Here's a jewellery store.

We were efficient at hijacking trucks full of anything people in the neighbourhood might like to buy. There were trailers filled with useful items like toilet paper. There were "reefers" – refrigerated trucks – full of meat or cheese or peanut butter or olive oil etc. were especially profitable.

It's all knowledge and planning.

Owen knew some hippies who were selling coke and weed, so I sent him and another member of the crew to take them down.

Spence needed some money. He had his eye on a credit union, so I planned that one and sent my cousin Tommy and another guy to take care of it. It took thirty seconds in total. The bandits got $20,000. Spence and I took a cut of five grand each.

Shakey was always hungry for cash. He was using speed and playing with whores, so his needs were constant. I sent him and a friend of his to take down a jewellery store. They grabbed just over $200,000 in gold. I dropped the haul off with a fence and took a twenty percent cut, which we split three ways.

Then one of our guys, Skippy, spotted a truck filled with cigarettes. We took it in the middle of the night, sold the smokes for thirty percent of retail and walked away laughing.

One day I noticed a fur store on Spadina where the alarm wasn't working properly – for some reason there was a delay. We spun the lock on the front door, rushed in and took as many coats as we could in the forty-five seconds it took for the alarm to ring. That bit of business netted just over $300,000 in furs, which I sold for twenty percent, splitting the money with everyone involved.

You might not think so but even as I planned, tested and executed each score I was still clinging to the hope that I'd be free of crime one day, and able to concentrate full-time on boxing. Teddy McWhirter had given me the skills to step in the ring with anyone and hold my own. I had yet to be knocked down, or knocked out. I hadn't been stopped or taken a standing eight-count or been hurt in any way. The future looked good, although the toll of working on scores sapped me of energy best spent in the ring.

But so much of life is chance.

One night, while I was smoking joints with some whores, one of them blurted that she had a kinky trick who worked in the movie industry. He'd told her there was a growing need for makeup artists who could do prosthetic work. She was thinking of taking a course, which got me thinking.

Makeup, serious professional makeup, was a skill I could use. My skills at disguise were useful, but crude. So, I found a course at a modelling agency and signed up.

I was the only guy in a class of ten girls, and Marg Harlang seemed pleased that I was making something of myself.

A while later, I bumped into a pretty redhead named Cindy at the Paddock Tavern. She was in a bit of a jam. She wanted to get away from her pimp and she said she'd pay me if I pretended I was her man.

I already had a lovely woman who stood by me when I was in the slammer – and I didn't need the hassle of managing a whore but she was easy to look at and it was possible that the relationship might prove fruitful.

Her pimp was a tall white guy I'd spent years in prison with. When he walked in I took him aside and told him the bad news – his woman was now my woman.

That's the nature of the game. One minute you had a woman sweet as pie who treated you like a king and paid your bills. The next minute, you were on your own, looking to start over.

I moved Cindy into an apartment a block away from mine, and hired two lawyers to handle my upcoming trial. I wasn't entirely happy about being labelled a pimp, but neither did I see anything wrong with managing business for a girl who chose to make her living pulling tricks.

I didn't see anything morally wrong, not with my family background. I hadn't put her in the game, and I wasn't the one encouraging her to continue, I was merely looking out for her interests. All in a day's work for a man on the edge of society, who also happened to have relatives in the business.

I often took Cindy with me to makeup class, to practice on her. A kick, really – the other girls were no different, looking to catch the attention of men or women to further their interests. Plus, I was the only player in the city who could do a makeup job on his woman before she hit the streets.

Cindy, you might like to know, got in touch via Facebook some thirty years later. She was still attractive and still had that youthful sparkle in her eye. Soon after we parted company, she left her old life and started a business making floral arrangements for special occasions.

I got full parole, as I expected, but it was clear that I needed more money than Cindy could provide. We parted company and I began to take stock and get busy.

One job from that time stands out because it had all the hallmarks of my work, using tricks of the trade I'd learned thanks to a government rat, Warren Hart.

We decided to take the bank in Kensington Market. It was the only bank there. Everyone used it, so it was always full of cash, so much that on Monday mornings the Brink's truck would arrive and just back up to the front door whereupon they would unload sacks of cash for a full fifteen minutes.

I'd had my eye on it for years.

I hired eleven guys for that job.

The Market is a compact couple of blocks. It was easy enough to block off all the streets with stolen cars in such a way that nobody – not even the cops – could get in.

I parked a van in front of the bank to protect the guys inside. The idea was to go in the front and come out the back, escaping through the laneway. At night, the cops would never catch us.

I filled the van with tires, and I put a bomb inside, rigged to go off on a timer: hit a switch, and the bomb would explode a minute later. The noise would be a shocker. The burning tires would give us a smoke screen.

When that bomb went off, I would call the fire department and tell them how to get in, which was through a parking lot. I wanted a diversion, not a conflagration, and the presence of the fire trucks would also impede the cops.

I had a second explosion planned to go off as we escaped: another pile of tires, soaked with gasoline, which we would detonate using certain chemicals. Toss, and *boom*.

Brian's job was to call time.

Shit happens. He called time too soon and the guys on the inside only managed to get two boxes of mostly cheques. All we made for all that work was about what an average doctor would make for a day's work saving lives when any one us could have lost ours. It was the least amount of money and the most number of guys I ever used on a score.

The only pleasure I got from that job?

I was standing by the brick wall in the Projects. From there I could see a cop standing on top of his car, jumping up and down, screaming into his walkie-talkie.

One of the things he said? "I seen three black guys with guns." I know what he said because we were tapping into their conversations.

Around that time, the cops were calling us the Nightmare Bandits, not just because we often worked at night, but also because we really were a nightmare for them.

I read a warning later from a cop psychologist who was quoted in the news, along these lines: "Whoever did this has to be approached with caution. He doesn't want to be caught. He's thinking at another level, several steps ahead of anything you can think of."

In other words, be careful.

That was useful to us in another way. It sent a message to the other gangs about how organized and determined we were. If we could seal off the Market and take it down, think of what we could do to any gang that challenged us.

A while later, my cousin Shakey was on my case to rob a jewellery store. He wanted his little brother Mike as one of the gunmen. I was greedy for some easy money, so I gave in and began to plan the score.

I spent a couple of days driving around the city, looking for a location with minimal risk for Shakey. I wanted something easy, so that Mike would not feel the need to shoot anyone.

Shakey had ideas of his own.

There was a jewellery store near Queen and Spadina. That's a busy corner with lots of citizens. Cops from 14 and 52 Divisions were always patrolling around there. Nobody wants to work under those conditions, especially with an untrained and untested guy. Shakey assured me his brother was capable enough.

The score had to go down flawlessly. Two robbers had to pass muster at the door and be buzzed in by security. My skills as a makeup artist had to be top drawer.

A third robber would be behind the building outside of store's back door, equipped with empty bags, a hammer and a shotgun. When the front-end robbers got into the store, their job was to jack up the owner immediately, run to the back door, get it open and grab the hammer and the bags. That was to be followed by the smashing open of the cases and then stealing as much as possible before running out the back and escape down the lane. Textbook, really.

I sent Shakey to the Malabar costume house on McCaul Street. He came back with three masks. With a little modification, two of them made perfect disguises. But the third one, a gorilla head, made me wonder about him.

I thought we should wait and get another mask.

Shakey argued that, as the back-door man, only the store owner would see the gorilla mask, so it didn't really make a difference what he wore. His brother Mike and a second gunman – we'll call him Billy – agreed.

I shrugged; everything was set. The cars were stolen and waiting in place. There was a fence down the block, waiting to buy the gems. All the alibis had been taken care of.

They were the ones taking the risk, so I gave my approval.

But crime often fails for reasons beyond anyone's ability to foresee complications; in this case, things began to go wrong right off the bat.

Mike didn't come to the back door quickly enough, so Shakey ran around the front to see what was going on, wrestling with his gorilla mask while at the same time hanging onto his shotgun, running along the sidewalk of the busy street.

He got to the front of the store just in time to see Billy and Mike make their entrance, so he rushed around to the back in front of hundreds of shoppers, ready to take care of his end of the robbery.

I repeat: In his gorilla mask. In broad daylight. With a shotgun.

In spite of all that, the score went off without anyone getting hurt or arrested. I took the jewellery to the fence and put the score behind me, thinking that would be the last I'd hear of it. But the Hold-Up Squad doesn't forget about victims who've had guns waved in their faces, and they were turning over every lead they could in order to find the robbers; that is, us.

Now here's a thing, and it has an echo: Diane was working at the Magic Pan restaurant in the Eaton Centre. I was taking her to work one day, as usual, with the idea that I could case the Birks jewellery store at the same time. O.J. was in the back seat, having begged a lift downtown.

As we made out way east on King Street, at Jameson – a nasty little corner – two detectives walked into the street and approached the car, waving at me to pull over.

The copper on my side levelled his gun at my head, shouting: "Don't fucking move or I'll blow your head off." At the same time, I could see a detective had his gun trained on O.J. Both cops walked alongside the car through the intersection until I pulled to the curb.

They searched the car and they searched us and they found nothing. The copper said, "Okay, everything is fine, you can go." And they walked away. Just like that. As if it was normal.

O.J. was rattled. He said, "If I ever ask you for a lift again, tell me 'no.'"

Here's the echo.

A week or two later, on a wet Friday night, I was driving to the Paramount Tavern with Diane when O.J. saw me on the street and flagged me down for a lift. I wouldn't have acted as a cab driver for anyone except O.J., so I stopped, backed up, flipped the lock and he opened the door so my woman could jump into the back seat.

He hopped in next to me, pulled out a bag of weed and passed it back to Diane. I eased into traffic, with my window down, listening to O.J. talk about this and that, mainly about bands. I turned left on Queen Street and was sliding down Portland when another car pulled up alongside us.

Before I knew what was going on, I was looking at the barrel of a 12-gauge shotgun, inches from my face.

Detective Pat Kelly was leaning out of the back window of an unmarked car while another detective held him around the waist to steady him in case he had to shoot.

He sneered at me. "Ricky, pull over slowly or I'll blow your fucking head off." O.J., who had his head in the bag of weed, thought we were being jacked up. Without bothering to look, he said, "Fuck them!"

I said, "You tell them that."

I leaned back so he could see Kelly's shotgun.

O.J. panicked. His pockets were full of pills. He began stuffing his mouth full of weed with one hand, and with the other he was spilling and scattering pills all over the floor of my car and out the window.

I pulled over slowly. The cop slammed his car into park and jumped out screaming, gun pointed at us. Kelly leaped out the back but he caught his heel on something, his shoe flying off as he stumbled forward.

Steady on, boys. Let's be professional.

And then a gaggle of other cop cars came squealing up, hemming us in, and there was a shotgun aimed at my head again, and I saw Kelly's shoe on the street in the rain, and I wondered why I couldn't have a normal job like most people.

"Ricky, get the fuck out with your hands up!"

I eased my way out of the T-bird, followed by O.J. and Diane, all of us with our hands up. Uniformed officers surrounded us.

One of the uniforms, a rookie, ran past me to cover Diane and O.J. It was a stupid move. Kelly yelled at him to duck, because he was going to shoot. The rookie dropped to one knee, and Kelly came up to me and pressed the 12-gauge into my chest. Kelly turned his head slightly and yelled at the rookie. "This fucker is a marksman. He'd blow us away if he had the chance. Don't you ever run in front of my gun again."

Oh, please, let's all just relax.

When we were cuffed and patted down, Kelly unloaded his shotgun and placed five fat shells on the roof of his car, grabbed me in a headlock and walked me roughly around to the trunk. His thoughts mirrored my own.

"Ricky, you fucking asshole, why don't you find another job? This shit is crazy, man." And then he added, "I know for a fact that you were the gorilla. We'll kill you if we get the chance. Pack it in before it's too late."

I didn't want to tell him he was wrong. I just looked at the guy and grinned.

Kelly ordered the rookies to take O.J. and me to 14 Division, and then he jumped into the T-bird with Diane; they headed for my place, followed by the unmarked car, to search for evidence.

On the way to 14 Division, O.J. said, quietly, "Ricky, I don't say a word when we hit the cop shop." He was implying that I shouldn't say anything, either.

I took it as an insult.

When we got to the police station, we were stripped, searched and put in separate interrogation rooms. After an hour or so, I heard O.J. telling the detectives he was a pimp and not a robber, that he didn't know anything about any robberies. Every time they asked him a question, he spun them an answer until, finally, they finished with him and came for me.

I took note of my surroundings. There was blood on the walls and on the floor of the room I was in, but I wasn't worried about being beaten. I had boxed professionally. I was a street fighter. Also, they knew I had no fear and that changed everything.

Detective Kelly had a brown envelope that contained everything that I'd been carrying. He dumped it out on the table – a wad of cash, maybe a thousand dollars, along with my parole card, my driver's licence, and twenty tickets to a boxing match that George Chuvalo was promoting; I'd taken the tickets to help George out.

Kelly picked up the tickets and looked at the other cops. "You guys want to go to the fights?" They nodded. He reached for his wallet. I waved him off. I didn't want his money.

He started by asking me where I was on the day of the gorilla mask robbery. I stared at him.

"Come on, Ricky, play the game, don't be a prick. I've got to file a report. Give us something to write down."

I said, "Pat, can I call my lawyer, Michael Morse?" He made a fist and for a second I thought he was going to hit me. He sparred at the Lansdowne Gym. I knew some of the fighters there, and I knew he could hit. I didn't give him the chance.

I made a fist of my own and smashed it into my face as hard as I could, and then I ran my fingers across my lips to let him know I wasn't going to talk under any circumstances.

The other cops seemed surprised.

One of them said, "Pat, anyone who beats himself up worse than we would has got to be crazy."

Kelly said, "He's not crazy." He took the tickets out of his pocket, threw them at me and left the room.

He was finished for the moment. I was free to go home. Picking up my belongings, I stuffed them in my jacket. As I was leaving, I saw them turn O.J. loose.

"Pat, where's my car?" I asked.

"It's at your place," he said. "You want a ride home?" A little cop sarcasm. I declined his kind offer.

Outside the station, I had words with O.J. "You played me, man – if it happens again, we're going to be rolling and rocking. You were going to keep your mouth shut, but I heard every word you said. What did you hear me say?"

He hadn't heard me say a thing.

I left him standing there and hailed a cab. When I got home, Diane was putting the apartment back together in the wake of the search.

I still had to report to the halfway house at night. They did half-hour checks all night long, to make sure we were still in our beds.

One night I heard the woman on duty open the door and I saw her peek in. I could tell in the half-light that she'd been crying. I put on my robe and went downstairs to ask if she was okay. She was a university student, working on her sociology degree. Her cheeks were wet as she ran her fingers through her Afro. She said she hadn't been paid for two months, and she was behind in her rent. She was such an idealist that she was stressing out over the thought that she might have to abandon us to save herself.

Oh, great – Josiah Henson House, the first black halfway house in Canada had money management problems.

I took $500 out of the pocket of my robe and gave it to her. She said she'd pay me back, but I stopped her short. There was no way I wanted anyone to know I'd paid her to keep me locked up.

"Think of it as a secret grant," I told her. "One you don't have to pay back."

Four days later, the Mounties swooped in and shut the house down. Apparently, the supervisor had conned the government into giving him a cheque to cover a year's expenses; he then took the money and ran off to Dominica. Turns out he donated it to the island's communist party.

All the other parolees went back to the Don Jail to wait for space to open up elsewhere but, because I was four days away from my release date, my parole officer let me go.

I wasn't free because I was still on parole, but I was free enough. Diane and I hopped in the car and snuck off to New York, then to Cleveland and Detroit.

We were stopped a couple of times and let go. I could have been slapped with a parole violation, but in those days nobody was worried about a Canadian convict having a peaceful good time, and there was no such thing as Homeland Security.

After my little vacation, I went back to work. I began to make a bunch of bombs. I wasn't sure why. I just thought they might come in handy. I also began to collect a stash of guns and ammunition. Because you never know.

Bert Novis knocked on the door one day. He was with another detective. I let them in. They looked around and found a metal box with 1,000 rounds of ammunition, all calibres. Having ammo – even that much ammo – was not against the law, but he took it anyway and said I had major heat – his.

He wasn't telling me anything I didn't know; they were on us all the time. But what does a cop learn from a box of bullets? He knew what kind of weapons we had access to. He knew that some of the bullets were armour piercing.

And I knew it meant there would be increased heat.

I'd been making plans to rob Brink's trucks. I'd follow their routes, watching drops and pick-ups, but my plans went out the window in a hurry one day. As I was watching a driver make deliveries, I spotted someone in a parked car watching me with binoculars.

I called my brothers and asked them to do a little counter-surveillance. Turns out I was being watched by Brink's security. They were watching us, and they were tailing us, which meant that I was not only being watched by all the Squads - Hold-Up, B&E, and Organized Crime – but by private security as well. They all had guns, and they all had the power to shoot a guy like me. It was tiring. I had to be alert at all times. But I was soon to get a rest, not one of choice.

A few days later, I was picked up on possession of burglar's tools and taken to the Don Jail. The fact that I'd applied for a locksmith's course– and had some books on the subject and a set of picks – didn't seem to matter.

Or maybe it was all that mattered.

They transferred me to Kingston to wait for a bail hearing. When my turn came around, the judges asked the Crown if there were any break-and-enter charges to go along with the possession of the tools. The Crown shrugged, the police glared, and the judge tossed the charges.

You can see how the game is played, and why some people become cynical – do me for something I've done, not for something you think I might do.

Diane was waiting for me in the van when they let me go. I hadn't had a woman in five weeks, and there were things I wanted to do before we pulled away. I guess the guards saw the van rocking and, before too long,

I heard a handful of rocks crash down on the roof. I opened the door and looked out.

A guard called down from the prison wall, "This ain't a hotel; get that van out of here." I got back in and went back to rocking, but I was not rocking long before four guards walked over and banged on the doors. They said I better get off the property or be charged with trespassing.

I wasn't too concerned, but I didn't want to face the parole board again. We headed for Toronto.

DIRTY TRICKS

Back on the bricks, I decided it would be best to stay away from banks, so began to target credit unions, which were not sophisticated security-wise.

There were always guys lined up waiting for jobs. I kept busy casing places, testing getaways over and over again, gathering equipment, making disguises, stealing cars and rehearsing scores. Call it my executive phase.

There was a stretch when we hit two or three credit unions a week, sometimes doing two a day, until we'd hit about twenty. Then there was a job I did in the west end of the city, a high-end jewellery store, unusual because I was in on it myself.

I was wearing full makeup. Brian was to come in after me. Carrie was to wait at the back with the getaway car.

The woman behind the counter was a big Hilda, maybe 200 pounds with a thick Slavic accent. She was fussing at a mirror, and she hardly noticed me. "I'll be with you in a minute, sir."

And then she realized it was serious.

"Take the money and go."

I told her I didn't want money. All I was after was jewellery, but I guess she thought I was going to rape her. Everything happened in a hurry.

She came at me, screaming; her son who lived downstairs ran up and grabbed me from behind. I spun, knocking him down.

We left the getaway car and escaped into the nearby subway station. If we'd had loot with us, we'd have used the car. I had a special route marked out.

What was so special?

We had laid "spike belts" throughout the rest of the neighbourhood. I got that one from Warren Hart: lengths of garden hose, stuck through with sharpened spikes.

There were pictures in the paper the next day of cop cars disabled with flat tires, some of them rammed by civilian cars. A real mess, just as I planned.

Up to that point, the cops had been calling us the Nightmare Bandits, for obvious reasons: we were bandits, and we were their biggest nightmare. After that, we were known as the Dirty Tricks Gang.

If you care to look, there is a length of spike belt at the Toronto Police Museum on College Street. And yes, I am aware of the irony that the spike belt became a tool of policing.

A while later, I went to Montreal to kick back with Levern. When I came back home, I found out that four men with thick briefcases had picked the locks on my apartment and had spent a couple of hours inside.

I ducked out right away, making sure I wasn't followed, and went to a surveillance store to pick up a couple of devices to sweep for bugs. Spy vs. spy.

I didn't find any bugs, but I kept my mouth shut about crime while I was at home. I thought it important to stick to my usual routine, so I went to the gym to work out. This time, I sparred six rounds with Trevor Berbick, the World Boxing Council (WBC) heavyweight champ.

It might have been a sparring session, but I used everything my trainer taught me, working him to the inside with all my skill. He gave me a compliment when we finished. He told me I was the best inside fighter he'd come across. I guess I was; after all, we had the same trainer.

Berbick was not technically proficient, but he had what you might call bug strength, almost super-human. It's the kind of strength a mother uses to lift a car off her child's body.

Before we sparred, he took off his necklaces and a ring and he gave the bling to three Portuguese kids to hold for him. When he went to get his stuff back, the kid who had the ring was gone.

Berbick lost his mind. "Where's the other kid?"

The two remaining kids said, "We don't know. He wasn't with us."

They were shit-scared, but it was clear that the two kids didn't know the third one. Berbick soon calmed down; a ring worth five or six grand, what was that to him?

He was a champ, but I had held my own with him because I'd been trained to technical proficiency. All I will say about our separate paths is this – there are boxers who get breaks.

But he really was the strongest fighter of his time.

After sparring, I went to beat on the heavy bag, but the gym phone rang before I got there. It was Diane. "Get home now!" was all she said, and all she had to say. I rushed in and saw her put her fingers to her lips. She led me to the living room and pointed at the floor.

I saw a wire leading under the carpet and into my study, where I found a tiny microphone. I hauled out my harmonica and began to wail. *Nobody knows the trouble I've seen, nobody knows my sorrow.* I yanked the bug out, stuffed it into my pocket and went back to the gym.

Later on, I called my brother and took him back home with me. Diane was gone, and the place had been tossed, but I found a note on the television. "Give back our thing and we'll let your woman go."

It was signed by a detective whose name I choose to forget. He left his phone number. When I called, he told me the cops had found a joint in the apartment.

Diane was under arrest for possession, but if I returned the bug he'd drop the charges. Dwane drove me to the station where I was escorted to the detectives' office. The place was almost empty.

My brother thought we shouldn't have come. He wanted to confront the chief, Harold Adamson, about the treatment we were getting.

He had a point – the cops would not have been so anxious to get their bug back if it hadn't been planted illegally. All I wanted was Diane.

"A deal is a deal," said the detective.

A minute later, Diane was free. She was also hopping mad. I dropped the bug on the table and the three of us were leaving when a cop raced down the hall and stopped us.

The cop was waving a piece of paper. "You can't let him go."

"I'm letting him go," the detective said. "We had a deal."

"It's from the top. You go fucking argue with him 'cause I'm not," said the flailing cop.

The detective sat down at a desk and made a phone call. I didn't like the look on his face.

When he hung up he said, "Sorry, Rick, but the chief said no deals with you. You're under arrest for possession of narcotics. This just came in from Ottawa. Read it."

Narcotics?

He pushed the paper at me. It read that any person on parole who was charged with any offence had to appear in court for a show-cause bail hearing.

There would be no more bail handed out in cop shops any more. To get bail, it was now necessary to appear before a judge. The law had just been changed.

Lucky me, I was the first to know.

I was angry and disgusted, and the detective looked unhappy. He put his word on the line, and I'd acted in good faith.

"Look, Ricky, I don't bullshit. My word is my word. I'd cut you loose, but my hands are tied."

He gestured upstairs, where the chief had his office. "Sometimes he can be a real prick." As if that was somehow supposed to make me understand.

My brother took Diane home and I was locked up in the cells for the night.

The next day in court, I waived my right to a bail hearing, not wanting to drag the matter out any longer than necessary. The judge got the point. He ordered a speedy trial, remanding me over for two weeks.

After a night at the Don Jail, a special OPP squad whisked me off to Kingston. I always got special treatment, even for minor offences.

The guards who knew me shook their heads as I shuffled in for the usual strip search and introduction procedure. At least I came prepared.

I'd picked up several bails of Daily Mail tobacco at the Don, and I handed them around to anyone I thought could use a smoke.

"You're coming back and forth so much, we should reserve a room for you," noted one of the guards.

He thought that was funny.

Two weeks later, my lawyers advised me to throw myself on the mercy of the court. They also advised Diane to plead guilty, and that is the deal they sold to the Crown. Diane was fined a hundred bucks, and they cut me loose.

Not that simple, actually; I had to go back to Kingston, where I was released within an hour.

This time I took a bus back to Toronto, to give myself time to think. And I was thinking that the only way out was to raise my game, make enough money to get out of Toronto, and start a new life somewhere else.

I remembered a conversation with Domenic Racco. We walked the laneways around his father's bakery for old times' sake, and also for privacy.

I was addicted to knocking off jewellery stores and banks. It was now a full-time job, and it wasn't fun anymore. As for boxing, I was climbing the rankings but my fights were getting harder and harder.

In fact, I was burning out, and Domenic sensed that.

He said, "Ricky, in our world it takes all your energy to avoid arrest, stay out of prison, and keep from getting murdered.

"And on top of that you've got boxing, where it takes all you've got to avoid getting knocked out. How can you divide your attention between the two, and hope to succeed in either? I think you should choose one or the other."

I knew he was right, but that didn't make the choice any easier. Boxing could bring me fame and maybe fortune, if everything went my way. Crime was a ticket to fast money.

If I needed to be reminded of the risks involved in the latter choice, I got one in a hurry. Domenic Racco was taken for a one-way ride a few weeks later and shot to death by thugs he knew from Collins Bay.

I was so tired of ducking Bert Novis that I began to joke that he and I should share an apartment, to save us both a little time looking for each other. Here's how close we were: I was preparing a bank job at the corner of Spadina and Adelaide. On the day, I cased the area, just to make sure. Something caught my attention – a big woman smoking a cigar and sitting in a small car.

I radioed my brother and told him to do a little counter-surveillance, and we waited for him to report back. A few minutes later, my brother rolled up on his motorcycle and said the woman smoking the cigar was Bert Novis in disguise. He was picking up tricks from me.

I called the job off.

I was going to have to up my game – not only was he learning from me, but now every bank job in the city involving more than one guy was being attributed to the Dirty Tricks Gang.

I started doubling my precautions and began to rely more and more on elaborate disguises. I made myself up as an old white man, with a partially bald head and an ugly pitted face, wearing cheap baggy clothes. I walked slowly with a cane, mumbling as I passed my parents sitting in front of their house. They didn't recognize me.

For a time, Owen had his eye on a bank that I knew had been taken for $100,000 by the Boyd Gang in 1952. Yes, I'm a student of history and, no, the Boyd Gang's final bank tally never came anywhere near to ours.

The bank was in an industrial area, which meant it would be fat with money the day before payday. In this case, the big money would be in the vault, and it would take longer to retrieve than the minute or so it usually took us to do a job.

I'd learned the need for speed while walking the yard with bank robber and author Stephen Reid of the Stopwatch Gang – our scores outnumbered theirs. In this instance I figured a few seconds more wouldn't hurt.

Owen said the job would be his last. He was tired and wanted to move out west with his girlfriend. My motivation was similar but different. Diane was pregnant.

It's a bit of a game, crime: We had cunning on our side, but the cops had bench strength; we were on duty at all times, but they could change shifts and call in a whole new team in order to freshen up.

The score was set for Thursday, March 12, at 11:00 a.m. By way of cunning, I had worked out the disguises and the wigs, put the guns together, stolen a couple of cars, cut a hole in a fence the robbers would use as an exit to a third car, and thought about contingency plans in case anyone fucked up.

Fucking up was not an option – conspiracy to rob a bank carries a life sentence; committing the robbery is also life; using a disguise to commit a crime is worth fourteen years and possession of illegal handguns could tack on another five.

What I didn't know was that Owen had taken a peek at the bank a couple of nights earlier. He'd been spotted by Bert Novis, giving the cops two days to lay a trap. This time they weren't playing games.

I am convinced that their plan was to set us up in order to kill us. There was precedent for this, although you won't get any cop to admit it. The Toronto hold-up squad was formed in 1959 to stop a wave of Montreal bank robbers from terrorizing the city. Some of those robbers were shot dead as a message to others that Toronto was not just a piece of cake they could nibble on when they wanted a taste of something sweet.

In my opinion the hold-up squad, as it was in those days, broke as many laws as they enforced.

We had no idea what we were in for.

The morning of the robbery, we met at Brian's. His car had broken down; instead of stealing another, he elected to ride with me. We met early, so that I could work on everyone's disguise. And here, I want to point out again that my methods were achieved through necessity as well as design.

I put the scores together and chose people with the necessary skills to do the job, but I tended to stay back. Sometimes, as my alibi, I'd go to the gym to train.

I'd only meet up with the robbers after the score was done. That way, the cops could watch me all they wanted but they wouldn't learn much.

The participants this time were Brian, Mike and Owen the Crook. Skippy had a crew of about half a dozen lookouts who would make their way to the bank in their own cars and take up positions in places we'd chosen earlier. The actual robbers would take a stolen van and two stolen cars, parking them in pre-determined spots for use in the getaway. Brian and I would go unarmed.

I wanted The Crook to take a .30 calibre, sawed-off automatic rifle in order to supply a little fear inside the bank. He opted for a smaller handgun instead. Mike also declined a big gun, also refusing the elaborate mask I'd made for him. All he wanted was some phoney scars and a fake beard.

Owen also said no to full makeup, preferring some scars and a pair of sunglasses. He was bearded at the time and said he'd shave after the job was done.

I should have insisted, but I suppose it wouldn't have made a bit of difference one way or another. What's the use of planning fine detail if no one's going to take direction?

We went to The Gingerman in the east end for breakfast and then we went to work. It wouldn't do anyone any good to know I was disgruntled.

It took Brian and me twenty minutes to get into position. I checked my watch. The timing was critical. I had a few minutes to walk around the train tracks.

I climbed a boxcar in order to survey the surrounding area. I could see all the way down into the Don Valley where I spotted some cop cars gathered far below. But I wasn't worried. I knew the layout of the roads and was sure they couldn't get to the bank before the job was done.

Brian checked his watch and called up. "They're in." He counted off ninety seconds and said, "They should be out." I began walking along the top of the train, watching the valley below. I could see the cop cars peel away and come screaming up the valley road. Brian called again.

"They're late."

I climbed down and headed for the van. Brian said, "Let's go. Something's not right." I held up for a bit. I had never left anyone on a score in my life.

"I'm not leaving them. Sixty more seconds."

Brian got in and drove the van around the train and over the tracks. He waited, revving the engine nervously. A minute later he began to take off, spinning the wheels in the dirt. I had to leap at the door, yank it open and hop in while he was peeling away.

Ten feet in front of us a man with dark hair in a brown suit crouched down and started shooting. There was none of the usual "Stop, police, you're under arrest!" There were just bullets thudding into the van as we flew past.

Instinctively, Brian drove off the dirt road and careened the van down an embankment onto another dirt road that ran parallel to the one we'd been on. His instinct saved our lives.

We weren't far from Bayview Avenue, a big north-south artery; Brian headed toward it as another cop jumped out of an unmarked car and started shooting.

We bounced onto the road at high speed and Brian swerved to avoid an oncoming car, leaving us facing oncoming traffic.

There was no choice but to hit the gas and aim the van at the cars coming toward us, in the hope that they'd clear off and give us room. But a couple of yards down the hill there were three more cop cars and six uniformed officers waiting for us. They drew their weapons and waited to shoot as we bore down on them. I had one of those slow motion, high-speed, jaw-dropping, stop-time revelations. We'd been set up to be killed.

As we raced past, they opened fire, and I braced myself for the pain of burning bullets. Miraculously, they all missed.

Brian headed for an overpass that would take us either north, towards Bloor Street, or south to the lakeshore.

He asked, calmly, "Which way?"

Calm is a Zen thing, or maybe it's just common sense. If you're in a crisis, and all hell is breaking loose, things will not get better if you panic.

I knew what to do.

I replied, just as calmly, "Turn right, along the river."

He spun the steering wheel so sharply I thought we'd roll over. There were three marked cars gaining on us. One of them got within a few feet, and the cop who was riding shotgun reached his arm out the window and began to shoot. The rational side of my brain took over for an instant.

"They've got nothing on us. Isn't it better to stop than to get killed?" Brian shot me a look. So then I got clever.

There was a little umbrella on the floor between the seats. I picked it up, rolled down the window and pointed it back at the cop as if it were a .12 gauge.

He backed off a bit.

There was a roadside flower seller at the intersection of Rosedale Valley Road and Bayview. Brian hit the horn as we skidded around the corner. The flower seller jumped up just in time as we crashed through his stand leaving a spray of flowers in our wake. The wreckage stopped traffic – snarling it and blocking the cops behind us.

We were clear now, and Brian hit the gas hard. At 100 mph, we neared another intersection.

"Directions?"

"Up Park Road."

We skidded, nearly hit another car, raced up one street and merged into another. Whew. Now I knew we could lose the cops if we blended in and slowed down.

We were driving along Yonge Street, heading toward Yorkville, when another thought took hold. "Stop the van. We can run into the subway." But Brian was in a world of his own. He kept on going. And then a cop jumped into the middle of the street, holding a gun. I aimed the umbrella at him and he crouched and cowered.

His gun? A walkie-talkie.

I gave him the finger as we sped past.

We found ourselves on Bellair Street in Yorkville, our progress blocked by a delivery truck. Brian hit the horn and the driver gave us the finger. I hopped out, ran over, jamming the umbrella in the trucker's chest.

"Move the truck or I'll blow your head off." He looked at the little umbrella, confused, but frightened to have a guy my size yelling in his face. He froze.

"Move the fucking truck."

And then I saw the cop with the walkie-talkie, only this time it really was his gun, and he was screaming for everyone to hit the ground.

Brian jumped out of the van and ran to the side of a building, climbing up the metal staircase to the roof. I jumped over a fence between two houses, ran across Cumberland Street, crossed a parking lot and headed for Bloor Street as fast as I could.

I dumped my leather jacket in a trash can. A German shepherd dog snarled as I jumped over its head and made my way past a lady holding its leash.

I blended in with a gaggle of students, aping their behaviour, laughing when they laughed, stopping when they stopped to look at something.

For a moment I thought of ducking into the Royal Ontario Museum to gather my thoughts and catch my breath, but I was spooked when four cop cars sped by heading for Yorkville.

I ran into the subway, looking around to see if I was being followed, and boarded a train just as the doors closed. I was planning to get onto the Yonge line.

As I was waiting to transfer trains, I overheard someone say, "Did you hear the news? There was a bank robbery this morning, four people shot dead." It hit me like a blow to the chest. There had been eight of us in the robbery.

Who'd been killed?

I got off at Eglinton subway station and called Diane. I told her I needed an alibi. She wanted to know why I sounded so upset. I didn't want to let on. I never wanted to upset her before, during or after any crime I'd committed.

She came down and met me in the station. We headed upstairs together and I told her to look at her watch. Then I pushed her up against a restaurant window, hard enough to make some noise. I shook my finger in her face.

The point was to be memorable.

A couple of waitresses took note of us, and of the time. I knew they'd be potential witnesses.

Diane walked away.

I called Brian. No answer. I couldn't have been the only one to make it out alive.

There were loose ends everywhere.

I boarded a bus and headed for Brian's. The bus passed by the bank that we'd just hit; there were cop cars all over. I was thirty-one years old, and I have never felt more lonely, or more helpless, in my life.

I got off near Brian's and circled around to make sure I wasn't being followed. Then I went up to his apartment, only to find that nothing had been moved since we'd left for breakfast.

I put the makeup in its case and set it by the door, alongside all our coats. Then I washed the dishes. When I was done, I took a soapy rag and wiped down every place I thought there might be fingerprints.

I left the makeup case by the door, thinking I'd come back for it later, after I'd dumped the coats in a garbage bin.

As I was leaving to go back downtown, I glanced at a newspaper box on the corner. The papers had rushed an early edition to print. The headline read: "Robbers Shot Dead In Police Trap."

Among the dead, my friend and confederate, my ally and my trusted right-hand man, Owen Crookendale.

The Crook, no more.

I was heartsick. I still am.

I called Skippy's mother. She answered, and I asked if he was home. She burst into tears. "Isn't he with you?" I hung up.

Thankfully, the news was wrong. Skippy had been arrested and let go the same day. There was no evidence to hold him.

Then I called Mike's place. His girlfriend Tammy picked up. She, too, burst into tears and asked if he was with me. Again, I hung up. Each call was a risk. I found out Mike was just wounded.

I needed time to think and I jumped on a bus to kill time. Newspapers were open on people's laps. They were reading the evening updates, talking to each other.

Owen Crookendale was dead, two others in critical condition at an undisclosed hospital, guarded by machine-gun-toting cops. Three more of the crew were under arrest. The police stated they were looking for several more armed and extremely dangerous people.

The *Toronto Star* ran full pages of the crime scene but no pictures of the wanted men. I stared out the bus window, wishing I could go back to Grade One when I first met the Owen and change the directions of our lives. A cop car blared past the bus, skidding around the corner.

There were things I had to do. I got off at the next stop, spotted a pay phone and called Dwane's number. He picked up and started to talk. I cut him off. He hadn't read the news or turned on the TV.

"Let's meet, zone two colour blue," I said, using our special code for locations, which was as natural to us as any longitude and latitude directions.

Five minutes later I was standing in a laneway facing him.

He had a newspaper under his arm.

"I can't do this alone," I told him. My brother looked at me and swallowed hard.

Owen's father lived a block away, and we went over to tell him his son was dead.

A NEW START

A gang is a gang. We had to keep moving forward. Instead of robbing banks, I shifted my attention to stealing property. I recruited my best nighttime workers from the west end. These were guys who didn't use guns to rob during the day, rather sledge hammers, lock picks and crowbars to break into factories at night. We had to move forward, there were mouths to feed and a gang to keep rolling.

We had been operating on the cutting edge of business, using scanners and walkie-talkies to secure entire blocks; the technology helped us to penetrate deep inside factories and get out again before the cops could get near us.

Most of the time I stayed far back, well out of the action I had organized, but there were times I risked it all and went inside. My brother hated it when I did because I was the brains, the mastermind; he couldn't see any point in the risk. He was right, of course, but it was a complex thing. Stealing was what I knew best, even if it was not what I enjoyed most.

The only parallel I can think of is the junkie with his needle – I hated the grind of looking for a score and setting it up, just as a junkie hates to stab his arm with a spike. But just as the junkie loves the high, so I loved to beat alarms, pick a lock, find a weakness, and walk out clean.

What made it hard is that I was working fourteen-hour days. I was not just setting up scores, I was still boxing. Not only had I never lost, I had not been knocked down. I hadn't even taken a standing eight-count.

Through boxing I met Roy Gumbs.

Roy was a beauty of a middleweight from St. Kitts, and my trainer had arranged for me to go to Halifax to work in his corner for the British Commonwealth title. As it happened, Roy wanted me in his corner in another way: he asked me for a gun, so that he could shoot sports promoter Irv Ungerman who had apparently ripped him off after a fight.

I wasn't interested, but I wanted to defuse his anger. I said, "If everyone who wants Irv dead took a shot at him, I could take his body to the scrapyard and get a fortune in lead – there's a long line of guys who feel like you."

Roy set his grievance aside and won his fight. He went on to win the world middleweight title. We would meet again later, and we'd both suffer for it.

One day Dwane and I headed to a warehouse in the east end: The plan was to move a million dollars' worth of stolen video equipment over to a warehouse in the west end.

As we passed the Toronto East Detention Centre, I pointed to the fifth floor and said, "If we get busted, that's where they'll put us."

We stopped our car beside a factory and looked across several parking lots to the truck we were planning to use, which had been rented in my brother's name.

Everything seemed normal.

Just to be safe – you can never be too safe – I drove around the parking lot looking for cops. The coast was clear. We pulled up beside a truck that was filled with a fortune in stolen merchandise.

Dwane got out and slipped his gloves on ready to go to work, but as soon as his hand touched the door of the truck, cops burst out of the factory, surrounding us, pointing guns and screaming at us: Hands up!

I had no idea how we'd missed them, but I had no intention of going back to jail so I threw myself across the seat of the Lincoln and punched the gas pedal to the floor with my fist.

The big car surged forward, with a cop running alongside, pointing his shotgun down at me. Luckily for me, he didn't shoot. He couldn't keep up with the Lincoln. Once I put some distance between us, I sat up and grabbed the wheel just in time to miss a row of parked cars.

The chase was on. I thought I was in the clear until I tore around a corner and found myself face to face with four cop cars. When in doubt, hit the gas.

I wheeled around and raced past them, hitting a hundred miles an hour, until I was boxed in, outfoxed by superior numbers, superior planning and loads of weapons.

How did they catch us?

Try good police work, coupled with a little luck. They knew we had a warehouse, and they ran the plates of every truck in the vicinity until they hit on the one with my brother's name on it. A big payday for them, because in addition to nailing Johnny Bayliss –who rented the warehouse – they got everything in the truck, plus a ton of high-end stuff we'd taken from three of the largest electronic firms in the city.

They took the three of us to 42 Division and put us in separate rooms. I sat and waited. They liked to make me wait. I was watched over by two rookie cops.

Eventually the door opened and a tall man with greying hair walked in. He entered with authority, flanked by two detectives. He walked up to me and stared at me for a full minute.

"Ricky Atkinson. We meet again. This time, I'm the head of the precinct and you're still the badass you always were. Do you remember me?"

No, I did not.

He said, "I worked out of 14 Division back in the late Sixties. Because of you, I used my gun for the first time in my career. How could I forget you?"

A quick deduction – if he had shot at me back in those days, then he must have been the cop in the laneway in Kensington Market, when I was fourteen years old. He leaned forward, and it was odd the way he said what he said next.

"You had a gun on you that night?"

I suddenly got it – he knew he'd come close to killing a bunch of kids, and he'd been wrestling with it ever since, wondering all those years if he'd been right to shoot.

"It was raining really hard, thunder and lightning and all that stuff," I reminded him. He exhaled, as if I'd punched him in the chest.

"Do you know what you're under arrest for?"

I said that I did.

"Then there's nothing more to talk about." He turned and walked out, followed by his detectives, and that ended the questioning. Not long after, we found ourselves in the East Detention Centre.

After four months of waiting while the legal manoeuvres were played out, I pleaded guilty to three break-and-enters and admitted stealing over one million in goods. I was hit with a year apiece for each.

My brother and Johnny got two years.

We were classified for Joyceville, because Kingston was now considered a protective custody prison.

I wouldn't be going back there again.

JOYCEVILLE, THE HAVEN, PITTSBURGH

If this turn in Joyceville was my sixth time in prison, I had lost count of the number of times I'd won in court. And if it always stung to lose, this time it hurt more because of my daughter. Melissa was now two years old, and I adored her.

I knew Diane would bring her to see her daddy, but I also knew I was stuck inside for at least two years.

That's a hell of a life for a grown man to lead.

There were ten black prisoners in Joyceville, but there was no Black Inmates and Friends Association, so I got busy. I wrote a proposal and got it to the warden. Soon we were in business; our weekly meetings grew to include fifteen prisoners of all colours and creeds.

I was an old hand at life inside, so I also got the grievance clerk's job, which gave me my own office, and some freedom inside the prison, mediating complaints.

I was also elected to chair the inmates' committee.

I kept myself otherwise occupied by training boxers in the gym, painting and losing myself in books. It was all about tuning out the world, doing my time day by day and hoping for a break that would get me back to the big city.

Thing is, you can't keep your head down all the time.

There were changes to federal prison policy, resulting in a proposal to double-bunk prisoners. Seems the feds wanted to make more room for people who were pinched on cocaine offences. It was the Eighties, and those numbers were on the rise.

My duty, on behalf of my fellow inmates, was to lead the way against injustice. I got the guys in the shop to agree to stop building double bunks. I contacted lawyers who filed injunctions, preparing to fight the good fight. For my troubles, I was unceremoniously shoved in the hole one morning without warning, and then I was shackled and driven to Millhaven.

Ordinarily, every inmate who is being transferred to a higher security facility must be given adequate notice to allow lawyers to appeal such a decision. However, an emergency transfer can be implemented for the good of the institution. Security head Dave Page explained the implementation process as he tightened a set of chains around my hands and feet.

Why were they moving me?

According to the warden's report, I was involved in the drug trade inside Joyceville, an allegation that was an all-purpose bit of bullshit allowing him to ship me out, no questions asked.

I found out later that my removal had set off a sit-down strike – everyone at Joyceville refused to go to work, at the cost of a day's pay. No small matter, since it's almost unheard of for entire population of prisoners to agree to do anything together.

I sent a thank-you card.

Millhaven was going through a period of turbulence, amounting to a murder a month, topped off with fights, stabbings and constant lockdowns. The lockdowns were a violation of the rights of the entire population as a result of the actions of the few. Generally, they were lifted after a roundup of suspects and a sweep for weapons.

Due to the constant state of turmoil, even seasoned lifers were afraid to go out in the yard. Many prisoners refused to leave their cells at all, except on mandatory work detail.

While I was there, I decided to study sociology and business law, both courses offered by Queen's University. I also spent a lot of time walking the yard with guys who were in on organized crime beefs, and with guys who led bike gangs – an education of another kind. In case you haven't noticed, if you want a man to earn a master's degree in criminal behaviour, the best thing you can do is send him to jail.

My negotiating skills were put to use more often than I might have liked. As I've said, prison is like high school. There are cliques – the blacks, the racists, the bikers, the mob guys, and the native guys. You hang with your own. You take care of your own.

This is where my skills got a particular test. One morning one of our guys, Shakey, whispered that a gangster from Ottawa had just stabbed and killed Coco, the man in the cell next to his.

Shakey had heard the killing go down. He also heard the killer, a guy named Rocky, arguing with his gang over the dead man's cash and his stash of pills.

Shakey was worried that Rocky might kill him because he was a potential witness. Shakey's death would ensure Rocky's safety, providing that he could be killed without anyone noticing.

It was still early, and the guards had yet to discover the body, but word spread up and down the ranges like lightning. Everyone started stocking up, storing food, grabbing art supplies, securing contraband and just generally getting ready for the lockdown.

I hate this sort of shit, the spiral of death and retaliation, and I knew that killing Rocky would not be the end of the affair.

I had a better idea.

Our crew armed up and we went with Shakey up to his range. I approached Rocky and with a nod to Shakey I said, "He knows, and now I know. If he says anything, we'll kill him. Is that good enough for you?"

My word is my bond, and everyone knew it, so Rocky – his hands recently wet with Coco's blood – shook on it with Shakey, and the air eased out of the balloon. I also considered another option to get rid of Rocky. His love of pills made that easy: twenty Valiums could get anyone killed in Millhaven.

I know it seems insane, but that's how life is in prison, and I didn't dwell on it. I simply point it out as another kind of leadership – when there are risks to everyone, everyone needs assurances.

Once again, I underlined that my word was my bond, and my authority was reinforced. Neither me, nor my crew, were to be trifled with.

When the guards found the body, all hell broke loose. A prisoner named Donny Oag picked up a vat of home brew and, with his face twisted in rage, he dumped it on the guards. The alcohol ran downstairs to the range below, where inmates scooped it up with whatever they could. Better to be drunk and locked up than it is to be sober and locked up.

In the aftermath, there was outrage in the media about the prison being awash in illegal alcohol, but the outrage did not prevent family visits. Diane continued to come with our daughter Melissa, who was clueless to the tension around her. She was just happy to see her daddy.

One morning in August 1984, I heard over the radio that a police officer named Douglas Tribbling had been killed in the northern part of Toronto where there are a lot of electronics warehouses. As usual, there was talk about the death penalty for cop killers. I ignored the news, although a few of the inmates cheered.

This death would haunt me in the future.

I stuck to my routine, keeping out of trouble – boxing when I felt like it and studying when I could. It wasn't long before I was asked to move to Collins Bay to make room for someone who needed Millhaven's particular climate of pain, punishment and maximum security.

The Bay was not a rest home, but it was better than Millhaven. I trained a few guys in the gym, including Mark Leduc, who went on to win a silver medal at the 1992 Olympics. He was a brave man, and it took bravery for him to come out of the closet a year or so after the Olympics.

I was such a model prisoner that, when I put in for a minimum-security bunk, they sent me to the Pittsburgh farm camp, adjacent to the Joyceville pen.

Pittsburgh was a 4,300-acre farm with a slaughterhouse. It provided nearly all of the vegetables and meat required by prisons in Ontario and Quebec.

And yes, it had greenhouses for flowers.

Not only did I like working with my hands in the clean air, under the warm sun, but I was also interested in hydroponic growing techniques, which could come in handy if I went into the marijuana business. At the very least, I figured I could get a farm with Diane, where we could grow herbs for the restaurant trade in Toronto, if the marijuana thing didn't work.

I was a man ahead of my time.

My immediate job, however, was preparing cows for slaughter. It was my job to decide which seven cows would end up on death row on any given day. It was also my habit, while they waited to head down the ramp to their fate, to read the Bible aloud to them.

I didn't hunt. I didn't kill insects. I just knew people had to eat, and these poor cows were a link in the chain of survival. Hearing a voice calmed them and helped me hone my speaking skills. I'd grown up a lot since the days when I was hitting the poor beasts with my fists.

As my parole date neared, Diane brought Melissa for a visit. She had plans to take me on a pass, but she was late. I was called to the administration office.

Diane had rolled her car.

Luckily, the cars behind her were filled with doctors on their way to a convention in Kingston. They saved her life. The guard on duty let me call the hospital. Melissa was okay. Diane's neck was broken.

The doctor I spoke to said, "Come and pick up your daughter, and let us work on your girlfriend."

Not that easy. I couldn't just grab a cab.

The warden was a man who cared about the men under his control. He drove back to his prison on a Friday night, after work hours, and signed off on the changes to my travel permit.

The hospital was in Trenton. As soon as I arrived, Melissa rushed into my arms and said, "Mommy's head came off, and the doctors are putting it back on." One of the nurses overheard her and explained what happened.

Diane's scalp had been torn away, exposing her skull. She'd need hundreds of stitches to make it right, plus her neck was broken. The good news is that there was no nerve damage.

However, Trenton didn't have the equipment to take the kind of x-rays necessary for her operation, so they sent her by ambulance to Sunnybrook Hospital in Toronto.

I followed with Melissa in my father's car. My brother sat quietly beside me.

A prisoner's life is bound by rules, regardless of the circumstances. I couldn't just head for the hospital. Instead, I had to report to a halfway house. And so it was hospital by day, and halfway house by night for four days, after which I had to head back to the farm.

I've made hard trips but that one back to the farm was the hardest – mandated to leave my woman and my little girl when they needed me the most. They sent Diane home with a pocket full of drugs and a halo screwed into her skull.

She didn't take the drugs because she wanted to keep a clear head for our daughter.

And I wanted to get out of jail for her.

Two weeks later, I had a shot at parole and I fought hard for it. I dodged questions for an hour, lying when I had to, and presented a solid release plan. I got day parole to a halfway house on Yonge Street. My parole officer was my old supporter, Marg Harlang.

I barely had time to adjust when the pressure of making a living asserted itself. The guys wanted me to go back to setting up scores. My plans to grow herbs and live a quiet life in the country with Diane seemed gone for good.

ANOTHER HARD CHOICE

Once again, I had to decide what to do. I had a daughter who needed me, and a woman who needed my help. The decision was made for me when I was walking home one day and a cop pulled up beside me.

"Hey, you!"

I kept on walking. The cop car sped up and cut me off. Two officers got out and walked over. One of them grabbed my arm.

"Hey, when I call you, you stop."

The same old crap again.

I pulled my arm free and said, as calmly as I could, "You didn't give me a direct order. 'Hey, you!' could have been directed at anyone. And the next time you detain me and restrict my movement, I'd better be under arrest or I'll sue you."

They moved in close, with their hands on their pistols.

"Who the fuck do you think you are?"

I handed over my parole card. They looked at it, levelled their guns at my chest and said I was under arrest.

"For what?"

"For being an asshole and walking down the street suspiciously." I swear that's what he said as they cuffed me and pushed me into the car.

When we neared 14 Division, the cop who was riding shotgun turned and pointed his pistol in my face.

"You're the tough guy they talk about at the station. Let me tell you something. There's a new generation of cops out here now, and we don't fistfight like the old boys. We shoot assholes like you."

He kissed his gun and gave me his hardest look.

It was all I could do not to laugh at this fine example of the new generation. If he was stupid enough to think I'd take his bullshit and do nothing, well, I had to set him straight.

"Officer, if you shoot me you'd better be able to justify the shooting or you'll go to jail and be somebody's bitch. However, if someone was to shoot you, I don't think they'd care much if they went to jail or not, because most likely they'd have just gotten out of one."

He was surprised that I had the balls to confront him. He stuck his gun back in its holster and turned around. You could almost hear the wheels in his little brain spinning.

He was quiet all the way to the station. I might have scored a point, but I had just made an enemy, someone who could set me up on a phoney pinch or, worse, figure out a way to kill me. I did some thinking of my own.

It was beginning to look like I'd have to get out of town.

Inside 14 Division, one of the older detectives asked the new generation what I'd done. "He was walking down the street suspiciously." I almost laughed again. The detective looked at him like he was an idiot.

"Search him and let him go."

"But he thinks he's a tough guy."

"He's one of the toughest guys I know. So if you want to fight him, go ahead, but I'm too old for this shit."

I was searched and set free.

As soon as I could, I called Marg Harlang and told her what had happened. I asked her to write me up a transfer to Vancouver. She refused, on the ground that my parole was almost over and when it was I could go anywhere I wanted to.

I might have been content to let it rest, but a few days later I was heading into the Projects when I saw two salt-and-pepper detectives stop my brother. They didn't see me.

The black cop detained Dwane while the white cop searched his car. I saw the white cop reach into his pocket and drop something on the floor, which he then retrieved.

"Put the cuffs on him. He's under arrest. Look what I found." He was holding a little jar of hash oil.

I knew the cop. I left cover and walked over. He turned in my direction and ordered me to stand back. I kept walking towards him. He pulled his gun.

I'd had enough of that. "Officer, whatever you found on him is nothing compared to what they'll find in your car one day."

"Don't threaten me. I'm a cop."

I pointed to the hash oil. "You're a cop? I don't think so."

We stared at each other for what seemed like a minute. He pocketed the hash oil and ordered my brother released. But as he was leaving he drew his finger cross his throat and grinned.

That did it.

I wasn't going to survive in the city with cops hounding me, and there was no way Marg Harlang was going to help me get out of town. I went back to doing what I knew best.

What was there to lose?

I set up a gang consisting of Johnny Bayliss; my cousin Tommy Musgrave; Jimmy LeBlanc from the projects; Franz, also known as Bump, who'd been my cook in Collins Bay; Derek Cruz from Millhaven; Andy Ferguson from Beaver Creek; Chris Dorsey, one of Levern's brothers from Blind River and, of course, my brother Dwane.

The crew was multiracial. We'd all done time, and the rules of the game were that you had to carry a gun to get what you wanted. There were twenty others I could call on who knew how to swing a sledgehammer or wield a crowbar to break into factories or steal transport trucks.

The money started to roll in.

I paid no taxes. I opened no bank accounts. We kept nothing smaller than twenty-dollar bills. The fives and tens, we didn't bother with; we threw them away.

I paid cash for everything and never kept a receipt.

There was nothing in my name – not my car, not my house, nothing. We ate out often at places we knew, where we could slip the owner a wad of cash under the table so that we could come and go without a trace.

As usual, I rented garages all over town. In the garages were stolen cars, locked up tight. Locked in the trunks were little safes filled with cash and boxes full of guns.

I bought the best surveillance and communication equipment I could find. It gave us an edge; either I was going to end up with enough money to get out of town when my parole was finally up, or I was going to shake hands with The Crook, wherever it was that dead bandits went.

My thoughts were evolving; there was nothing I wouldn't consider if I thought it would help. On one bank job, I used a big Doberman to guard the front door and had Cruz call him to come when the job was over.

I was very proud of that dog, the way he raced around the back of the bank, through some bushes and into the getaway van. I knew he wouldn't squeal if he was caught, and he was happy to be paid in steak.

There was also the thrill of improvisation: on one job, Tommy ran out of a bank on St. Clair Avenue, leaving his accomplice alone. Instead of fleeing, he ran into the bank next door, where he made another efficient withdrawal. He ran back into the first bank just in time to exit out the back door where the getaway team was waiting.

After that bit of nerve, we often did bank doubles.

There was also a lot of nighttime action in factories all over the city – cleaning them out, loading the goods into trucks and making deliveries to an eager line of fences.

Night work has its perils, of course, but it was a useful course of action when the daytime heat was too much. It also had another advantage. When done properly, a break and enter done at night left no trace as to the age, colour, size or demeanour of the guys who did the score.

This was in the days before security cameras.

My father had a renovation business in those days, and I rented a warehouse in the west end. Sometimes, quite naturally and quite innocently, my father used my warehouse for storage.

It gave us a cover. At least I thought it did.

When a group of men moved into the empty space above us. It didn't take us long to figure out that it was the law.

We talked about moving, but there were no safe places for us, so I mimicked the cops. I stuck a bug up a heating grate so we could listen to them, and I bought a couple of big fans to run while we were talking.

Even so, whenever we had serious business to discuss, I took my guys for a walk along the railroad tracks. We talked when the trains went by to defeat the parabolic mikes that I knew were aimed at us.

There was a worm in the apple, as often happens in gangs. Carrie was the only one of us who'd never been to prison and, for some reason, Carrie decided that Bump was a rat.

Trust is paramount. Paranoia kills gangs.

I acted quickly and called a meeting under a railroad bridge in the west end, and did what leaders do.

"Your life is on the line," I told Carrie. "If you can't convince us of the truth of your allegations, then Bump has the right to kill you today. But if you can prove your allegations, well, it won't be pretty for Bump. Are you prepared to proceed?"

Carrie didn't make a very compelling case, at least not in my mind, so I put it to a vote. Not one person thought there was enough information to accuse Bump of being a rat.

Bump pulled out a bowie knife and moved on Carrie, who drew a knife of his own. I wouldn't have been sure how to handicap the fight. Carrie had hand-to-hand combat training in the American army. Bump learned all he knew in prison.

In the end, it wasn't much of a fight. They slashed at each other for a bit, both men drawing blood in a half-hearted manner. I stepped in and stopped the fight. Carrie got the worst of it, several slashes to his upper body.

I explained calmly and clearly what was going to happen. I told Carrie he was out of the group until the green paper came out. A green paper is a document outlining evidence to be presented in court, including any statements made by anyone questioned by police.

"If the green paper proves your allegations, we'll take care of Bump. If not, you're on your own."

Carrie asked me for a lift to the hospital. I refused, because that would have shown that I'd taken his side. He hailed a cab instead. Again, this is the stuff of leadership. Apart from the choice of weapons, you can't tell me it was any different from the fights that go on in boardrooms.

I sent Bump to the Bahamas to get him out of the way for a while, giving him the job of getting rid of $50,000 worth of money orders that we'd stolen from banks. Shit happens: Bump took a friend and the friend ripped him off. When Bump got back he broke into his friend's house, stole some video equipment, and offered to pay me back with that.

Bullshit. I wanted cash.

He begged me for a bank job to earn the money. I went low-tech for the planning on this one. I took an Etch-A-Sketch and turned the knobs until the message was clear.

An Etch-A-Sketch. Don't laugh. It was a useful method of communication. All I had to do to erase my words was give it a shake. Perfect. The message sent to the crew: "Who wants to work with Bump on a bank job?" There were several takers, even though Bump didn't have much experience.

I didn't much care. I just wanted to get paid. I'd been casing half a dozen banks with my brother, and didn't foresee any problems.

The first of these was a small bank in the west end. The female tellers held enough money for me to get paid back in full. Tommy would be the counter-jumper. Bump would watch the door, and cover Tommy's back: Andy's job was to keep six.

I had Andy walk me though his part in the job. As the outside man, he'd be in radio contact with the man on the door, and he'd also keep an eye on the street. It became clear he didn't know the streets and was not fully aware of all the options. I ordered him off the score.

I put too much time into the planning of jobs to jeopardize anyone, even an idiot.

The next morning, I met my brother at a prearranged spot. He showed up in a white, mint-condition 1965 Lincoln Continental. I was puzzled.

His bike was a better bet, allowing him to slip around in back alleys and between cars, making it easier to weed out cop traps, but Dwane had found his bike kicked in and useless where he left it the night before.

Fuck that white Lincoln shit.

I threw him the keys to a black van and jumped in beside him. This was unusual because I'd stopped going on actual jobs a long time ago. Dwane was puzzled. "There's no need for both of us to ride together."

I said, "Just drive. We'll be okay." I wanted to see Bump at work. That's another executive function; you need to know the strengths and weaknesses of your team in action.

We picked up Tommy and Bump at the Royal York subway. Tommy was smart and reliable. I trusted him enough to know he hadn't been followed, so we headed for the bank. I had a couple of stolen cars in place, and all looked good. We rehearsed the details of the score as we drove.

Tommy was uncertain about Bump carrying a loaded gun. Personally, I never have carried a gun without bullets on the off chance that some-body might decide to be a hero. In this case Bump was an amateur, and this particular bank was full of women. Tommy tossed the bullets.

As it happens, while all this careful planning was going on, we were being followed. Why? Because Andy, on his own, had driven by the bank that morning to take a look, and he'd been followed ever since.

So much for my trust in his skills.

With the location confirmed, the cops called in a chopper they had waiting on standby. The Dirty Tricks Gang was about to walk into another ambush.

We very nearly avoided trouble. Dwane smelled something not quite right. "The woman at the bus stop let the bus go by. She's right across the street from the bank. That guy up the hydro pole is supposed to be a line-man but he hasn't touched a wire in over a minute. And there's a man standing by that Corvette over there. It's not his car. I think it's a set-up; your call."

I took the radio in hand and sent out the usual signals to call it off, and I repeated them just in time to see Bump and Tommy approach the bank, intent on the job at hand. Why? Because, like an idiot, Bump hadn't pushed his earpiece in all the way. I now had a dilemma, just like the one I had the day Owen was killed. Leave the robbers and save my ass or risk it all again.

Things went sour in a hurry.

One of the tellers threw a roll of coins in Tommy's face. An old man grabbed Bump, who pulled out his empty gun and reflexively pulled the trigger until he realized it was useless, so he whipped out his knife.

Tommy pushed the teller out of the way. When he opened her drawer, he could tell by the way the money was stacked that it was a set-up. As soon as they fled, they ran into the fake lineman, who had climbed down from his pole and was now pointing his gun at them.

There was no way to help. Nothing to do but get the hell out. Dwane hit the gas pedal and we raced past the Corvette. The idle man, who was idle no more, pointed his gun at us as we flew by.

I thought we were in the clear until a cop car boxed us in. He jumped up from some bushes with a shotgun. I had a grim flashback to Owen.

I tore my shirt open to show him that I was unarmed. Of course I was unarmed; I was the just a six guy, blocks away from the action. I didn't need a weapon.

I stepped out with my hands up and there was the young, clean-shaven Sergeant Gary Silliker, behind him was another cop with a machine gun.

"Get on the ground."

I stayed calm. "No. Am I under arrest?"

There was a moment between us where I looked him in the eye. I had the feeling that this was a set-up, and the outcome was to be me, dead.

I swear I saw his finger tighten on the trigger.

"Get down or I'll shoot."

I was pretty sure that what he meant was, "Get down so I can shoot." Dwane, who was in the back of the van, piped up and said, "You shoot him, you better shoot me." I never broke Silliker's gaze. He exhaled.

He couldn't do it.

The cop who'd stood by the Corvette caught up then and cuffed us, told us we were under arrest and searched us. They found nothing, of course, but I would soon discover that one of them planted a gun in the van.

Meanwhile, Silliker radioed in for help. "We've got the Atkinson brothers; send us backup."

Silliker whistled lightly and looked at his watch, as if he was marking the day and the time. The weather was warm and sunny. All was right with the world except for the Atkinsons.

I remember that he said to me, "We're going to get Tommy in two minutes." Two minutes later, the police radio crackled.

"Shots fired. All units – shots fired."

Silliker put the radio to his lips.

"Is he out? Is he out?"

A calm voice over the radio replied: "He's down and he's out." Some of the cops slapped hands.

"That's one funeral you won't be going to," Silliker told me. "Now let's see if you miss Andy's, too."

Killing Andy Ferguson would have caused the cops a lot of problems. He was the nephew of Archie Ferguson, a chief in the Ontario Provincial Police and head of the OPP's organized crime section. Also, his father was a former prison warden.

It was not my place to school them in lineage. They hustled us into a car and drove off to 21 Division. The radio crackled again.

"Shots fired. Shots fired."

The driver radioed back. "Is he out?"

"No, subject in custody."

Andy might have dodged a bullet, but I was sure Tommy was dead. Silliker seemed to enjoy the news. He turned to me and said, "If you had even flinched, I'd have blown you away."

"Fuck you."

When they brought us into the station, one of the sergeants looked up sourly. "What's he doing, grinning at me?" I took that to mean that I was supposed to be back at the scene, dead on the ground.

None of the other cops – there were fifteen or twenty of them – would look me in the eye. They all looked at each other as if seeing a ghost.

I may be wrong but my instincts are pretty good. It looked, it felt, and it smelled to me as if it had been a set-up all along.

Bert Novis emerged from his office, pulling me aside.

"Tommy got shot, but he'll live. Bump didn't get hurt." Then he said something that stopped me cold.

"Your dad is here. Want to say anything before we let him go?"

I nodded. We turned a corner, he opened a door and there was my father, trying to explain to a cop that he didn't know a thing about my activities.

"Dad, you don't have to say another word to these guys."

He jumped up and faced me. "You and your brother okay?"

"Tommy's shot, but he'll live. We're okay, but we're off to jail, dad."

"Anything you want to say to your mum?"

I just shook my head. Novis led me into a room filled with cops in plain clothes and in uniform, all of them looking at me wordlessly. Time to go to the interrogation room.

"You want a coffee?" Novis asked.

"Yes."

"I'm not buying."

I reached into my pocket for some change, enough for two cups. When he came back with it, he said, "Your brother hasn't fucking changed, has he?" The big cop put my brother's coffee down on the desk next to mine. I stared at them until both cups grew cold and then I tossed them in the garbage.

Yes, well, neither have you, Bert.

"I'm not the lead detective on this. Silliker is in charge. If you have anything to say, you've got to say it to him. Do you want me to call him?"

I looked at him as if he'd just said the stupidest thing in the world.

"I thought so. I guess I'll see you in court. Good luck."

A gang of cops wielding machine guns had arrested my father. A case of overkill if ever there was one.

When Tommy got out of the hospital, I learned that his trouble began when he braked at a light to let a woman cross the street. A cop car pulled up beside him and fired a bullet at his head. Tommy took the bullet in his outstretched arm and fell to the floor. Thinking quickly, he rubbed blood on his face and played dead, which is what I'd heard over the radio. Dead, not dead.

In time, I also learned something else. Because the cops correctly figured out that we were up to something, they had disabled Dwane's bike the night before the job.

I hate being outsmarted.

MOMENTS IN THE
LIFE AND TIMES
OF RICKY ATKINSON

Dwane, Russell and me with Martha Polnik, my maternal grandmother. 1970.

My father, Sonny Atkinson, and my mother, Anne Andruschuk. 1954.

After my paternal grandfather's funeral: his wife (centre) surrounded by 14 of my aunts and uncles, in front of their house in the projects. Circa 1977.

My first three-day pass, out from
Frontenac Institution. I'm best man at
Dwane's wedding in August, 1975.

My uncles and cousins, all Commonwealth Boxing Council champions.
Promoter Irv Ungerman is seated beside Clyde Gray, after his title win in November, 1979.

With Ronnie Ward (Mad Dog) at Millhaven Institution, the day after he fought a younger guy with a knife, in the yard . One never knows when your life might abruptly end while in prison. 1988.

At a Prison Social event, Mission Institution. My daughter, Jennifer, visits from Toronto. We enjoy games of chess. 2009.

Joyceville Institution, 1993. Guns and crime are replaced by creative endeavours in stained glass, pottery, and the sweet science of boxing.

With Sonny after his appearance on the *Contact Show* for which he brought 10 kids to Joyceville Institution. 1995.

My first birthday out of prison after eight years. Restrictions were so tight I had to celebrate with Brian Judge, co-producer of the *Contact Show*. 1996.

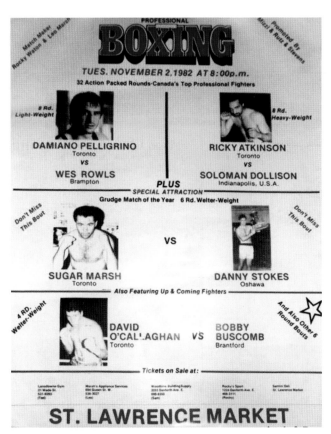

Headlining the card: Ricky Atkinson vs. Soloman Dollison. 1982

With George Chuvalo. 2014.

With Angela, Christmas at Bath Institution in 2003. It was a short four-hour visit before she left for Vancouver. A few months later I was transferred to Mission Institution (British Columbia), and six years later I was released.

With Angela, after arriving from Toronto to Vancouver, 30 days prior to her diagnosis of terminal cancer in 2013. She died one year later.

In Memory of

Angela Casey/Mezzacappa

November 15th 1950 – October 29th 2014

IN AND OUT, OUT AND IN

Once again I found myself on a bunk at the West Detention Centre. I called Diane. My daughter picked up and said, "Daddy, come home." That was a heartbreaker. I told her I couldn't come home because I was behind the fence.

She knew what that meant. Ever her father's daughter, she came up with an instant plan.

"Daddy, you climb the fence and Mommy and I will come to get you and we'll run away together."

I thought my heart would stop.

I had failed her and I knew it.

When Diane took the phone she told me that my big Doberman had been seized at the warehouse. There was no way the cops would get a word out of him.

And then she told me she was pregnant again.

Everything was more serious now. That seemed to be the constant in my life; always more serious, higher scores, higher stakes, greater risk, no matter what it was.

We were escorted back and forth to court by cops with machine guns and the newspapers had a field day with the Dirty Tricks Gang. Everyone inside knew we were facing hard time. They all gave us lots of room and respect, although some of the newcomers – the ones doing short bits – didn't get it.

There were fights. We won fights.

Prison, like anything else, is an opportunity for teaching and learning. I took one of the new guys aside, because I knew his brother from Joyceville. He felt he could muscle anyone he wanted without a thought for the future. He brushed me off. He should have listened. He was sent to Millhaven and he was there for a grand total of six hours, four of them dead, before they found his body.

Another of the inmates, a West Indian, stopped me on the range and demanded a cigarette. I was lost in thought – courts, Diane, lawyers. I told him to take a hike.

"Man, when me ask for de smoke, you fetch it up."

I clipped him on the jaw. He was shocked, and looked to his crew. They were smarter than he was. They just stared. I said, "Fuck off, or I'll kill you."

"Man, you no kill me. You go jail a long time."

One of his guys explained. "He don't care. He's facing thirty or more." My poor sap sucked his teeth and said, "Thirty nothing, man. He do twelve months."

His crew wised him up. "That's thirty years, asshole." The sap got it then, and it hit him funny. His eyes bugged out, he snapped his fingers and jumped up and down.

"Blood clot', man; me kill myself, do so much time. Why, man, why?" Why indeed.

Maybe he really wanted an answer because after that he followed me like a puppy, wanting to know what I thought about what would happen to him; after all, he'd been pinched with a couple of joints.

The province assigned Crown attorney Glen Orr to our case. Orr was tall and gangly, like a farm boy. In court, he had a habit of pulling on his suspenders and leaning back when he talked, drawing laughs in court with his homespun humour, even though he always asked for maximum sentences. He was formidable, even for our high-priced, court-savvy team.

They may have called us the Dirty Tricks Gang, but the cops had a few tricks of their own. They slipped undercover cops onto the range, into the court cells and even the paddy wagon. That shit didn't fool us. They also bugged our cells, and we had to be careful because prison was full of rats who'd stoop to anything in order to catch a break.

Speaking of rats, it wasn't long before I ran into Bobby Marsh. He'd risen to the position of president of the Toronto chapter of the Outlaws motorcycle gang.

In a touching display of something, one of the guards took me aside and told me that Bobby was talking to the cops; his testimony ended up convicting eighty Outlaw bikers. He even set up his own brother.

I kept my distance.

After four months of remands and court dates, we found ourselves before Judge Cecil John "One Day" Cannon. He had a reputation for moderate sentencing. I thought I'd seize the moment with a little improvisation.

"Your Honour, I'd like to plead guilty to all my charges."

The cops and the farm-boy Crown attorney went into a frenzy of huddles and hot discussion. Orr stuck his head up and said, "Your Honour, he can't do that." All the cops, sensing some sort of ruse, nodded furiously.

"Really?" said Cannon.

He turned to me and said, "Mr. Atkinson, have you been coerced, threatened or promised anything in return for your guilty plea?"

"No, Your Honour."

"Then I accept your plea."

There was a sudden rush of cops making calls, lawyers running up to the prisoner's box to whisper with their clients, families scratching their heads and wondering what was going on. The others must have figured I was onto something, because one after another they pleaded guilty too.

My boldness was rewarded when the date the judge set for sentencing just happened to be my daughter's birthday.

I figured I'd do okay. Although as the sixth guy, I was nowhere near the actual robbery. I faced the full weight of that charge because I played a role in the event and had a history of robbery and breaks and enters. The gun wasn't mine. It had been tossed in the van after the fact, but I was charged with both possession and use of an unregistered prohibited firearm.

Here you should know that the detective who planted that gun went on to rise high in the ranks. He'd sue me if I mentioned him by name. But he broke the law, and he conspired with the others to gun Tommy down.

He knows who he is.

On the day of sentencing, I decided to throw another curve ball. I was so ticked off about the planted gun that I told my lawyers I'd changed my mind about that charge and I wouldn't plead it out.

I was persuaded not to. My lawyers were tired of the judicial circus that was in play, including armed security who harassed anyone on our defence team. I figured one illegally placed gun wouldn't mean much in view of my impending double-digit sentence. I would regret my decision not to fight that gun charge shortly afterward.

Just before things started, Bert Novis shocked everyone in court when he walked over, shook my hand and wished me good luck. He must have known something.

Here's how it played out: Andy Ferguson, who had pleaded guilty to a crime he'd had nothing to do with, got six years.

Bump got six years, plus one more for a gun planted by the cop who shot Tommy.

Tommy, whose shattered arm was still in a sling, got eight years. On top of that, he had to listen to the judge praise the cops who shot him because they had saved the citizens of the city, blah, blah. All this blather, in spite of the fact that the gun had no bullets. However, now the gun was in court, and now it was loaded, which meant he got an additional year.

Dwane, acknowledged as a lookout, got six years.

I got twelve plus one.

Some luck.

I also got a shock in the morning when I read the *Toronto Star*. It was reported that the gun planted in the van had been stolen from a store on Yonge Street fifteen years earlier by Johnny Bayliss. The cops said the gun had been used to kill a York Region constable named Douglas Tribbling, with the inference that I'd be charged for that as well. Thing is, Bayliss didn't steal the gun.

Owen and I stole it. It was the gold derringer I gave Johnny and his wife as a wedding gift.

Mind you, I had a rock-solid alibi for the shooting – when Tribbling was killed, I was doing time in Millhaven.

Before long, I was snatched, shackled, cuffed and whisked off to Whitby, where there was a special handling unit for the worst of the worst, i.e., guys like me.

Meanwhile, the cops went around picking up anyone they could think of, trying to get someone who was willing to tie me to the murder. In aid of that effort, one of my cousins, the one we called Mad Dog, had his hair set on fire by cops who took him to Cherry Beach and tried to beat and burn him into telling them that I'd told him that I killed the cop.

I'm not making this shit up.

Eventually Diane and my mother were allowed to visit. I got one of the guards to pass my mother the document stating that I was in a Provincial Special Handling Unit.

This is sad knowledge but my mother knew what your mother does not: you can't put a federal parolee in a SHU without a special board determination that certain restrictions are warranted. My mother called the head of provincial prisons and said that there would be a lawsuit if I was not removed from the SHU. Two days later, the Ontario Provincial Police gave me a free ride to my next stop.

Millhaven, ho hum, been there, done that. Not exactly, but the place was familiar to me. I knew I'd be mixing with the general population within the week. It happened faster than that. The day after my arrival, I was greeted by a fellow with a big smile on his face.

I remembered the last time I'd seen Detroit hit man, John Hogan.

Owen and I had been tipped off about a score at a party house where there was a lot of hash and cash. We got the address with the help of a little torture applied to a pusher we knew. I slid a ski mask over my face and pulled out my 9 mm. Browning. Owen, armed with a .38 and a meat cleaver, stood behind me as I knocked on the door.

When the door opened a crack, Owen pushed me through. I grabbed John, pressed my gun to his head and hissed that if he moved he was dead.

I frisked him quickly, taking his gun and pushing him into the room where the party was. Over the loud music and distracted laughter, I yelled out to the assembled, "Shut the fuck up or he dies."

That got everyone's attention.

I could hear movement in one of the bedrooms. People were hiding dope or finding guns. I couldn't tell.

"Everyone out of the bedroom now!"

Owen covered the room as bikers came out in various stages of undress, accompanied by two attractive naked women, all of them with their hands over their heads.

In all, there were some twenty guys in the apartment. It occurred to me that I knew them all, either from Millhaven or from the street.

They recognized Owen right away. He wasn't wearing a mask. Me, they knew because I was with Owen, and I was big. Who the fuck else could it be?

What would you have done? I let John Hogan go and handed him his gun with a disarming smile. Biker Big Bobby B. was six-feet-four and built to last. He came over to me and said casually, "Ricky, what brings you here?"

As if it was a social call.

I said that I was going to rip them off until I saw who they were, so out of respect I called it off. I also gave him a useful piece of information about the runner who gave him up.

No harm done. Big Bobby gave me a chunk of hash and a drink. The party picked up as if it hadn't stopped; turns out the party was for a friend who'd just got out of the Haven.

I shook that guy's hand.

Bobby asked me to stay but I was too hyped to relax, and I could tell that the doorman wasn't too happy. So we left.

But John was standing right in front of me, smiling now.

By this time, Dwane and the others had been moved along to the Bay. I was classified for the Super Max and was in the general population the next day. I knew a guy there, a bank robber named Jeff Mitchell. He pulled some strings to get me onto 2-B range, which was loaded with all sorts of high-profile prisoners, guys I knew well or respected. It was just the place for me. I settled in and started to relax for what looked like a long thirteen years.

Jeff and I bonded, in a way. Every night, no matter the weather, he and I would walk the yard and shoot the shit. Sometimes we were the only ones foolish enough to brave the rain and snow or the packs of convicts looking for trouble.

Diane came up to see me, carrying my new baby boy in her arms. I was lucky to have visitor privileges – not everyone did. Millhaven had family units where you could spend as much as three days away from the prison population.

A few months after one of those visits, my classification officer passed along word that Diane was pregnant again. In eight months, I had a gorgeous daughter, Jennifer. We named her after my mother's sister.

One of the first to congratulate me was Bill Dendy, who was on the Citizens' Advisory Committee. The CAC started a couple of years earlier after a guard had killed a convict. Its role was to monitor guards and inmates and act as a kind of liaison.

Bill kept me up to date on the politics of the prison and suggested I run for one of the inmate committees. We knew that was a way, maybe the only way, to a lower security prison. If you could demonstrate a little maturity and take a little responsibility they might lower your classification from, say, max to medium and that in turn would significantly improve your living conditions on the inside.

It was a plan.

Here's something you may not know about prison life, because it isn't really talked about. In several of the places I was inside, guys asked me how much I'd charge for killing them.

Why? A guy might be too damn tired to see his sentence out; maybe he doesn't want to hit the fence and take death by copper; maybe he doesn't want to fuck with the rock, whoever that might be.

The going rate?

One guy offered me his television, which I could auction at bingo. He was a creepy little Vietnamese guy, very bad; no one liked him. I turned him, and all the others, down.

Most guys, when they get desperate, take care of the matter themselves. One day Carl Hines tapped on my door and asked if he could come in. Carl had been a friend of my father's; he'd been my baby-sitter a couple of times when I was a kid.

"I'm out of here in an hour."

He was saying goodbye – the long goodbye. Carl was accompanied by Mad Dog – not my crazy, hair-setting-on-fire cousin, but another friend of my father's, and Carl's best friend inside. I turned to him. He shrugged sadly.

"Done deal," he said.

A little while later, Mad Dog whispered through the bars that Carl was dead. There is an emergency button in each cell. I hit mine and the guard in the security bubble hit a button of his own, opening my door. I went and looked in Carl's cell.

He was hanging from a rope attached to the bars in his window. There was nothing we could do. We left him hanging there and said nothing –to give the rest of the inmates a chance to pass by and pay their respects before the next security check.

The lockdown after a riot? Several days. The lockdown after a killing? Days. The lockdown after a suicide? A couple of hours.

Time slipped by, and by now you already know how I made time work for me. I minded my own business and I took care of myself as best I could.

One day Mitchell, whose lawyer was also my lawyer, came back from court with news – he'd heard there were more charges coming my way. I assumed it was for the cop killing. I wasn't worried, at least I wasn't worried until I heard that there was talk of some sort of super trial in the works and that the high court was being readied to accommodate a large number of prisoners, probably my crew.

Still, I was puzzled. Nothing made sense, unless someone had ratted us out. Weeks passed and the rumours were gathering like storm clouds. To make matters even worse, one or two guards mentioned that they knew the dead cop. He'd been their friend.

I made some calls, and the next day there was a full-page article about the dead cop in the *Toronto Star*. The piece ended by noting that the man suspected of shooting him, i.e., me, had been in jail at the time.

At least that was out of the way.

A couple of days later I heard the sound of helicopters. It was rare that anything flew near prisons. In those days, the guards would surely have shot at anyone bent on intruding from above. Suddenly there were all these cops with machine guns. The joint was locked down, and I was taken to administration.

The warden said, "Richard, this is very unusual."

Well, yeah, it was. But not for me, I always got special treatment. A convoy of cop cars and vans sat outside the gate and there, in the midst of fifty coppers, was my old nemesis, Bert Novis, puffing smugly on a fat cigar.

The whole gang of us were shackled, loaded up and shipped off like wildebeests straight to the bullpen at Toronto's Old City Hall, where we were guarded by more cops with machine guns. Nothing like this had happened since the Boyd Gang.

Everyone asked me what was going on? I remembered the old Sherlock Holmes calculation – if you eliminate all other possibilities, what remains is the answer.

"Who's not here?"

Answer: Carrie Burke.

We were prodded into the prisoner's box. Everyone was there in court – Diane, the rest of the girlfriends, Dwane's wife and all of the lawyers involved.

"I feel like the safest person in the city; every police officer seems to be in this room," offered the judge. "I hope the citizens of Toronto have someone out there to protect them." Ha, ha, what a joker.

Glen Orr stood up, stuck his thumbs under his suspenders and said, "Your Honour, when the wolves are in their cages, the lambs of the city are safe in their mangers."

Oh, clever. But not so clever that any of the assembled worthies could figure out how to start such complicated proceedings with so many individual cases.

I've been around that block.

I stood up and said, "Your Honour, firstly, I would like to know what I'm charged with and secondly, I'd like to waive my right to a bail hearing, as will all my co-accused, with the exception of Jimmy Leblanc, who is not serving a sentence at this time."

The judge took a breath and said, "At least someone in this courtroom is thinking clearly."

Orr was still at the movies. He walked over to the prisoner's box and slammed a thick book on the table in front of me. The noise of it jolted the crowd.

"These are the charges against you, Richard Atkinson."

The scribes started scribbling. The book contained 313 charges, all of them robbery-related.

And so began a round of trips from jail to court and back again, always in the company of a caravan of cops with machine guns. Depending on the length of the proceedings, I might be held over in the Don Jail. Every time that happened I had to lobby to get back to Millhaven where, in the interim, I could visit with Diane and play with my kids.

Millhaven was bad, but at least I didn't have to deal with the strutting and the bullshit from the short-timers.

If there was a bonus of any kind, it is that conditions at the Don were now so bad that every day spent there meant time taken off your sentence.

A lot of guys couldn't handle being cooped up in the misery of the Don, so they copped to big beefs just to get the hell out of there.

Mostly, while there, I was kept in the hole. I was a particular hassle for the warden, because any time I was moved out of the building, the Task Force took over control of me inside his jail. It meant the joint was put on lockdown and the warden's precious routine was disturbed.

At Millhaven, I helped organize the prison's first kids' day social – it was a big deal, with everyone involved. We raised money for a clown, and for a pony for the kids to ride, and we figured out some games and so on.

It was looking good until one day while in transit, one of my co-accused did something stupid and caused a guard to point his weapon; this was deemed so dangerous that the drivers refused to take us back and forth to Millhaven. I was going to miss the social I'd worked so hard for, and miss a chance to play with my kids.

I am a man of fairly even temperament, but this sort of nonsense is simply mean-spirited and soul-destroying. They parked me in the East Detention Centre.

When faced with a problem, you solve it with the tools at hand, no matter what they are. So, I went on a hunger strike.

Hunger strikes aren't easy.

Each day the guards left a tray of food in my meal slot and it took every bit of will I had to resist until the food was taken away. I took three Styrofoam cups and glued them to the wall of my cell with toothpaste. I made spit balls out of writing paper and used them to mark the passage of time.

Three cups, because I knew I had three weeks of starvation before organ damage set in. After one week, I got a visit from the jail's psychologist. After two weeks a senior regional psychologist came along, with prison officials from outside the jail for good measure. The stakes were high. Higher for me than for them.

Then came a crowd of doctors, nurses, administrators, guards and the warden, assessing me like I was some creature in a cage, which I suppose I was.

The psychiatrist opened with a question: "Are you trying to blackmail us just to get out of here and back to Millhaven?"

This was not your usual psychiatric bullshit; straight, simple and to the point. I gave him the answer I'd been rehearsing in my head.

"I'm facing an unprecedented 313 charges related to bank robberies. The Crown said he wanted three years on each charge. If I'm convicted, that gives me over 900 years of federal time. I doubt, with my attitude and with my record, that I'll make parole, so that means at least 600 inside one of these holes. Ask yourself if I really give a shit about dying today or tomorrow. I just want to hold my son in my arms. I have no choice but to go all out, all the time, even if it means hurting myself. Or any one of you." They looked at me as if I were a mixture of toxic chemicals ready to explode at any moment.

An official from the government said, "Does anyone have anything to add?"

The warden said, "He's not going to control my jail. I don't care what he does."

Then the head nurse spoke. "I've known this man for several years. He's very disciplined. He often fasts and meditates, sometimes for days on end. He behaves himself unless provoked. I believe he will stick to his convictions."

The warden huffed a bit. "He's still not running my jail."

There was some silence. Then they turned, almost as one, and left me alone.

I was about to say they left me in my pain and misery, but the thing about a hunger strike is that only the first week is painful. After that, peace of mind sets in and the pain seems to go away.

Two hours passed, more or less. This time, the mob of guards sent to attend me was smaller and one of them carried a tray with juice and cereal.

"Eat this and tomorrow morning, you go back to Millhaven." I knew this guard as a straight shooter. He'd been a beat cop on Spadina.

They all watched me eat.

The next morning, I had a ride in an armed convoy, which dropped me off at Millhaven. A week later, I was playing with my son during the kids' day social.

A few days later, I was sitting around with the other committee reps when a young native prisoner approached and asked what would happen if he punched out the warden.

The question came as no surprise. The warden, Rémi Gobeil, was equal in his approach to both guards and inmates: everyone hated his guts.

He liked to creep around the prison in his off-hours, spying on his guards who might have been napping or playing cards in one of the control bubbles. Rumour had it that he'd park outside the gates and watch to see if the perimeter checks were being made on schedule. He berated guards if their uniforms were sloppy, docking their pay if they appeared without a hat or tie, or if their shoes were scuffed.

The native prisoner, Randy Charbonneau, had simply had enough, having been jacked up and sent to the hole for infractions as insidious as an untied shoelace.

I said I'd never heard of it happening before, but we all knew that if you struck a guard you'd get your ass beaten by that guard and others. It also meant another year or two tacked onto your sentence. Thumping a warden was probably worse.

I'm not saying we were talking to the warden on purpose but, as luck would have it, Billy McAllister and I were doing just that one day when Randy walked by us. The warden barked at him to stop.

Billy and I stepped back.

Then Randy was all over the warden, throwing punches hard and so fast that Gobeil took half a dozen shots to the head before he began trying to fight back.

I looked up to the guard towers in time to see the slots fly open; firearms pointed at the combatants. One of the senior uniformed staff looked up and shook his head.

The rifles disappeared.

The guards intervened, grabbing Randy roughly and cuffing him while the warden stood there, bleeding from the nose.

As Randy passed in front of us on his way to the infirmary, he said loudly, "I want the committee to escort me to the hole." That was one of the concessions we had won; it was a way to prevent gratuitous beatings.

A little platoon, then: Billy and I, six guards, a nurse and Randy shuffling off to the hole. The keeper whispered in my ear, "Who pays for this guy's steak dinner, the committee or our union?"

The warden vowed to extract revenge even as guys lined up, one after another, dropping off smokes and goodie bags for us to give to Randy while he was in the hole.

And then I got a bit of information: someone said that one of my crew, Franz, had called Carrie and told him that I'd given permission to kill his family. The cops listened in and they jumped on the chance to bust Carrie's father for stolen video machines. They threatened to put him in the same cell as Franz.

Carrie had been a loyal soldier for years, but he believed that the tape changed things, so he rolled over into Witness Protection. He not only sang about crimes he'd done with me, but he lied about other crimes in order to help the cops manipulate the courts. Things were crumbling fast.

I repeat: that's life in a gang. You never know when someone's going to roll over. It's the joy of working with a brother, and the horror of a rat's betrayal.

If it's true that the only way three can keep a secret is if two are dead, then I know there are criminals who will kill their partners when the time is right in order to stay safe. I examined my co-accused one by one.

There was more going on than just Carrie.

I couldn't figure it out.

A second rat?

Franz began getting on everyone's bad side. He pulled a blade on Andy. Andy sucker-punched him and snatched the knife. I had to put a stop to the bullshit, all the internal strife. Somehow, the next day, Franz ended up in protective custody getting his jaw, his arm and his ribs repaired.

A preliminary hearing is generally a quiet affair. The Crown, in its typically methodical manner, presents what it considers to be sufficient evidence to show that its case is solid enough to go to trial. The defence makes arguments and leads challenges. This preliminary hearing, however, was something to see.

Any case involving multiple defendants and hundreds of charges is bound to have an elevated judicial profile and bring out the heavy artillery. Indeed, the courtroom was packed, and behind the judge's chair there was a cop with a machine gun who stared at me as if I'd eaten his breakfast before he'd gotten out of bed. Then the doors of the court flew open, and I knew the summer of 1988 was going to be more than long and hot.

My cousin Mad Dog, the one who'd had his hair set on fire, was escorted to the front and sworn in. For an entire week, I had to sit still and listen to him testify, in excruciating detail, about crimes he'd never committed, about people he'd never worked with, and money he was paid that he sure as hell never got from me.

In the middle of one of his stories, Andy noticed a cop flashing signals to Mad Dog, as if to help him remember certain things.

Andy spoke up: "Your Honour, if you play baseball at all, you will get a kick out of the signals that shithead over there is giving to the rat on the stand."

Judge Kerr looked around and threatened that anyone caught flashing signs would spend the afternoon locked up in the court cells with us.

The papers had a lurid field day reporting how Mad Dog had stabbed his mother, stabbed his father, kicked the baby out of his sister's stomach, cut a guy's toes off with a pair of hedge trimmers, and bit the toe off Dolores in a fight.

Allow me to clarify: Dolores was Jerry Patterson's drag queen brother, and I don't know about his toes but the rest of him looked like Mike Tyson in a miniskirt.

Mad Dog mentioned setting fire to buildings, cutting people for no reason, and he told the judge that he'd even stabbed himself at the Paramount during a fight with his girlfriend.

The judge was right to ask him why he'd done such a thing.

"I had to stab someone, Your Honour,' Mad Dog told the court. "I didn't want to stab her so I shoved the knife in my own belly, to ease the pain." And of course, he also told the court of the time the cops had set his hair on fire, while trying to get him to admit I'd killed one of their own.

The reason Mad Dog turned rat was to get out from under a robbery beef. He held up my cousin Merle's girlfriend. That put him in shit with his wife. The cops said they'd put him in my cell at the Don, so he asked for Witness Protection. He was willing to turn on his family in order to save his marriage.

Thing is, he was my cousin. I'd put up my house to bail him out, and Diane was the one who picked him up and drove him to the government offices on University Avenue, where he signed his little deal with the devil.

I will not attempt to describe how I felt.

Ian Scott, the Ontario Attorney General, brushed off reporters who asked him why the government would make a deal with such a man. Eddie Greenspan, the best lawyer in the country, asked who was worse – a gang that never hurt anyone or an informant who hurt many?

Scott's response?

"We put away a criminal genius who was running the most sophisti-cated gang in the country. We think it was a fair trade."

Our lawyers were confident that they could knock Carrie and Mad Dog off the stand. And then Mad Dog – only his mother called him David – stood up, pointed at me and cried out, "I'm a walking dead man."

Judge Kerr asked, calmly, what made him think that was so.

"I know for sure that man has put a hit on me," Mad Dog told the court. "I'll be dead in two years."

I hadn't put a hit on him but at that moment, if I could have, I'd have thrust my fingers through his eyes and into his brain.

Not that it would have done any good – if you testify at a preliminary hearing and die before trial, your testimony still stands.

Mad Dog's mother joined the hysteria. "My son's a dead man! My son's a dead man!" She fell to the floor, sobbing, causing Mad Dog to exclaim, "I love you, Ma!"

My cousin Cecil and my aunt Flo rushed to Mad Dog's mother and picked her up off the floor. All the lawyers in the room figured that the outburst was the result of coaching by Glen Orr – pretty smart for a country boy.

My lawyer leaned over and said, "If she puts that act on in court, in front of a jury, your ass is cooked. No jury would believe a son would put his mother through all that agony for $1,250 a month in Witness Protection payments."

There were other tricks besides the theatrical. One day a woman came into court and – before she was sworn in – she started counting all of us in the prisoner's box.

She was counting out loud, which I found curious.

Finally she pointed to Johnny Bayliss and said in a thick, Eastern-European accent, "That's the one, the dark one, he's the one who robbed me."

Judge Kerr swore her in, and when she was on the witness stand he asked her why she'd been counting. She wasn't too bright, but she was honest. She said she didn't know the robber, but the police had told her to pick out the seventh guy, the dark one. The judge very nearly leapt off the bench and ordered her to find the cop who told her that.

She returned a few minutes later, looking confused and scared. She told Kerr that she couldn't find him. On hearing that, the judge instructed us to change positions in the prisoner's box any time we felt like it. His demeanour changed so dramatically that Orr suggested he was acting for the defence. And so, we played musical chairs any time we felt like it.

Here's what was put on the table – forty years for the others, and sixty years for me, with a minimum of seven years inside. All in all, it was the longest sentence anyone had ever received for a bank robbery.

I advised my lawyer to tell them all to take a hike.

They came back with a deal – forty years for me, and thirty for the others. Again, I told my lawyer to tell them to fuck off.

They came back offering thirty and twenty years, as if this was some kind of reverse auction.

I didn't bother to respond, so they threatened me – if I didn't take a deal, they really would come at me full-bore, seeking three years for every single charge, or 939 years in jail.

The absurdity of this hit home, but I didn't waver.

In the end, it was suggested that I plead guilty to twenty charges for a total of twenty-five years. To sweeten the deal, they'd give my brother twelve years, and less for the others.

The system works in mysterious ways. My lawyer passed me a hand-written note from another Superior Court judge. It read: "Rick, you have a friend in the building; seek mercy, not justice. There is no justice for you. Please eat this note."

I chewed it, and I chewed things over.

I have known Brink's bandits who shot people and got shorter time. I also knew that if I fought back, there was a good chance I'd rot in prison for the rest of my life.

After a night's reflection, I told my lawyer if they agreed not to oppose my parole when it came due, I would take the deal. The next day Superior Court judge Hugh Locke thanked me for saving the province millions in legal costs, but he chastised me for wasting what he called my intelligence, my leadership ability and my organizational skills on crime. He said I could have run a Fortune 500 company if I'd applied myself differently.

He was right, of course.

He sentenced me to twenty-five years and wished me luck. Luck had nothing, and everything, to do with it. Ever since, I've wondered if that note was a trick played by the cops.

The next day I was back in Millhaven with eight of my crew, each of us looking to our own futures.

I promised myself I'd never do another robbery again.

The Dirty Tricks Gang was no more.

There's no point doing nothing.

This time, I concentrated my jail time on religious studies, passing the Salvation Army's correspondence course in record time with the highest marks in anyone's memory.

I passed another course equally quickly, and then took a religious studies course offered by Western University. Why religion? I enjoy history, and I knew a bit about the power that cult leaders enjoy. What is a cult if not a gang?

I put in for a transfer to Joyceville so that I could be with Billy McAllister. They turned me down, saying that there was an "incompatible" in Joyceville. An incompatible is someone you'd fought with, someone the administration presumed you'd try to hurt, or someone who'd ratted you out.

The prison rat population was growing exponentially.

I was curious. As with everything, the system could be gamed. Once, when I was in the Bath Institution, a young Jamaican prisoner approached and said, "I want to tell you this before someone else does. This is my first time in the adult system and I got your name from a list floating around reception in Millhaven. I asked my classification officer to send me to minimum security because you were going to kill me over a drug debt from the Don Jail."

I asked him why he'd do such a thing. He said, "I was scared to come here. I thought I could pimp my classification officer to get into a lower security."

Why didn't it work?

"My classification officer said you had two relatives in the same range I was on, and if you really wanted to get me, it would have happened already. She called me a liar and sent me here."

What this kid told me filled me with unease, to think that others for their own benefit, and without my knowledge, were using my name.

I asked Bill Dendy from the CAC to check with my cousins in Joyceville, to find out who the incompatible was. Turns out my cousin Merle was there. He told the warden at Joyceville about how he'd ratted out Mad Dog, and he thought I might want to get him for that. I was shocked, but Merle wasn't the only one who knew how to pimp a prison official.

I wrote a letter to Merle, and sent copies to the warden and the head of security. I thanked him for ratting out Mad Dog, and told him I wished he could have come to our trial so that he might have shed some light on Mad Dog's viciousness. I signed off, calling him a friend and a relative, and telling him he had nothing to fear from me or my crew.

Merle was released not long after that. People who didn't like him very much chased him out of Toronto. He headed for Vancouver, where he wound up dead on a highway with a needle stuck in his arm.

Life goes on. I turned my attention to boxing lessons, committee work and making stained-glass items that I traded as a way of getting my children into Christian summer camp programs.

CONTACT

Billy McAllister had a bright idea.

He wanted to create a crime forum filled with lifers from Joyceville, along with judges, lawyers, criminologists, religious leaders and politicians, in order to talk about all the issues associated with crime and punishment. I was the committee chair, so he and I worked closely on this.

Reaction spread fast when the media found out. It got as far as late-night talk show host Arsenio Hall, who told jokes about it on his CBS network TV show. Ottawa's reaction was to shut us down.

Then a local reporter, Brian Judge, came to Joyceville and asked us to air our concerns on his television show.

This was something new.

Warden Jim Blackler thought that television might help dispel some of the misconceptions people had about prison life; he gave permission for cameras to film inside, and so began the first prison reality TV show.

Our first cameraman was Brian Smith; we called him Smitty, not very original. He was a Newfoundlander, cheerful and easy-going, doing a life-ten sentence for killing his best friend. I didn't ask why. It didn't matter

One of the network news shows came into Joyceville to do a piece on his case, and it looked like there was a chance his conviction would be overturned. During the taping, Smitty was diagnosed with lung cancer and given six months to live.

A sad story, how this thing works – if you maintain your innocence, your parole will be hindered; as a result, very few guys defend themselves for long. But Smitty never wavered. His cancer was his parole; they sent him home to die in Newfoundland, surrounded by his family.

I became more involved with Brian's show, which we called *Contact*. Turns out I was a natural at production, which required similar skills to those I'd used robbing banks – all that organization, all that planning, all those little details.

As I have learned, and as I continue to learn, things tend to be connected. My father was often in the news because he had taken it upon himself to clean up Alexandra Park.

He organized a bunch of fearless senior citizens and they went up against all the known crack dealers, asking the dealers to close up shop voluntarily, or be harassed out of business by the community.

Sonny was one of the toughest men in the city, but he was up against a group of young gunslingers who saw him as old, and who didn't know that his son was a mobster.

I got in touch and asked Sonny what he thought about bringing a group of Project kids into the prison to meet some of the inmates so that we could talk some sense into them.

Warden Blackler also thought it was a good idea so he called Sonny and they worked it out so that ten teens from Alexandra Park could come.

We called that program "Choices and Consequences."

One of the guys I asked to speak was a fighter I had trained. BamBam was gifted, and could have made millions in the ring. He was from Regent Park, but he knew my father well enough in his own way. He had been hustling dope in the Projects one day when Sonny and his crew of anti-dope crusaders confronted him.

"Your dad said that if I showed up in the 'hood the next day he was going to whack me with a stick," BamBam told me. "I laughed it off but the next day when I was there, doing my thing, he walked up to me and, without saying a word, he hit me on the head. Here I was, running down the street with my 9 mm. in one hand and a bag of dope in the other, trying to get away from a gang of old folks." One of them had a stick in his hand.

I asked him why he didn't shoot my father. He said, "How long would I have lived once I walked into this jail?"

"You'd be already dead."

BamBam eventually left prison. He left boxing and went into the computer business, where he made ten times the money he'd been earning hustling dope.

A lesson there.

Here's another: for Sonny, cleaning things up was personal. After my crew moved out of the neighbourhood, a younger generation moved in, drug dealers, for the most part. I think there were thirty-two crack houses in Alexandra Park at the time.

It was not pretty. People were breaking into cars to shoot up, and if you're stoned you're not always careful with your works. The result? My sister got into a car once, and she sat on a syringe. It poked her. As a result, she had to have an AIDS test, and all the other tests you'd take if you were stuck with a dirty needle.

That was it for Sonny.

He didn't want his daughter, or his grandson, to have to deal with that so he just said, "We've gotta get these dopeheads out."

The reason he was successful is that much of the criminal element in the neighbourhood was family, his family. Or else they were connected somehow to the family. The former drill sergeant was the patriarch of the clan and everyone, family or not, knew that Sonny a tough guy.

If he had another reason, it was that he wanted what had been promised to him, and to the rest of us when the neighbourhood was built – he wanted peace and harmony. He was fearless, he was smart, and he had a simple message: You don't fight with the people you have to live with.

Also, blood is thicker than water.

Another man I lined up for the show was Tim Bissonette, who ran a program raising money from prisoners for the Children's Wish Foundation. He was a consummate hustler who had spent time in Vegas. His cell was lined with pictures of celebrities, and he had a host of stories about Frank Sinatra, Liberace, Tony Curtis and others.

He was on top of the world until, in a moment of blinding anger over a deal gone sour, he shot and killed his best friend at a miners' convention at the Royal York Hotel in Toronto. He was sixty-five years old when he was charged with murder. That's a good story to tell kids who have trouble with impulse control.

Meanwhile, I was doing my time as well as I could until Diane, in the way these things go, decided she'd had enough. She was woman enough not to keep me from my kids, so I owe her that much at least.

But I am not the sort of man who can live easily without a woman. I wrote to Sharon, the beauty I'd seen when I took my first pinch at age seventeen. I'd never really been able to get her off my mind. She came for a visit, bringing her six-year old daughter Kristin. As time went by, I began to think of myself as a kind of stepfather and came to adore her as much as I did my own kids.

It's funny, but in a way I was living better in prison than most guys were on the outside: I had a TV show, I was the committee chairman, I spent my nights on my hobbies, I ate well enough, and I was hanging out with my brother and four of my cousins. And, after six months of visits, Sharon and I decided to get married.

The wedding took place on the outside.

One of our escorts was Dave Page, the former head of the SHU in Millhaven, and now head of security at Joyceville. He pulled me aside and said, "I'll be watching you like a starving hawk. Anything suspicious and you'll end up getting married in prison. You got me?" I got him.

It isn't just gangsters who have reputations to protect. Page was as hard-nosed as they come, and no way he was going to risk a paycheque on my account.

My best man was Ira Hussey, a rounder from the east end side of Toronto; he'd worked my corner at the Queen City boxing club. And of course my parents were there for the ceremony, and also my sister and my brother Russell. One of my gang pals, Skippy, showed up uninvited.

It was the first time I'd been outside in a decade.

After the ceremony, this unlikely band of celebrants attended a local restaurant, one that had been approved by Page. During the meal Sharon, a bit tipsy, stood up and mentioned how much rum was in the cake. Page smiled.

"No cake for you, boys."

At the end of the evening, Page and the other escorts pulled out their wallets to pay for what they ate. Just like old times Skippy hauled out a roll of bills and paid for everyone – except Sonny, who quietly refused.

I saw my mother kick him under the table, so that he wouldn't speak up and spoil the occasion. My father was a principled man, and Skippy was at the top of his list of bad guys. No way Sonny was going to accept.

Page didn't know or suspect a thing. He unwittingly dined courtesy of a gangster; my little secret, until now.

Afterward, Sharon and I went back to the prison and spent three days in the conjugal trailers. Sadly, that was the best of it. We butted heads often when we were alone or on the phone. After a year of marriage we agreed it would be best if she left me for good. It still hurts me to remember the look on little Kristin's face when we told her.

I was eventually transferred to Bath Institute, a minimum-security camp next to Millhaven. From there, it was easy to leave in the company of Bill Dendy or Brian Judge, on escorted passes to Kingston. Cablenet, which is now CogecoTV, agreed to broadcasting the show.

The assistant warden, Dave McDonald, bent over backwards to make this work, which was risky for him. He was part of the old Millhaven mob, and by giving us a hand, he was risking a lot of shit from the other guards, none of whom were interested in helping prisoners.

Then I was asked by the John Howard group at Collins Bay if I would interview the former federal Solicitor General, Warren Allmand.

I couldn't get there fast enough.

I spent two decades thinking about the man who had hired Warren Hart to report on so-called black revolutionary groups so that his office would look good when they made the arrests.

I found myself sitting face to face with the person who had, in effect, tricked me into destroying my youth. I began by asking if he had heard the show. He said he had.

I didn't waste any time: I asked him about Warren Hart. He froze. There had been no pre-interview. He was not expecting this. Recovering quickly, he asked what I meant.

I explained my involvement as a teen with Hart and the Black Panthers. Allmand chose his next words carefully.

"Warren Hart was good for the Canadian government, but bad for Richard Atkinson."

The air went out of my sails.

I don't know what I'd been expecting; an acknowledgement, maybe, that as a result of his scheming I'd been duped as a young man and propelled down a course of terror that fouled up the rest of my life?

Fat chance.

Allmand was a professional politician. I was a professional in my trade as well, but there was nothing, especially not a TV interview, that was ever going to make things right.

Let me explain what was bad for Richard Atkinson from my point of view. The government hired Hart to infiltrate the black community. Hart found us. We weren't political radicals or revolutionaries, but we were a crew.

He turned us into terrorists.

He conned the government, and he warped us. Remember, we were just teenagers, full of sap and sass. He turned us into soldiers who knew how to plan, how to make bombs, and how to improvise destruction.

I am not joking here. One night Hart asked us, with our fresh young minds, how we might take out the Prime Minister. I didn't know this at the time, but he had a tape recorder and microphone hidden in his briefcase.

I said it would be possible with a small, remote-controlled airplane carrying twenty-five pounds of explosives. If the whine of the motor was a concern, then you could glide it in, and by the time anyone noticed, it would be too late. That's me, blue-skying, at age sixteen. I should have been thinking about track and basketball and girls. Instead, I was being turned into some kind of weapon.

Here's another thing to consider: suppose he'd had us act on that plan. Suppose we'd succeeded. Who'd have been complicit? Not just Hart, but Warren Allmand. And the government of Canada for that matter.

If I derived any satisfaction from the taping of the Allmand interview, it was in the filming itself. Two Dirty Tricksters, Jimmy LeBlanc and Tommy Musgrave, were working behind the lens. Instead of taking orders from me on robbing a bank, they now devoted their efforts to getting the perfect camera shot of the man who had set me up.

We were the first gang in the world to leave a prison, head for the office of the Commissioner of Prisons, bag an interview and head back to jail, where we were tucked in for the night.

There were other similar pleasures, especially the interview I did in Millhaven with Officer Springer. He was an old-school guard. Once, during a break in filming, he offered to get us coffee. The cameras was still rolling when he threatened me not to tell anyone he'd picked up coffee for a bunch of convicts.

He went on, feeling relaxed and expansive – the guard, letting his guard down. Eventually he bragged about cracking me on the head with his billy club when I was seventeen years old, on my first day in Millhaven.

I never used that admission against him, but his confession made me understand why I had such anger towards guards. Maybe that understanding brought me a small measure of peace.

The commute to the TV station was a privilege, of course, but over time the steps I had to go through became an annoyance. Brian Judge asked me if I could be transferred to the Frontenac farm camp, which would allow me the freedom to walk or take a bus to the station on my own with no escort.

I got the transfer and Warden Fred Sisson agreed to let me come and go, almost as I pleased. Sisson had been the senior in security at Warkworth when I was in my teens. He seemed friendlier now. He pulled me aside one day and said, jokingly, that he was about to retire to a town in Nova Scotia that was full of my relatives; he said he was staying on my good side because he didn't want his house burned down. No worries. Without men like Sisson there would have been no *Contact*.

The show also brought me back to Alexandra Park, where I returned one day to talk to kids about prison life. When I pulled up to the community centre, I was pleased to see that it had been named after my father. I was surprised to see the street jammed with reporters and television trucks.

Even CNN was there.

It gave the show, and my father's work, more exposure than we could have managed on our own.

As expected, a gang of cops from 14 Division stood at the back of the community centre, glaring at me and waiting for me to do or say something they could arrest me for.

I found out later that one of them approached my security escort and asked if he could shackle and cuff me, lest I escape.

I spoke to the kids about the horrors of prison life, and the need to think hard about the choices they would eventually have to make in life, so that their future choices wouldn't be taken from them after a rash moment of stupidity.

I hope some good came from that.

The show put me in touch with a lot of people I might not otherwise have met. It was also an opportunity to meet the heads of various groups such as BIFA, the Lifers groups and the Native Brotherhood, all of whom were allowed to visit other institutions for social or group functions.

That's how I came to meet women prisoners, and how I came to understand that the time they served was different than the time served by men.

The biggest difference for women doing time?

They tend to get dumped by their men a lot quicker than the other way around. Also, in some cases, men are able to beat their beefs because their women stand up and bear the brunt of the charges.

Listening to their stories certainly helped me understand my cousins Debbie and Joanne, who were doing time for bank robbery. The show was able to respond quickly when an issue came up that affected women in prison everywhere in Canada.

One night in the Kingston Prison for Women, a group of women in the hole went off, screaming and yelling at the guards the way men often do in the same situation. It was a normal incident in P4W until one of the girls tossed a cup of piss at one of the female guards. The warden responded by calling in an all-male Task Force.

Things went off the rails right from the start.

The Task Force snuck in at night, pounced on the sleeping women, tore their clothes off, searched them and cuffed them in their cells. They filmed all of this so that the tape could be used in evidence when the women were tried for assault against the officer who had the piss tossed at her.

After things settled down, the girls had the presence of mind to sue the Task Force, and Correctional Service, over the way they'd been treated. One of them, Joey Twins, offered us her disclosure – everything the prosecution had gathered as evidence to use against her – including the videotapes. The judge, viewing us as a media outlet like any other, gave us copies of the videotapes and we decided to do a show based on the incident.

We had a scoop.

Corrections Canada went into an immediate PR frenzy trying to cover their asses. The head of the Task Force wrote to say his unit would resign en masse if the show went to air. Brian and I also got threatening letters from the Auditor General, claiming that the government owned the tapes and that, if we broadcast them, we could be sued for copyright violation.

More seriously, it was hinted that if we went ahead I could be shipped across Canada to parts unknown.

Fred Sisson told me that Ottawa was breathing down his neck. He certainly had the power to stop me from using the P4W footage. I have a hunch he felt safe, given that he was so close to retirement, but I think he also knew that airing the truth was a good thing, even if it might cost him his job. He simply said, "My wife wants to know if I'll have a job after the show airs."

"Show airs at 8:00. Don't miss it."

Context? Today, inmate shows are everywhere but at the time we were the first. All eyes were on us, and there were daggers pointed at me from all sides. One wrong word and I could have been a dead man. Prisons were becoming insane asylums where inmates had a variety of weapons and guards didn't need a lot of provocation to shoot someone when they were pissed off.

That Thursday night Brian counted us down. "You're on live."

I turned to the camera, as relaxed as I had ever been.

"Welcome to another edition of *Contact*. Caller, go ahead."

I heard a familiar voice. It was one of the girls from the hole in P4W. In the background, I could hear other girls yelling out messages.

I knew from my own experience what it was like to be taken down hard by armed men so I asked a leading question, hoping for the best. "Caller, who would you blame for being pulled from your sleep, having your clothes ripped off and being searched by an all-male Task Force? The soldiers? Or the general who ordered them into the jail?"

She hesitated. "The warden has some explaining to do, don't you think?" A weak response.

I expected her to pin it directly on the members of the Task Force. But that's live broadcasting, and she had her own time to do. I spent the rest of the show soliciting as much information as I could, trying to fill in what was not shown on the tape. I also took several calls from members of the Task Force who were obviously watching and listening closely.

In the morning, Sisson called me into his office and thanked me for balancing the show. Ottawa called him. His job was safe.

I got a letter of thanks from the head of the Task Force, and another from Peter Milliken, the Speaker of the House. More important was my own revelation that even if I had the power to tip the show in one direction or another, the truth tends to be found somewhere in the middle.

On the basis of the Task Force episode, Brian and I were nominated for a television award as best producers of a live TV show. I was even allowed to attend the ceremony with Brian at a local hotel. It was an eventful evening, and not just because we won in our category.

In attendance was Marc Leduc, an Olympic boxing silver medalist. I'd trained him in prison, and he was a frequent guest on the show. With Leduc was his agent, Angela Casey, an attractive redhead who had many friends in the movie business and fashion industry.

I've always had a weakness for red hair. We parted, promising to keep in touch. When Angela heard that I was close to getting out, she wrote to me. I applied for and got an unescorted pass.

We arranged to meet in Hamilton.

She was the one.

Contact had no sponsors; Brian Judge was spending his own money, including his savings, to teach us the skills needed to produce live television. Fortunately, Cablenet let us use their facilities free of charge, and other volunteers pitched in to drive us where we needed to go. As a result of our newfound success we were eager to grow and to reach a larger audience.

Brian came up with the idea to sell an episode of the show, including snippets of the Task Force tapes. That spelled trouble for me. As soon as the episode was put up for sale, I was sent back to mopping floors and cut off from my broadcast career.

A month later, I was granted day parole in Hamilton. I was full of optimism, armed with plenty of TV experience, and an important award in hand. I figured it would be easy enough to bag a job in television. I was wrong. There was no work. Or maybe there was just no work for me. To keep busy, I volunteered as a cameraman at the TV station and soon I was travelling around town, enjoying my freedom.

One day I was passing by Bannister's, a strip bar, when the manager recognized me and rushed outside. I'd known him at the prison farm in Frontenac. He offered me a job on the spot; what strip club doesn't need a smooth talker with the nerve and skills to take care of trouble?

It didn't pay much, but it paid something. I jumped at it, even if it meant smooth-talking my parole officer.

Have I said one thing leads to another?

Six months later, a familiar face – and let's just leave it at that – came in and told me that Dominic Musitano, a Hamilton crime boss, had just died and mobsters from around North America were in town to pay their last respects.

I couldn't attend the funeral because of my parole restrictions but some of the people who came were men I knew from prison, and they came to visit me at Bannister's.

One night, the guy who'd told me about the funeral took me for a ride in his Mercedes. As we cruised the streets of Hamilton, he talked about the fortune he was making in the dope business. It didn't take long for him to make his pitch.

"Ricky, with your connections world-wide; with your family, and with all the people you know all across Canada, you can make a million a month if you want to. I'll take whatever you can get into the country."

Me, an importer?

He reached into the pocket of his Lou Myles suit and handed me an envelope. "This is for you; consider the direction you want to take in life." I didn't open the envelope until he'd dropped me off. It contained $5,000 and a telephone number.

All my old instincts kicked in. I was making peanuts in the strip bar and nothing at all working as a volunteer in television. While that made me feel good it paled in comparison to the thought that I could command an army of crooks and make millions in months, especially when it took years to make any money at all as a square john.

What was all that jive about choices, and consequences?

As I was rolling things around in my head, my mother called. Sonny was dying and he didn't have long to live; a few months, no one could say how long but surely less than a year. He'd been a powerful force in my life.

I remembered the day when he told me he hated white people. He had also said, "You're not the only one who knows gangsters. You're not the only one who was at the top of the game." Why did he get out?

He said, "I put it all aside for you."

That floored me, in a way. I hadn't known. We were father and son, but unbeknownst to me, our lives ran on parallel lines. We were similar in many ways, but the lines never crossed.

He led a life I might have lived.

And I led a life he might have lived.

But if we were never really close, now there was no time left to make Sonny proud of me. Sure, I could easily have knocked off a bank truck and showed up in a designer suit, driving a new car, throwing money around; none of that would have impressed him.

I knew I had to help my mother, which meant I needed to be back in Toronto. At the same time, if it came to that, I'd be in position to reconnect with my old criminal contacts.

I put in for a transfer and was back in Toronto within a week. I picked up a job as a bouncer in a blues bar and slowly let the city wrap itself around me.

Angela had an apartment in the Victoria Park and Lawrence area. When I was not with her, I was with my kids, and with my mother and father. Along the way, I tried to open a bank account with $2,000 of my hard-earned money.

Yes, it was hard-earned. Still, the bank refused me. I fumbled around with my brand new Social Security card and the head teller recognized me from a TV interview I'd given. I called a reporter friend of mine and told him I had a story. The next day, there was a full-page article in the *Globe and Mail* about the city's most prolific bank robber who now couldn't open an account.

The reporter noted that I'd never had any problems with withdrawals.

It was almost time for Sonny's annual outdoor party, a beer bash in the neighbourhood to raise funds for the community centre. Everyone knew it would be his last.

I'd been absent from all the others, but I'd organized hundreds of social events in prison and I knew how to plan a gathering, so I pitched right in.

The day was bright and warm and hundreds of friends and family showed up for a day of drink and song. It was a bittersweet treat for me to see what I'd missed for the past ten years – my kids, playing with other family members the way all kids should.

At the end of the day I volunteered to help strike the event, as I'd always done in prison. Sonny said I should take his car and drive something over to the community centre a few hundred yards away. I told him I'd carry it. I didn't have a full driver's licence, and I didn't want to get pulled over for something so petty as a driving violation.

It was one of those little things that could have, and would have, landed me back in jail. Maybe I didn't spell that out to him. Sonny exploded. He toppled a barbecue he'd been pushing and started yelling.

"You fucking hard-headed bastard, why can't you do as I ask for once? All I want is for you to drive this over to the community centre!"

I held up my hand for him to stop, something I'd never done before. He stilled his rage, waiting for what came next. Time stopped around us as people waited to see what would happen.

My instinct was to pick up a pipe and smash his head in. At the same time, I wanted to run away and hide so as not to see the anger in his face. I chose my words carefully.

"Dad, I came here to help. Nobody yells at me. Not you. Not anyone." He was about to speak. I held up my hand again in warning. "Yell at me once more…"

There was no need to finish the thought. I looked at him as if he were a stranger. He opened his mouth to say something. No words came out. Turning his back on me, I felt the full force of his disre-spect.

For a moment I wished that I could take the whole thing back, that I could change time and do some of the things that make fathers proud of their sons. I was thinking these thoughts when I carried my burden to the community centre as I said I would.

There, I saw a framed copy of a *Toronto Star* story from the time I'd come to the neighbourhood to talk to the kids about life in jail. With the article was a picture of me. The caption read: "Prison sucks – make the right choices."

The next day I stopped by the community centre again. Sonny and I had a moment together. Whatever had happened between us, we both knew that I was my own man, living my life on my terms.

As he had done.

CHOICES AND CONSEQUENCES

Even though I felt that Sonny and I understood each other, I still felt awkward and uncomfortable in his world. I sought out a couple of high-rolling mobsters who owned bakeries around the city – men I'd done time with in Millhaven. As soon as we met we were joking and laughing easily about old times, and the bad taste in my mouth from Sonny's barbecue was disappearing.

As I was about to leave, they kissed my cheeks. And here it came: "Ricky, there's lots of shit going down. You've always been family. We need to know if you're with us."

Choices?

I said, "You're like brothers to me. Don't hesitate to ask for what you need done."

"We know you need money," they said. "We'll have a stag for you in a couple of months. You should be able to pick up thirty or forty grand. Are you okay until then?"

I was too embarrassed to tell them I was broke. I simply nodded and said I was good. The only complication was that we were all still on parole. Even meeting like this was a violation. They were family, but I stayed away from them until the night of my stag.

Angela and I rented a place in Parkdale, in the west end of Toronto, next door to the black halfway house I'd stayed at decades earlier. This was my turf. All I wanted to do was make enough money to ease myself into legitimacy and become untouchable from the cops.

That's all any crook wants.

You get a taste for the business, and it's thrilling at first but after a time, if you are successful, that's all you want – a score so big you can get out of the game forever.

I thought at the time that I could beat the cops with cunning and smarts. I might as well have had a target on my back. They saw me as a threat. They were watching.

I began by stocking up. I accumulated guns, and hid them in false compartments in the walls of the apartment. Behind the building, I buried a couple of high-powered rifles near the train tracks.

Before long, a biker I knew called me to a meeting. He wanted to make sure I understood the political situation. We shook hands, and he offered me a drink and a joint.

I refused both; live clean.

He said, "Ricky, your name is flying around the city. Our club house is near Regent Park, and we're hearing you run Regent Park." I had relatives there, but I hadn't been in that part of town for ten years.

"Here's the thing," he said. "We're taking over what we can. Planting flags wherever we can. But there was a meeting with our national president, and we decided to leave Regent with you, even though it's in our area. We believe you're not hurting our thing with your thing.

"This might change in the future, but we don't want a war with those young hotheads hanging around there right now." Saying that, he clapped me on the back. "We hope that maybe we can work together one day, once you're settled in."

I hid it from him, but I was stunned.

If my name was being passed around like that, odds are the cops had picked it up on a wiretap. I headed across town to get to the bottom of things. Within minutes, at the corner of Parliament and Dundas, a young black kid rode over on a bike, sizing me up. I burned a hole in him, and in those few seconds I was surrounded by hard young black teens.

"Hey, mister, what you want in this area?"

"Fuck you."

The one who spoke gasped as if I'd punched him, and the others sucked their teeth. "You a cop, man?" I eye-fucked them.

"My name is Ricky Atkinson. You got a problem with that?"

Two of them rode off and came back seconds later with twenty others, all of them smiling, some of them reaching out to slap hands. I didn't know any of them, but I recognized that some of them were cousins and I pulled them aside.

"You guys mention my name to the bikers?"

"Fuck them white-boy bikers."

One of them pulled aside his coat to show me he was carrying a small, fully automatic machine gun. They had no idea what they were up against.

They held a small piece of real estate that didn't generate enough money to fight over, except for other little groups of teens holding equally small pieces of turf. I didn't want anything to do with them.

"Listen, fuck up. I will only say this once. I just got out of the joint. I got fifteen years of parole to do. I don't need anyone, especially family, dropping my name every-fucking-where. You dig?"

The leader of the little crew sucked his teeth. "Cuz, we ain't putting you out on front street, man. Anybody says we talking about you is a bitch-ass punk and all you got to do is say who is lying on us, man, and we will cap his ass right quick."

I got away from them as fast as I could, but I knew I was screwed. My name had to be resonating around every cop shop in the city. If I was going to survive another month, I had to get a crew around me quickly.

Most of the gang leaders I met with over the next few weeks had just one word of advice: drugs. "That's where the money is," they said. "Forget everything else."

I wasn't so sure.

My preferred scheme involved the use of fraudulent credit cards to steal millions of dollars in gas, which I thought was preferable to the business of drugs and pushers.

The trouble with drug dealers in those days is that they weren't really criminals, or at least I didn't think of them as criminals. They were just people selling a product with high demand and higher profit margins.

And anyway, salesmen are dreamers, or at least most of them are. They were not hardcore like I was. Most had no pedigree, and no code of ethics learned the hard way from made guys and men of honour.

You couldn't trust them. They might have amassed fortunes, but as a rule they were wimps who would sob at the thought of facing an armed gang in Millhaven.

The credit card scam was going to take some time to set up, and until it was in place, I needed something to do. I did know a bit about drugs. Many of my family had dabbled in them at one time or another, although none were hardcore addicts. For most of my relatives, the drug of choice in the Sixties and Seventies was speed.

Why speed?

The men used it to fuel their sex addictions, and the women used it to dull the pain of sexual abuse, to ease the pain of turning tricks and to take the edge off poverty.

When the market for freebase cocaine exploded in the black community in 1979, dozens of people I knew were suddenly using. Some of them became addicted for years to come. I had no use for drugs and I didn't like the game, but I had no moral objection to dealing.

Today maybe that's a distinction I don't want to examine too closely.

Within weeks a guy offered me $25,000 to introduce him to a trucker who would run some loads of Mexican weed across the border for him. Let me put that in perspective – I'd make $25,000, tax-free, for making a simple introduction.

It only took me a couple of days to find the right guy.

The three of us met at an expensive hotel, the introductions were made, and an envelope was passed to me under the table.

According to the law, that was a drug infraction. It could have sent me back to jail, but at that moment I didn't think of myself as a dealer – I had no idea what was going to happen, or where, or how. I hadn't seen any drugs, and I hadn't profited directly from any sales.

Neither of the guys I introduced ever mentioned the other to me again, and I quickly forgot about them. Easy money.

Then Harry the Greek called a meeting. He knew more about selling hot gas than I did; he offered to help me if I wanted to pursue the idea. I was still thinking that drugs were something I didn't want to get into, too dangerous all around. At least, if I got caught committing fraud, I'd only get a few months.

The assurance of the Greek's backing was good, so I called a meeting of my own with a Chinese crime boss on Spadina Avenue. I needed his help with the credit cards.

He looked on it as easy money. He was willing to give me the best cards he had; and he'd help me finance a drug deal, or buy anything I might bring into Canada.

People trusted me. I was a rounder.

Before things went any further I needed to put together a professional crew so I approached Ross Dankwarth, a lifer and former inmate committee chairman who was with me at the Keele Street halfway house, and old friend, Reggie Mallot. I got them to put together a small gang to run the credit cards and get the trucks I needed.

Rather unexpectedly, someone else I knew gave me 60,000 Ecstasy tablets and asked me to set up a distribution network. He'd made the pills himself, in Amsterdam, but he didn't know how to hustle them there, and hadn't felt safe selling them overseas. Ecstasy was new in Canada at the time, so I went to the library and read everything I could.

Then I took ten envelopes and put ten pills in each and mailed them across the country to guys I knew. Within days, my phone was ringing. I was offering lots of 1,000 pills at twelve dollars a pill, knowing that they sold for twenty-five dollars wholesale on the street, and forty dollars a pop in bars.

Trouble is, nobody I knew was willing to take 1,000 pills at a time. I gave the Ecstasy back after a month. At least I was beginning to feel like I was back where I belonged, running a crew, making my own money. Best of all, the credit card scam was going to be something that had no violence attached to it and it would be hard for the cops to catch me at.

Sweeter still? Bert Novis retired and fraud was generally under the radar of the Hold-Up Squad.

I want to stress that I wasn't thinking about the personal repercussions, or about the loss of revenue to the companies I was about to defraud. I wasn't thinking the harm I might cause to my family, or the fact that I might be misleading the kids I spoke to in public about the horrors of prison life. All I could think about was the money, and the freedom that it would give me.

That's the hook for most crooks – the lure of that one last score, and with it the freedom to live a normal life without being worried or bothered by the cops. Yes, and as a goal that is no more realistic than the lure of the junkie's last high, the glorious eureka moment just before he quits for good.

A friend called me to a meeting at a small blues bar in Parkdale. He introduced me to a friend of his and the three of us sat at the back, away from prying ears.

"This man here is my right arm and my partner over twenty years," my friend told me. "He handles the money and I take care of the logistics. I've told him about you."

This-man-here was a Bay Street suit, a high roller. I looked at him and asked if he'd ever done time. The stranger said, "No, I've never taken a pinch. I've never been in jail. But I've been doing this all my life, since my days at Rochdale."

Rochdale, the university student-housing experiment where I spent some of my youth robbing hippies, had quickly turned into a giant, chaotic drug hot spot. It's now public housing for seniors.

The suit might not have taken a pinch, but my friend had been caught with the biggest load of marijuana in Canadian history at that time. He and the stranger were at the top of the soft drug trade again, having negotiated shipments of drugs and money moved around the world with the cooperation of army generals.

If they needed me, they were desperate.

"Ricky, we bought a ship for half a million dollars, and a load of hash for a million. The ship was supposed to go to Amsterdam but we lost our contact there. The ship has already left Pakistan – we need it to land somewhere within sixty days. Can you help us get it into the country?"

That kind of help has a price.

"How much hash is worth a million bucks to you guys?"

There was no room now for errors of any kind, especially errors of math. They said, "We have 18,000 pounds of very good smoke." The street value of that much hash was around $32,000,000. I knew I had to establish a credible fee.

"That will cost you $300,000 once the ship hits the shore," I said without hesitation. They looked at each other, then at me, and then back at each other. They nodded.

"When do you need an answer?"

"Yesterday."

We shook hands. I was happy at the prospect of making a third of a million bucks, just because I knew some guys who knew some guys.

I drove to the gym, looking for a Portuguese mob enforcer who was training there. He had connections on the docks in Vancouver and I asked if he could help. As it happened, he was flying out to see his daughter that same weekend. He said he'd give me an answer once he got back. I didn't ask him who, or how – those questions always arouse suspicion in people who get by on their gut feelings.

But I felt I couldn't wait.

It was winter and a snowstorm was gathering. When I got home, I could smell the spaghetti dinner Angela was preparing. I had an idea. "How would you like to go to Montreal for supper?"

"Supper will be ready in an hour or so."

"Put it away, this is important."

That was all I had to say. Angela didn't ask how I made my living. I was in on a boxing gym. I knew people. I was never broke for more than a day. I never looked at a bill in a store, and we were never hungry. She trusted me.

If we couldn't land that ship on the west coast, it would have to come up the St. Lawrence Seaway to the port of Montreal.

Fifteen minutes later we were heading up the highway, along with everyone else trying to beat the storm and make it home. By the time we hit Kingston the snow was falling hard and Angela was holding the dash, her knuckles white.

I wasn't afraid. I know how to drive in snow. My mind was locked on finding someone who could handle 18,000 pounds of hash. My one big score, the great white whale I was searching for.

As usual, it was not as simple as it sounded.

My phone rang when we hit the Quebec border. A Russian gangster wanted to meet first thing in the morning. I asked where. He said Montreal. I laughed at the coincidence. Russians are not afraid of snow.

We met for lunch and he asked if I could get him a load of weed to sell in the Toronto market. Coincidentally, my hash guys had hundreds of pounds of Mexican weed. Of course I could help.

Normally, coincidence tends to worry me but I trusted the integrity of the Russian. We ended the day with our women in an expensive restaurant.

In the morning, the sun was shining, the roads were cleared, and it took us six hours to get back to Toronto, plus another hour to get to a friend's house outside the city. What friend?

One of the heads of the Irish mob.

Irish, Russian, Portuguese, Chinese. Toronto is nothing if not multicultural. We talked in his basement, with the taps gushing and the washer and dryer tumbling – covering our voices in case there were wiretaps.

We quickly struck a deal. The hash could come in once the Seaway was clear of ice and as soon as the docks opened, in about sixty days. My friend's fee for avoiding customs was 6,000 pounds of the hash; everyone gets a cut when there's business to be done.

I met the hash guys the next day and gave them the news. Everyone was happy: they had a buyer for their load. No muss and no fuss. For setting things up, I was going to make $300,000.

Stop. Right. There.

I repeat: most criminals tend to think of scores in the making as if they've already happened; nobody likes to think of failure. But big crime is like the lotto – the odds always favour someone else. The odds favour cops, and guys in suits.

Since I was doing the hash guys a favour, I asked them for one in return: could they toss me $50,000 until the ship came in? My friend began a long and careful whine – he had to cover the cost of the ship and the customs guys. He had to pay the crew to sit on the high seas an extra month until the ports unfroze. He had to lay out cash along the network that set up and moved the load. At the end of all this he said no.

Plus, he said, money was tight and he'd just bought thirty houses in the Toronto area. He threw me a bone. He owned a historical property in the city's east end. I could buy it from him or I could rent it and run it as I wished.

The sale price, for me, was $400,000 even though it was on the market at $700,000. Really, the last thing I wanted to do was flip a house with twenty-eight rooms.

Ross asked a trucker friend of his from Beaver Creek if he wanted to invest in the gas business. The trucker jumped at the chance to make some extra bucks. He said he knew some trucking companies out west that could use cheap gas, adding that he could come up with a couple hundred grand of his own to invest depending on the profit margin.

In the meantime, Ross asked his parole officer if he could earn a few bucks working at my gym. He was shot down because his parole officer thought Ross would be running illegal card games at night, as happened at most old-school gyms. I was working out with Trevor Berbick at the time. He was on his way to the heavyweight championship of the world.

Roy Gumbs, the former middleweight champ I'd cornered for once in Halifax, called from St. Kitts. He had more on his mind than renewing our acquaintance. After we chatted for a while, he asked how I was doing financially.

That was a subtle question, and I replied with equal subtlety that I could use some help with the gym. He said he was connected in Vegas, maybe he could help me out by providing fighters for the promotions I came up with. Just before he hung up, he alluded to a conversation we'd had ten years earlier, and said he wanted to talk some more.

We had talked about taking over an island in the West Indies. The idea wasn't fanciful. Roy had worked as a cop in St. Kitts. He knew the politics, and who to pay, and who to threaten to get what he wanted.

He thought we could create a criminal stronghold, including running the police and even the government. He talked about some guy who pulled all the strings as someone really special in the criminal underworld.

Several days later he surprised me by walking into my gym. We spent some time together talking, and then took a walk in a nearby park so that we could continue our conversation without fear of interruption.

Roy pulled out a newspaper from St. Kitts and handed it to me. I took it from him carefully, knowing it might have been just a newspaper, but whatever was in it was important. He pointed to a story about Charles Miller.

Miller had an iron grip on the island. The article spoke of politicians and police inspectors being murdered and intimidated into giving up control of the island to a gang of thugs. Miller was wanted everywhere, so he stayed on the island, surrounded and protected by an army of mercenaries. The story mentioned that Miller had been a former CIA agent.

I handed the paper back to my friend, thinking how the years had changed him, and how they probably had changed me as well. I asked the question, even though I was pretty sure I knew the answer.

"What does this guy have to do with you?"

"I can get you anything you want. We can also take any amount of money you've got and clean it."

If this thing, whatever it was, played out properly, then I wouldn't have to climb up the ladder a rung at a time, ducking cops, and dealing with pushers I didn't like. I'd be on top and untouchable.

Roy made me an offer, a demonstration of good faith; that's how I saw it at the time, good faith. He said he had some blow that was ninety-four percent pure, and he'd sell me a kilo for $4,000. At the time, you couldn't buy that much for that little without leaving the country to get it yourself.

It looked like this was going to put me right up at the top in a hurry: I had visions of making millions a month without doing much more than concentrating on finance – arranging boats, planes and human mules to bring the dope from the island to Canada – easy enough to do with the connections I had.

Roy flew back to his little kingdom.

I thought it would be easy, and it certainly looked that way, but I was still on the fence about calling him back. There were calculations to be made besides planes and boats and the cost of doing business. The path that could lead to riches ran awfully close to the path that could lead to death, or at least to a long stretch in jail.

One of the reasons for my caution? Billy McAllister had just got out of prison when an old friend he hadn't seen in ten years set him up on a drug conspiracy. He ended up in a Florida jail serving "life sentences." I didn't want the same thing to happen to me.

Guess what?

The lure of the money won out. I called Ross and Reggie and explained the change of directions I was taking. It was fine by them.

What I didn't know is that both of them had been selling dope to Ross' trucker friend behind my back, to earn a few bucks to keep them going. The lesson?

Never trust a pusher.

Ross suggested I meet the "Trucker," to see if he wanted to get in on the gas fraud business and to feel him out on any dope deals I might have in mind. The Trucker had reasons for wanting to get close. I thought those reasons were financial.

By now, a lot of things were falling into place. In addition to the hash deal, I had another deal to bring 5,000 pounds of weed into Canada from New Jersey. At the same time I also had an offer of hundreds of pounds of cocaine from Columbia. And a friend in Brazil who had control of the docks wanted me to go into farming with him, just outside of Rio, as a way to launder money. It was not so far-fetched. After all, I had experience with farming, thanks to all my time in prison.

There are some things common to all business transactions, legitimate or otherwise: you spend a lot of time in meetings, you talk, and in the end you have to trust. In the world of legitimate business, if you aren't careful, you lose your shirt. In the world of crime, if you aren't careful, you lose your life.

I had Ross talk to the Trucker about bringing in the weed from New Jersey. The Trucker seemed reluctant; he'd rather run a load of blow, which would mean more money faster. He said he wanted to meet me. He had a lot of nerve.

I decided to test him.

We met late one night in a parking lot. He was eager enough to get in on the stolen gas scam, which was still coming along slowly, but he was even more eager to run cocaine; fewer trips, less risk, more money.

He said, "Listen, Rick, with you I'm in the big leagues. I can do a run or two of cocaine and retire. I don't want to a lot of little runs with weed."

A run or two, and retire. That is the dream.

But he had it a bit backwards. I wasn't in business to satisfy him. I had plans of my own, and I blew up at him.

"Who the fuck do you think you are to school me? You may know Ross, but who else do you know?"

I didn't want an answer, and I didn't care at that moment what he might have known. I walked back to my car, ripped the door open, and drove home in the face of a snowstorm. That was the test. I needed to know how he'd react. I had seen my share of undercover cops sitting in the various prisons I had been in, trying to catch me. That made my leery of everyone and everything but I was also greedy and desperate – two things that bring down every rounder.

The next day, Reggie gave me two names of guys who did business with the Trucker while they were all in Beaver Creek prison camp, so that I could check them out. I knew both of the references from jail, and soon set up a meeting. They confirmed they'd done a couple of deals with the Trucker a few years back, without repercussion or concern, but both stressed it was just small kilo weed deals.

I had Reggie set up another meeting.

At this point I knew I had an advantage, psychologically, given how the last meeting had ended: the Trucker might figure that he had made me mad, but he wouldn't want to keep me mad with the prospect of a deal in front of him.

He had money and he seemed genuinely eager to invest, which to my way of thinking meant I could use him. I asked him how he felt about taking $100,000 down to St. Kitts to buy some blow. He could bring it back through the airport with the help of my connections there. This run was a tester, part of a larger plan to bring back as much as 500 kilos a month until we got rich or got tired of playing the game.

"This is the kind of action I love," he said, leaping at the opportunity. "When do I go, and what do I get for my investment?" I asked him to wait a bit.

We met again a week later and I gave him a sample, two ounces of the ninety-four percent pure that had come to me from the West Indies. He called me the next day to say he was willing.

Christmas was coming. I avoided his calls because I wanted to spend some time concentrating on my family. This would be the first Christmas for the kids with me out of prison.

Instead, Reggie talked to him weekly, telling him everything was okay, assuring him that he'd just have to wait, that I was the boss, that he couldn't and shouldn't rush me, etc.

January and February came and went and with the arrival of spring break, the whole city seemed to want to party. And then Rodney called and said he had some blow he wanted to get rid of; he had airport connections, and he wanted me to use the Trucker.

So he wanted to make some money, and I wanted to test the system. I sold the Trucker a pound. Rodney's stuff was not as pure as it might have been – certainly it was not as pure as Roy's – but he took it anyway, which made me suspicious.

Here's how my thinking went. Although he was a whiner, and I disliked him, I would have some respect for him if he'd declined a weak deal.

On top of that, I was pissed at Rodney for disrespecting me with garbage dope. I thought about ripping Rodney off, or having him taken care of in a more brutal way, in order to save face. As soon as I thought of killing someone over a drug deal I snapped awake. I knew that if I stayed in the drug game I would end up killing scores of people who didn't have the principals I had. I didn't want to start with killing Rodney. On the other hand, I had plans for the Trucker and decided right there and then to rip him off and get out of the dope game for good. I thought I might be able to take care of both of them with one slick move.

I'm not bragging about this. That's how my mind worked at the time, and that's how the business works, even now. Your ego and your nerve form the basis of your reputation, and you can't let your reputation suffer.

I came up with a scheme to get the Trucker to come up with a pile of dough. I knew if it worked I wouldn't have to sell any blow to make any money.

I told him I wasn't too happy about Rodney's shitty dope, and promised to make it up to him. I asked him to take enough money down to St. Kitts to buy ten kilos of cocaine at $15,000 a kilo; all he had to do was sit under a coconut tree and wait for my man to meet him.

But he'd have to front the money.

I assured him that he would be treated with respect, and that he would be in safe hands. I also said that the airports in St. Kitts and Toronto were ready to turn a blind eye. I wasn't kidding. Roy had taken care of St. Kitts. Rodney had a guy at Pearson who had ways to get past Customs, and I had an ace card if I needed one, in the form of a crooked Customs agent. I told the Trucker that he could trust me with his money and his life, or he could forget it.

Greed got the better of him, as I knew it would.

Meanwhile, Angela was pressing me to get some kind of legitimate work, and with her media connections she set me up with a couple of TV shows. I was booked to talk about the days of the Dirty Tricks Gang, my life in prison, and the progress I was making with my sideline – talking to kids at risk.

I ended up doing an interview with Erica Ehm, who had been a bright young VJ on the MuchMusic channel. She was doing talk interviews. And I was still talking about going straight and doing right.

After the interview, while she and Angela chatted about old times and toured the studio, I got impatient about the St. Kitts deal so I excused myself and made a call.

I got Roy and told him I was sending someone to meet him. I faxed him a photo of the Trucker and left the rest to him. Not even Roy knew what I was up to.

If this were a movie the foreboding music would come up here.

I drove my mark to the airport, cautioning him that the RCMP sometimes took over the jobs of airport workers in Toronto, often for a week at a time, to curb any interest airport employees might have of importing on their own.

"If anything happens, I'll pay you back and find another way to bring the dope into the country." He nodded, and I continued. "Look at it this way – you get a paid vacation in paradise, you'll meet some really cool people, and you won't lose a cent no matter what happens."

He boarded the plane and I knew I had him.

In St. Kitts, the Trucker sat under a coconut tree in the heat, clutching a gym bag full of Canadian $100 bills, looking at every black man who passed by. That would have been a lot of black guys.

And at the prearranged time, the champ came jogging along, throwing punches in the air. Roy stopped to stretch and struck up a conversation with the nervous stranger; nothing unusual, islanders are friendly.

When the Trucker turned the talk to boxing, and when he mentioned my gym, the connection was made. Roy looked after him for a week, taking him fishing, golfing, and partying at a place called the Monkey Bar.

As part of my master plan, I walked out of my back door and across the way to the Canadian National Exhibition grounds, picked one of the dozens of pay phones there and called Roy in St. Kitts. I explained that there was a problem at my end, and he was to keep the Trucker's money, and to send him back with nothing.

Roy put the Trucker on the phone. I said, "Plan B, my friend; don't worry about a thing." He was in no position to question me.

I met my Toronto airport connection and told him when the Trucker was coming in, and I asked him to observe his arrival from a security point of view, and to let me know if anything was amiss.

I said he'd be coming in clean.

That night, I got two urgent calls, one from the Trucker, and one from my security agent. They both wanted to meet right away. I met the airport guy first.

"Your guy stood around the baggage drop until the last bag came down," he explained. "He looked nervous, and he put our security on alert. He picked up one bag but left the last one rolling around like a hot potato. My boss was unable to wait any longer. He sent us out to grab the bag and your guy. We took him into custody.

"He claimed he didn't know whose bag it was. When we opened it we found cocaine. We let him go, but he's now red-lighted in our computer system. Turns out he's also got a prison record, with an address in Calgary."

I thanked him for his troubles and slipped him $500 in an envelope; after all, nothing's free in the drug world. This would not have been possible in the super security conscious post 9/11 world.

I arranged a meeting at a restaurant with the Trucker. He was pacing back and forth in the parking lot when I pulled up. I walked over briskly, showed my gun and told him I wanted him to put his hands on his car so I could frisk him.

He was shocked. Things were unfolding as I'd planned.

I said, "What the fuck, man, I told you not to bring anything back. What the fuck happened down there?"

He said he'd been told that Roy's boss, Charles Miller, had ordered him to bring back ten kilos in order to test Toronto security. He was too afraid to refuse.

"Yeah, well, you violated the terms of our agreement. I'm not taking responsibility for your loss. The only consolation I can offer is that I'll pay you back your hundred grand on our next deal. But you'll have to step up to the plate and come up with a million dollars."

I was rewarded with a blank stare.

"You tasted the product down there. It's as good as it gets; where else you gonna get anything that pure? I've got several ways to get it into Canada. I've talked to Montreal; the docks are open for us there. I've also got people in British Columbia. And, I have an ace card at the airport. It's still good to go. If you don't do anything stupid like you did this time, all will be okay and you'll be a rich man."

He said, "I'm not going to take any chances with a million bucks in cash unless I meet your airport guy. And we have to go into this as full partners, no hidden agendas."

I pretended to consider his proposal.

I knew I had him hooked. I was going to rip him off anyway, so I didn't think it mattered one way or another if he met my airport connections. If that helped loosen him up then it worked in my favour.

"No problem. You'll meet him. You've already met the other end." I drove away, still a little pissed at Roy for causing me a minor problem, but certain that I could still set the Trucker up for a million-dollar rip-off.

I didn't go directly home. I went back to the CNE first, to that bank of pay phones where I put in another call to Roy.

"You fucked me. My friend didn't make it through the airport." I didn't bother to hide my anger.

Roy asked, "Is he in jail?"

"No, but he lost the bag."

Roy lost his patience, yelling at me over the phone. "What are you upset about? If you want us to give the money back, we will. But if that little weasel comes down here again, I'll send him back to you in a box."

This wasn't going well.

I said, "My friend, don't you raise your voice to me. I've always been a heavyweight. You understand what I'm saying to you?"

Roy calmed down. And so did I when he explained his side of the story.

He said, "My boss took the position that you don't know shit about what's going on here. He wanted to sweeten the deal with your guy. No disrespect for not clearing it with you first. I would have made sure you got cut into any profits that guy made. Why are you so upset?"

I was on a pay phone, calling another pay phone, so I opened up. "Listen, I have a plan. He's going to come back with a million dollars. I'll split it with you – I want you to take the goof down."

"You want to burn the bastard?"

"Yeah. But I don't want any problems in communication so you've got to come up here to see me. I can't come to you."

Roy's tone turned even more pleasant. "I'll be up this weekend. Let me tell you, my friend, there's no sweeter business than the one I'm in."

I batted that back. "You're in the wrong business, my friend. The future is in computers. After this play, that's where I'm headed."

This was news to Roy.

"I'll be up this weekend."

As it happens Ross was back in jail, having tested positive for drugs at the halfway house, so I called a quick meeting with Reggie and one of the Italian guys – a hit man I knew from Millhaven whose services I might need if things went wrong with the Trucker. My plan?

Roy would give the Trucker a suitcase with a million dollars' worth of pure dope, and one of his guys would switch it for garbage dope in the airport in St. Kitts.

Once the plane was in the air, I'd have my airport guy alert Customs. They'd seize the garbage dope.

That way, I could scream and holler about my losses and blame them on the Trucker, ending our relationship and keeping his money. If he got out of line, well, whatever happened would be his fault.

I have to repeat, I am not proud of this. The business was treacherous, and so was I because the success of this deal was going to set me up for the future. And I wasn't shitting Roy about the computer idea. I had already bought several of the most powerful machines on the market I had a hacker lined up who was willing to work for coke. If things turned out, there'd be no more hit men, no more bags full of dope, no more crooked customs agents or dealers. Just little illegal keystrokes, so small no one would ever notice.

A harmless bit of skimming.

Nickels and dimes a day, amounting to millions.

When I told Angela about Roy's arrival, she invited one of her girlfriends to meet him. Then she went shopping for a spread of the finest meats, fruits and cheeses.

Angela may not have known exactly what I was up to, but she wasn't stupid. I loved her, in part, because she didn't put her nose in my business.

I went to meet Roy's flight. The airport was jammed with visitors, it being the July 4th weekend – everyone was going home to spend the holiday with relatives. Still, I could sense something wasn't right.

In spite of the crowd, I spotted plainclothes cops everywhere. When I spotted Roy, I also saw undercover men perk up. Something was very wrong.

All I could think of was getting outside so I could run.

Roy spotted me and smiled. I walked him quickly towards an exit, and as we neared the door I saw an agent talking into his sleeve. Soon they were all doing it.

"I think we're going to be arrested."

Roy opened his mouth to say something but I hustled him outside. The airport limos were all there. The doors were open and the trunks were up but there wasn't a driver in sight. Damn.

My car was parked nearby.

We never made it.

Cops wearing balaclavas and combat gear poured out of two vans, armed with machine guns. Other cops came forward with handguns and shotguns. I looked up and saw snipers on the roof of the airport.

There was death in every direction when my head exploded. One of the cops smashed the back of my skull with the butt of his machine gun; when I tried to get up another one smashed me in the face.

"Get his gun! Get his gun!"

"He doesn't have a gun!"

"He always has a gun."

I came to my senses. "I ain't got a gun, asshole." Along with the rifle butts, what hit me then was that I was the real target of the arrest.

I'd been set up.

I was cuffed and yanked to my feet and tossed into the back of a waiting car as if I were a sack of meat, with two masked cops for company. "Sit still and don't move, or I'll blow your fucking head off."

"Fuck you."

It was all I could think of to say, knowing that I was probably looking at years of loneliness and – quite frankly embarrassment – ahead of me. The route they used took us past the CNE. When I turned my head I could see my house surrounded by cop cars.

At least there was nothing illegal at the house. They tossed it and arrested Angela anyway, but not before she offered them the feast she had prepared, so that it wouldn't go to waste. Always gracious, was my girl.

Once again back at 52 Division, this time surrounded by the RCMP and Toronto drug squad cops, ten of them. I was on unfamiliar ground; I had no idea how these guys conducted business. After a few minutes of silence – perhaps they thought I was going to spill my guts – one of them said, "We've got a surprise for you."

In walked the Trucker.

He took out his badge and stuck it in my face. "You're under arrest." As if I didn't know. He pulled up a chair and sat down facing me. "We're arresting people all around the world right now. We have seventeen warrants out for your gang. Everyone's going down. You're on top of the heap, Ricky, and you're looking at a life sentence."

I stared at him with my one good eye.

He continued, sarcastic and triumphant. "I thought we could trust each other but when we saw you with the Italian the other night, I knew you didn't respect me anymore and that really hurt my feelings."

Have I told you how much I love sarcasm?

"For my own safety, I had to close the operation down," he explained. "Too bad because with your connections we could have been running around the world for a long time."

I suppose I was lucky that he'd shut me down before I'd made moves into one of those countries where they execute guys like me for drug stuff.

"By the way, after we wrap this up I'm officially retired. I've had twenty years of this shit." He stuck out his hand and said, "My name is Clive."

He seemed proud of that.

"You only have one chance to get yourself out of this mess, but it has to be now. You know the Italian bakery you were at the other night? We'd love to nail those guys. You were in Montreal with Eddie Melo. We'd love to nail those guys, too. Cooperate with us and things can go really sweet for you. If not, well, you know what's going to happen."

I smiled and kept my mouth shut; anything I said could have been used against me in court. After a minute of silence, they locked me up for the night.

I rotted in the Don for a year until trial.

I was in for a surprise, but not the one my lawyer had warned me about. The cop I knew as the "Trucker" did not lie in court, nor did he embellish or add things I hadn't said on tape.

It is one of the few times, if not the only time, I had any respect for any of the cops who testified against me.

Here's the real surprise: all the pay phones at the CNE had been tapped. I also learned that if Roy had not said his real name over the phone, no one would have known who he was.

Worst of all?

My voice, on tape, talking from the phone in Erica Ehm's office, running my mouth on what I thought was a safe phone but which was tapped at the other end.

I felt like a fool.

When we finally got to court, I learned that I had been set up by the very head of the RCMP in Ottawa, who had watched me on Jane Haughton's show going toe-to-toe with one of his officers from Calgary about the faint hope clause for lifers.

The judge at our preliminary trial said he'd had enough. He could not find sufficient evidence to proceed with charges against fourteen of the accused. Thanks to Trucker Clive's testimony, he also withdrew charges against me of conspiracy to commit murder and conspiracy to rob an undercover police officer.

"I have never heard of anyone trying to smuggle cocaine into Brazil," noted the judge disdainfully. "So, I am also withdrawing that charge. What a waste of time and money."

The Crown shrugged. "That's the way it goes, Your Honour."

The Trucker – oh, hell, let's give him his due and call him The Copper – walked over to the prisoner's box and extended his hand. I refused to take it but I held no grudge.

He'd been smarter than me and he'd been fair in court. He was not the instrument of my own greed and stupidity. I was.

In the end, I received a twenty-year sentence for conspiring to import drugs.

As far back as I can remember, I've always been on the alert. But being alert is not enough. I've always questioned my observations, trying to see what it is I'm looking at, working hard to keep my instincts honed.

In crime, as in many other walks of life, if you see something dangerous you either cross the street or you deal with it. Sometimes you have doubts, and sometimes you doubt your doubts. It's wearying.

Every time things have gone wrong, it's been because I've ignored my instincts. Roy had said there was something wrong with the the "Trucker." The usual and the successful position: when in doubt, wipe him out. But I'd said Roy should just send him back up.

My mistake.

And let that be the last sentence in the story of the original Dirty Trickster.

EPILOGUE

When I was finishing my time in British Columbia, I met a young black gang-banger whose four-year sentence for possession of a stolen gun was almost complete. He wanted me to help him get ready, physically and mentally, for his return to the streets in Toronto.

It was an unusual, but not an unnatural request, because he knew I'd been there and done that more than once.

To help him I had to know him and get him to trust me so I began to teach him how to box. And as we went along I asked him to fill me in on how the kids his age operated in the Jane-Finch area of Toronto.

My uncle Biggy and aunt Vicky had lived there so long ago that that they were one of the first mixed-race couples in the neighbourhood. Now, of course, no one would raise an eyebrow at a mixed marriage.

Today it's gang central. He said there were a bunch of guys – he called them "walking-dead niggers" – that he wanted to kill. Why? Because they'd come for him one night and when they didn't find him they killed his sister and her child.

He'd managed to hit a couple of them and he was committed to getting the rest when he got out. I felt bad for him but his was a problem with no solution – he couldn't finger the specific guys so his only option was to take down the whole gang.

But gangs are fluid and organic – members come and go all the time, for all the usual reasons. That's why you can never kill your way out of all your problems.

I explained the odds – he'd either end up in prison for trying, or he'd end up dead when he failed. He bit his lip. He wasn't happy to hear what I had to say. He said, "Brother, I gots to get some more dead niggers before I go back home. I can't live with myself if I don't."

I tried another angle.

"Young brother: mob dudes, bikers and such, all shake hands after a war is over, even when family gets killed. Your shit needs something. What is it that you need?"

"Man, what I think? Niggers like me, from our 'hood? What we need more than anything is a leader so we can up our game, make more money, fight better wars and survive this shit."

I wasn't getting through. "Okay, say I'm your leader; top left." I touched my heart to show him I was sincere. He smiled and slapped my hand.

"You want me to teach you to make bombs so you can kill your enemy at a distance?" I asked. His eyes lit up at the thought but he shook his head.

"You want me to teach you about poisons you can make easy? You want to know how to improvise a drone from remote control toys to attack your enemy?"

He rolled his eyes.

"What about picking locks, cracking safes and robbing banks to get money for war supplies?"

It was as if he couldn't comprehend where I was coming from.

"You're a fucking caveman," he said. "Niggers don't know that shit any more. We just shoot and run."

I had no intention of teaching him any of that shit, but I wanted to see if there was a chance he could be turned away from the endless cycle of retaliation. Nothing doing. I slipped the boxing gloves off his hands.

"For you to succeed, you must free yourself from your ghetto and stop seeing yourself as a nigger."

He was startled, as I knew he would be. I was from another generation.

"What the fuck you talking about?"

I just walked away. I might have been doing time, but I didn't have time to waste. I had to get my own shit together.

I walked the yard alone that night, thinking about the young criminals I'd have to work with if I started up again, guys like him. My guys, in my day, all went to crime school. They were good at what they did. They had all the skills. These kids didn't want skills. All they wanted was a pistol and a pair of sneakers.

It became clear, in the darkness, that outfits like the Stopwatch Gang, The West End Gang in Montreal, the East and West End Boys of Toronto, and even my own Dirty Tricks Gang, had become something for the history books. We were old-fashioned, out-of-date, behind the times.

Shoot and run, hell.

Something else happened that steered me a bit more in the direction I was going to have to go if I wanted to get my own life back. I was still doing time in British Columbia and, as I had done before, I was making pots and running the pottery room.

Working at the wheel is meditative, productive and creative at the same time. It filled a need in me and, as a bonus, and maybe a clue to the future direction of my life, I was able to display and sell my pots in the galleries of Vancouver.

I was also in charge of the prison pottery program, which meant I had the key to the room. In prison a key, any key, is a sign of power, a luxury, and an indication of trust.

It also meant keeping my leaderships skills sharp, because the sign of a successful program is that anyone can join, even if you don't happen to like or get along with them.

There is always a kind of truce in the prison hobby shops. If you can't get along with others then you have to leave the program, it's as simple as that. And having something to do is precious – it's how you make your time go by.

Pottery is difficult to master. You have to put your mind in a state that is receptive to learning. It's Zen, if you will.

It is also a way to create something tangible that can be sold for cash or given away as a souvenir. So you adapt and that is a step toward redemption.

The benefits of discipline are not immediately apparent to everyone. One day I was changing the coils in the kiln when a slim, athletic brother walked in, talking shit and looking around. I knew who he was, brothers know brothers.

He was in for a double-tap – he'd killed two people in Ottawa – and was doing a pair of life-twenty-fives. He saw the pottery shop as a place to hang his hat while doing his time.

It took only a few seconds for me to figure him out – he wanted my key, and I was sure he was working out the politics of getting it. His name was Richards.

Young Richards made a show of pulling out a Crip flag, wiping his face and putting it in his back pocket so that it showed. All the while, he kept an eye on me to see how I'd respond. I pretended to concentrate on what I was doing.

Showing his colours was not a smart move.

An hour or two later, when he was sitting down, trying to make a bowl out of a lump of cold clay, I walked over and whispered in his ear. "Brother, you got to put your colours away as long as I'm running this shop." The smile left his face. He sat up slowly.

I had just challenged him.

Thing is, I was doing him a favour, even if he didn't know it yet. He was the only Crip in the place, which made him a man alone. Showing his colours was stupid. He might as well have been a Klansman in a hood, showing up at a powwow.

The next day he came up to me and said the administration had shown him a bunch of rules enabling them to take his flag away from him. That was predictable.

They also warned him there was a Blood in the population. He confided to me that he was going to track this Blood down, He went on and on about all the colourful ways he was going to put him in his place. I let him go on.

I told him a story.

Back in the day, when Millhaven was a seriously dangerous place, there was only one range that was safe: all the guys knew each other and they left their doors open.

One day, as a joke, a guy named Easy wrote "Crip" on his cell; to further the joke, someone else wrote "Blood" on his. And then a brother drew a line down the middle of the floor, with "Crip" on one side and "Blood" on the other.

Ottawa got word and stepped in. They summoned the Blood and asked, "Have you started an organization?" The explanation: no, just a joke.

Ottawa said it wasn't funny, and maybe it was not a joke: the line had better get scrubbed off the floor immediately. So it was.

I told Richards that I was the Blood.

His jaw dropped a bit.

That incident went on my file. It has followed me forever after like a long punch line to a bad joke.

Richards was looking at another thirty years inside, which meant he had no idea what life was going to be like when he got out. If he was going to act stupidly about his affiliation, then he was going to have to watch his back at all times, or he might not even live to get out at all.

It was as if a light went on.

He got rid of his colours and went to the administration and filled out the paperwork renouncing his affiliation. He began to do what I was doing. Smart time.

I gave that young man a knowing smile and went back to doing what I was doing then, which is what I am still doing.

Making something useful from a lump of clay.

My run as a rounder? All in all, I stole for a living and stole for decades, tapping every day for years, hundreds of thefts in clothes, furs, jewellery, and shoes. There were roughly seventy banks robbed; maybe thirty credit unions; fifteen warehouses with guns, another fifty B&E; thirty safes cracked, three gun store robberies, seven gun store B&E.

We stole meat, cigarettes and electronics out of factories day and night. We robbed twenty fur stores, plus another twenty coat-rack grabs. There were ten oriental carpet heists, thirty jewellery store smash-and-grabs, more than fifty safes cracked.

As for muggings, there were more than I care to remember, although I remember one. During a hold-up a guy asked me, point-blank, to kill him. He'd just lost his job and his wife had left him. I bought him a coffee instead.

The other side of the ledger of my success?

Half a life in jail.

Do I have remorse? Let me put it like this: I wasted half my life in jail and I lost time with family and all those who love me. I can't change that.

So I changed myself.

No more razors' edge. No more ducking, no more hiding, no more taking what is not mine.

I'm a taxpayer now.

I still think of Owen the Crook from time to time. I miss him. He was the kindest soul. If you ever wanted a guy on a bank job, he was the one, because he'd never hurt anyone. To this day, they talk about that part of him.

Of all of us, his parents treated him the worst, but he wasn't angry. For some reason, from kindergarten up, he was a happy guy. He could be dangerous, but he preferred to mediate: He'd say, "Smash 'em, but don't cut 'em." But he cut me once.

I still have the scar, just above my knee. He was explaining how a southpaw, in a knife fight, had an advantage over an orthodox guy. My cut was his explanation.

I see it, I think of him.

Brian Bush runs through my mind often enough wondering how he's doing, how's his freedom. Owen's dead and I'm still walking around with a sentence that can send me back to prison for the rest of my life.

Angela is constantly on my mind, she was the catalyst for change in me. I'll never forget standing on the dock, before I was sent away: She was there, in cuffs along with all the rest of us, even though she'd done nothing and she knew nothing.

She leaned over, overwhelmed by the presence of all cops, and all the crooks, and she whispered, "Are you finished with all this now?" I told her I was, and I meant it.

And this is why I still mean it. Because she said, "Then no matter what happens, I'll stand by you." And she did.

She never wavered.

I transferred to Vancouver in order to be near her; she came back to Toronto with me so we could start another new life together. She stood by when I was yanked off parole in Toronto and sent to prison because I'd taken a job painting a mosque, of all things, with Johnny Bayliss. I was not supposed to associate with felons, etc.

In all, she stood at the gate for twelve years, waiting for me.

Sadly, when I got out the last time, she ran into a combination of blows. Her brother died, but he left her a handsome inheritance, which might have meant freedom from worry. And then a death sentence: cancer.

I loved her, I took care of her, I fed her, I ferried her back and forth to doctors, and I buried her. I still grieve

I'm still true to Angela, and I'm still straight, because she was true to me. I could have used the tragedy of her death as an excuse for cutting loose and going on a crime spree to get back at everyone who deprived me of time with her.

I was a rounder no more!

I've learned to let go.

An old-school cop who used to chase me called and asked for a sit-down. I agreed to meet Eddy Blaha not far from his office in Little Italy. He retired from the police force and was doing the "Get you off your traffic ticket" hustle.

The cop chose the restaurant and I arrived early, taking a seat facing the door, wondering. The old cop comes in alone and takes a seat facing me. He's relaxed and familiar with the eatery, so I relax, too.

He leans forward. Instinctively I follow, having spent my life with an ear people liked to talk into.

He asked if I was finished with my run as a rounder.

I chose my words carefully.

"Eddy, I can't be bribed, bought or threatened, to take another run at Toronto's finest."

The retired cop smiled and leaned back, assessing me.

His tone took on a more sombre tone. He explained he had stage 4 cancer and wouldn't be around much longer. Alexandra Park was his old cop beat and he wanted to help me in my endeavours to help kids at risk.

He went on to explain that what his crew, which included Bert Novis, appreciated in me most was that I didn't use gratuitous violence during my criminal career. In fact, he explained, that was the reason they let me live to have such a long run at them.

I thought of the eighteen bullet holes in my car when they killed Owen Crookendale and the stolen gun tossed into my van when they shot cousin Tommy.

After chatting about old times the cop reached for his wallet. I waved my hand. I was in Little Italy where eyes saw everything. A solid member of Toronto Police force allowed me to buy him lunch. I was touched.

A lot of guys have written crime memoirs, and there's a theme common to most of them: drugs made me do it or I was dealt a bad hand, and now I've seen the light.

I can't stand whining.

What made me do it? I had so many chances to go straight, and I know in my heart what the judges knew – I was smart enough to run a Fortune 500 company.

I was addicted to the score.

Psychologists and penologists all say that the best indicator of future behavior is past behavior. I've been a square john for seven years now. Let that be an indicator of my next five years. I worked squares I never thought I ever would and enjoyed working at the Vancouver Convention Centre. I also enjoyed working outside of the city for a welding company. I even trained the plant boss how to box. I drove a forklift at another factory, experiencing the life of a blue-collar worker – getting fired and hired.

These days I'm training a university student and Canadian boxing champion on his way to glory in the ring. I love teaching the sweet science. When not doing that I'm busy running a pottery program for young adults and teens in the Alexandra Park Projects.

What grounds me is my mother. After forty-seven years away, thirty-two of them in prison, I'm back, seeing her more often and getting to know the fun side of the woman I call my Mom. I also take her to Bingo every Sunday, like clockwork, something my father would expect of me. I see my kids struggling to raise their kids, all of them going in directions different than the one I followed. All of them are doing better for their children than what I did.

I have aunts and uncles whose children and grandchildren have college degrees and no criminal records. My brother Dwane is a living example for me to emulate. He has been crime free for thirty-five years. Now retired from a career in construction, Dwane enjoys his children who have all earned master's degrees and are working toward doctorates in their chosen fields. It's a life change I now know can happen to all rounders, if they wake up and allow the system to work for them, rather than fighting against it.

What fires me up each morning is my passion for spending time in clubs learning more about the world of blues music. It was a large part of my past, it is my present, and it will be my future.

What keeps me smiling is looking for young rounders in groups of Kids at Risk when I'm giving a talk. Spotting them in a crowd and trying to redirect their energy to more pro-social stuff that avoids prison life and early death is its own reward.

Here's a final moment, if you want one. I was checking in at the cop shop recently and, as usual, the duty officer asked for my name.

"Ricky Atkinson."

An older officer at the other end of the counter overheard. He perked up. "Hey, this guy's a legend."

Almost without thinking, I said, "No man, you're the legend. You're still working. You guys retired me twenty years ago."

AUTHOR'S NOTE

Everyone steals in commerce and industry. I've stolen a lot, myself.

—THOMAS EDISON

The folly of most habitual criminals is their belief that they can use crime to reach the top of the social ladder, as Edison did.

At the end of the day, I look in the mirror and ask, "How can you call yourself a successful criminal when you've done so much time?"

A town is a prison if you can't leave it; likewise, a country is a prison if laws force you to remain in it. I've always tried to make the best of a bad situation while doing time in any prison, utilizing all the help the prison system offered, while mostly neglecting any help the Parole Board of Canada offered once I was released.

I now seek help from anywhere and anyone, believing in a quote by black author Ralph Ellison: "If you can show me how I can cling to that which is real to me, while teaching me a way into the larger society, then I will not only drop my defences and hostility, but I will sing your praises and help you to make the desert bear fruit."

It's time to sing praise where praise is due.

ACKNOWLEDGEMENTS

Many tried to pull me into mainstream society over time and all failed as I clung to the fringes of our society, doing it my way. I would like to thank all who took a shot at changing me into a more productive member of society. There were many.

My parents were there, time and again, when I failed at crime and also when I succeeded at other things. For that, I thank them.

I would like to thank the three women who bore the shame and expense of loving a rounder doing life on the instalment plan. I couldn't have done it without Sharon, Diane and Angela.

I would like to thank everyone who wrote letters of support over the decades to the parole board and especially to Glen Flett of Long-term Inmates Now in the Community (L.I.N.C.) and Joan McEwen, lawyer/author, who sat beside me at parole panel hearings fighting for my greater freedoms.

I would like to thank Wardens Jim Blackler, Dave McDonald and Fred Sisson for allowing Brian Judge to escort me outside of their prisons more than 460 times to film the world's first prison reality television show, *Contact*, which has evolved into www.prisontv.net. It changed the course of many lives.

I would like to thank Mel Bellissimo, founder of Decorus Spiritual Arts Academy, for his advice, friendship and employment opportunities. I would like to thank my children, Melissa, Sonny and Jennifer, and my stepdaughter Kristin, for never turning their backs on their dad after a life of him in prison.

Journalist, author and man-about-town, Joe Fiorito listened to me and applied his craft to my story. I thank him for his generous spirit and talent. Thanks also to Michael Callaghan and his publishing team at Exile Editions for assuming the challenges of this project.

Lastly, I would like to thank any cop, parole officer, or correctional officer who saw something worth redeeming in me and reached out to help. There were many. Just as I have not forgotten the abusers over the decades, I have not forgotten you.

APPENDIX

The Federal Prison Record of Atkinson, Howard Andrew Richard:

71/09/09	Theft Under $50; suspended sentence, 2 yrs probation
72/12/08	B&E w/Intent; 6 mos & 12 mos. indefinite
72/12/13	Poss Burglar's Tools; 2 mos consec to sent serv
73/02/20	Armed Robbery (x2); 4 yrs each chg consec but consec sent serv
73/02/21	Att B&E w/Intent; 1 yr w/conc sent serv
73/02/21	B&E w/Intent; 1 yr conc & conc w/sent serv
73/02/21	Poss Burglar's Tools; 6 mo conc
73/02/21	Poss Burglar's Tools; 3 mo conc
73/02/21	Failure to Appear; 3 mo conc each chg
77/08/09	B&E & Theft (x2); 20 mo each chg conc
81/09/02	Impersonation w/Intent; $100 I-D 10 days & 2 yrs prob
83/06/09	Poss Burglar's Tools; 30 days
83/08/05	B&E & Theft; 2 yrs & 3 yrs prob
83/08/05	B&E & Theft (x2); 39 mo each chg conc & conc sent serv
86/11/26	Robbery; 12 yrs
86/11/26	Use of Firearm; 1 yr conc
86/11/26	Poss Unreg Restr Weapon; 5 mo conc and prohib firearms 5 yrs
88/09/06	Robbery (x13); 25 yrs each chg conc
88/09/06	B&E & Commit (x 3); 25 yrs each chg conc & conc
88/09/06	Att B&E w/Intent; 25 yrs each chg conc & conc
88/09/07	Conspire to Traffic; 2 yrs less 1 day conc sent serv
98/08/26	Conpsire to Import Drugs; 20 yrs consec

Att = Attempted

Conc = Concurrent

Consec = Consecutive

Insts. = Instruments (as in burlar tools)

BE & Theft = Break and Enter plus Theft

Poss = Possession (as in Possesion unregistered restricted weapon)

Sent = Sentence

Ser = Served

The following withdrawn or dismissed charges were also noted:

71/09/09	Poss Stolen Property	Withdrawn
72/07/28	Poss Narcotics	Withdrawn
72/09/09	B&E & Theft	Withdrawn
72/12/04	Theft	Dismissed
72/12/04	Poss Stolen Property	Dismissed
73/02/20	B&E & Theft (x2)	Withdrawn
73/02/20	Theft of Auto	Withdrawn
73/02/20	Poss Stolen Auto	Withdrawn
73/02/20	Theft Under	Withdrawn
73/02/20	Poss Stolen Property	Withdrawn
73/02/20	Poss Stolen Property	Withdrawn
73/02/20	Poss Unreg Weapon	Withdrawn
73/02/20	Theft Over	Withdrawn
73/02/21	Poss Burglar's Tools	Dismissed
73/02/21	B&E w/Intent (x 3)	Dismissed
77/08/08	Poss Stolen Property	Withdrawn
78/04/18	Poss Narcotic for Purpose of Trafficking	Withdrawn
80/12/18	Poss Housebreaking Instr	Withdrawn
81/09/02	Poss Narcotic for Purpose of Trafficking	Withdrawn
82/04/20	B&E w/Intent	Discharged
83/03/03	Fail To Comply (Recog)	Withdrawn
83/08/05	BE & Theft (x2)	Withdrawn
83/08/05	Poss Stolen Prop Under	Withdrawn
83/03/05	Poss Stolen Prop Over (x2)	Withdrawn
83/08/05	Theft Over (x 4)	Withdrawn
83/08/05	Poss Burglar's Tools (x5)	Withdrawn
86/01/20	B&E w/Intent	Withdrawn
86/11/26	Poss Stolen Prop Over	Withdrawn
87/01/09	Conspiracy To Commit Robbery	Stay of Proceeding
97/10/17	Conpsire to Murder Undercover Officer	Withdrawn
97/10/17	Conspire to Rob Undercover of $800,000	Withdrawn

Ricky Atkinson will be on parole until August 26, 2035, at 9:00 am.